"Cohen delivered - this book is truly amazing. His podcast *Two Bi Guys* and the discovery of his own bisexuality are a powerful foundation for the rich oral histories of the men interviewed. Bisexual men really do exist, and this innovative, intersectional resource is desperately needed to challenge the bi-erasure they endure. I can't wait to use it in my own classes!"

Lisa Spiedel, associate professor, Department of Women, Gender and Sexuality, University of Virginia

"A fascinating read that sheds a light on a demographic that is so often invisible. With an eclectic group of people, Cohen showcases the lived experiences of bisexual men married to women, highlighting their similarities despite their numerous differences. Through grace, sensitivity and wisdom gained through years of activism and conversations with others in the community, Cohen imparts his knowledge throughout a series of oral histories as well as sharing his own life. Even as someone who is not in a relationship with a woman, I found these stories resonating with me in countless ways. I have no doubt that this book will reach so many who are so often scared of the limelight."

Vaneet Mehta, author of *Bisexual Men Exist: A Handbook for Bisexual, Pansexual, and M-Spec Men*

Bisexual Married Men

How much do you know about the lives of bisexual men who are married to women? Do you know any personally? Have you seen them represented in media or pop culture? Bisexual people make up a majority of the LGBT+ community, but they are still relatively hidden and misunderstood. Robert Brooks Cohen aims to address this invisibility by sharing a collection of interviews with Bi+ men who are or were married to women, helping readers find connection, understanding, and community.

Their experience is often erased as "not queer enough", but these men are queer, and they are challenging societal norms in important and innovative ways. Written by the host of *Two Bi Guys*, this book intersperses Robert's bisexual journey with the diverse stories of other Bi+ men to help normalize sexual fluidity and create more awareness and compassion. Each chapter is framed around a bisexual married man's story which touches on an important theme in many people's journey, such as coming out, monogamy, intersectionality, porn, marriage, parenting, and finding community, with Robert sharing his thoughts, research, and analysis. The book shares interviews with men and a few of their wives from a wide array of cultural and regional backgrounds, religions, family structures, and more, helping bisexual men find pride, validation, and joy in their sexual identity.

This book is written about and for bisexual and questioning men so they can see their experience represented. However, it is also for their partners, family, and friends – as well as students, researchers, clinicians with bisexual clients, and allies – so that they can better understand the unique challenges of this identity and provide meaningful support.

Robert Brooks Cohen is an author, screenwriter, and content creator. He received his MFA from New York University Tisch School of the Arts. He wrote for *Law & Order: SVU* and hosts the *Two Bi Guys* podcast. His work can be found at www.RobertBrooksCohen.com. He is from New York and lives in Los Angeles – a bicoastal bisexual.

Bisexual Married Men

Stories of Relationships, Acceptance, and Authenticity

Robert Brooks Cohen

Routledge
Taylor & Francis Group

NEW YORK AND LONDON

Designed cover image: © Getty Images

First published 2024
by Routledge
605 Third Avenue, New York, NY 10158

and by Routledge
4 Park Square, Milton Park, Abingdon, Oxon, OX14 4RN

Routledge is an imprint of the Taylor & Francis Group, an informa business

© 2024 Robert Brooks Cohen

The right of Robert Brooks Cohen to be identified as author of this work has been asserted in accordance with sections 77 and 78 of the Copyright, Designs and Patents Act 1988.

Library of Congress Cataloging-in-Publication Data
Names: Cohen, Robert Brooks, author.
Title: Bisexual married men : stories of relationships, acceptance, and authenticity / Robert Brooks Cohen.
Description: New York, NY : Routledge, 2024. | Includes bibliographical references and index.
Identifiers: LCCN 2023025826 (print) | LCCN 2023025827 (ebook) | ISBN 9781032473253 (hardback) | ISBN 9781032473260 (paperback) | ISBN 9781003385585 (ebook)
Subjects: LCSH: Bisexual men—Relations with women. | Married men.
Classification: LCC HQ74 .C64 2024 (print) | LCC HQ74 (ebook) | DDC 306.76/50811—dc23/eng/20230804
LC record available at https://lccn.loc.gov/2023025826
LC ebook record available at https://lccn.loc.gov/2023025827

ISBN: 978-1-032-47325-3 (hbk)
ISBN: 978-1-032-47326-0 (pbk)
ISBN: 978-1-003-38558-5 (ebk)

DOI: 10.4324/9781003385585

Typeset in Bembo
by Apex CoVantage, LLC

Contents

Acknowledgments

Just a few years ago, I never imagined that I could write a book like this, and even when I began this project, I didn't know what shape it would take. I did not do it and could not have done it alone, and I'm grateful to so many people who helped me on this journey.

To the editorial and production teams at Routledge, specifically Georgina Clutterbuck, for your collaboration and guidance in writing my first book, and especially to Heather Evans, who believed in this project from the beginning and has championed it throughout – I've never done it before, but I can't imagine working with a more supportive editor.

To my teachers and mentors over the years who instilled in me a love of psychology and writing, thank you all.

To Kegan Schell, James Engle, and the team at Navigation Media for supporting and promoting my career as a writer – thank you for understanding and believing in my voice.

To the Independent Writers of Southern California and Telly Davidson, thank you for your advice and many useful resources.

To Heather Genovese, thank you for helping me explore my identity, recognize my feelings, and stay true to myself.

To everyone who came out and embraced a Bi+ or queer identity before me, thank you for paving the way. I'm especially thankful for those I've met in various Bi+ communities and the leaders who organize them – BiRequest, NYABN, AmBi, LA Bi+ Task Force, Bi The Way, and others. The community support and friendships I've found in these groups have been invaluable on my journey.

To Alex Boyd, co-creator of *Two Bi Guys* – I could not have started it alone, and I wouldn't have been inspired to had we not connected at BiRequest and shared so much with each other. Thank you for the work you continue to do for the queer community.

To everyone who has listened to *Two Bi Guys* over the years, thank you for your support, engagement, and words of encouragement – it's what keeps me going.

To all the men who volunteered to be interviewed, and especially those who shared their stories for this book – you are all incredibly brave. I learned so much from your stories, and I know they will help others, too.

To my family, my biggest cheerleaders: my parents, who have always loved and supported me and who I can turn to for advice any time, and especially my mom, who has worked hard to collect and preserve the oral histories of communities she cares about and who inspired me to do the same; and my sister, who I can talk to about anything and whose courage and perseverance through difficulty inspired me to be my authentic self. I love you all so much, and I feel lucky to be part of our family.

To my wife and partner Moxie, who helped me understand and love myself at a turning point in my life, gave me the courage and companionship I needed to survive a pandemic, taught me what it means to be authentic within a marriage, and loved and supported me throughout our relationship and especially while writing this book – I love you always, dear, and I'm grateful for every minute.

And to myself a few years ago, thanks for being brave.

1

Introduction

The Hidden Lives of Bi+ Married Men

The first time I was intimate with a man, I was shocked by how familiar it felt. The touch of his hands and lips, the tingly feelings in my body, the quick emotional connection that can only come from being exposed and vulnerable – I'd felt it all before with women. I'd been taught (and I believed) that being with men was categorically different, but in an instant, my body knew otherwise.

I was 29 years old at the time. I had my first "girlfriend" at age 10, first kissed a girl at age 12, and I'd been dating and hooking up with women (exclusively) since then. It all felt natural and authentic, I had positive and loving relationships with people I cared about and found attractive, and the straight identity I had defaulted into felt fine.

Except for the other thoughts in my head. Except for the cute guys I was awkward around and didn't know why. Except for the gay porn I'd occasionally watch. Except for my group sex fantasies that involved people across the gender spectrum.

I wrote all that off as incidental and unimportant for a long time, but in my late 20s, I finally started taking those secret thoughts seriously and realized I didn't want to keep ignoring them – I wanted to explore them. I decided I couldn't turn 30 without knowing what same-sex intimacy felt like. I expected it to be a completely new, transformative experience, and it <u>was</u> transformative, but only because it was not new at all. It was so similar to everything I'd experienced with women, I couldn't believe I'd ever imagined otherwise.

DOI: 10.4324/9781003385585-1

I was suddenly confused and upset for a whole new set of reasons: how could I have been so wrong? Why had I avoided this for so long? Why did I think it would completely change who I was? What's so crazy about liking more than one gender? And how many other people like me are out there, hiding and compartmentalizing and suffering in silence?

I began to research bisexuality, a word I had heard but never really believed was an option, and everything began to make sense. I attended a bisexual discussion group in New York City called BiRequest, where people I'd never met talked about the exact same things I'd been struggling with for years. This experience helped me realize that sexual fluidity is not only normal but much more common than I thought. I also began to notice and understand the pervasive biphobia and bi-erasure in our society.

The clarity I gained from finally exploring my sexuality and then connecting with like-minded queer people completely changed my life and worldview. Since then, I've been on a mission to share what I've learned and help Bi+ people understand themselves and connect with each other, and this project is my next step toward that goal.

This book is about a specific but incredibly common subgroup of the community – Bi+ men who are married to women. I'll explain more about why I've focused on them later in this chapter, but first, the basics, or as we called it at BiRequest, "Bi+ 101".

BI+ 101: WHAT IS BISEXUALITY?

Bisexuality is often misunderstood, so let's start with some definitions of what it is and isn't. My favorite definition and the one that is most accepted and well-regarded by the Bi+ community itself was written (and updated over time) by Robyn Ochs, a prominent bisexual activist, scholar, and author. She defines bisexuality like this:

> I call myself bisexual because I acknowledge that I have in myself the potential to be attracted – romantically and/or sexually – to people of more than one gender, not necessarily at the same time, not necessarily in the same way, and not necessarily to the same degree.[1]

Many people think bisexuality includes equal, "50/50" attraction to men and women, but Ochs's definition intentionally avoids quantifying those attractions, focusing instead on the potential to be attracted to more than one gender. If it's at all possible for you to be attracted to more than one gender in any way, her definition of bisexuality can apply to you.

Ochs also separates romantic and sexual attraction, so it is inclusive of people who feel different types of attraction toward different genders (a very common Bi+ experience). For example, many men in this book have experienced sexual attraction toward more than one gender but romantic attraction only toward women, which is perfectly valid and fits this definition of bisexuality. Ochs also specifies that these attractions don't have to happen at the same time, in the same way, or to the same degree, allowing for attractions to be fluid, or changing over time, within a bisexual identity. In my experience, this is much more common in the bisexual community than attractions that are permanently fixed.

Some have argued in recent years that the "bi" in "bisexual" is too binary, especially as gender is viewed as more fluid and potentially non-binary. While the word "bi" does literally mean "two", the bisexual community has historically been inclusive of trans and non-binary people and attractions, and there is significant overlap among these identities. To address this perceived discrepancy, Ochs has added an addendum to her definition, writing:

> For me, the 'bi' in bisexual refers to the potential for attraction to people
> with genders similar to and different from my own.

So the "two" genders in "bisexual" (for those who insist on taking the word literally) now refers to genders similar to your own and different from your own. In other words, it includes everyone with attractions to more than one gender.

The term "pansexual" is another recent attempt to address that perceived discrepancy. "Pan" means "all", so people who identify as pansexual are usually attracted to all genders (or experience attraction "regardless of gender"). For most intents and purposes, this is equivalent to Ochs's definition of bisexuality. Personally, I identify as both bisexual and pansexual, because both definitions technically apply to me, but when someone else identifies themselves using one label or the other, I respect that choice. Everyone should be allowed to identify however they are most comfortable, for whatever reason.

In this book, I will also frequently use the term "Bi+" (usually pronounced "bi plus"), which is a newer umbrella term for all "fluid" identities. Where "mono-sexual" describes people who are only attracted to <u>one</u> gender (which usually includes most straight, gay, and lesbian people), Bi+ is an attempt to unify all <u>non</u>-monosexual identities, including bisexual, pansexual, and others, and to be inclusive of new labels or other marginalized identities.

While the differences between these labels can be important for individuals, it is also vital to recognize the fundamental similarities we share and to have language that unites us, because as we'll get to later in this chapter, Bi+ people are regularly marginalized, erased, stigmatized, and persecuted. Labels are a useful tool to understand an individual – they are the beginning of a conversation to get to know someone – but Bi+ is a valuable umbrella term that prevents our community from becoming too fragmented by our incredible diversity and that can help us collectively resist the stereotypes and assumptions made about us.

I will also frequently use the word "queer" in this book, a word that has recently been reclaimed from its derogatory roots. For me, "queer" is equivalent to the full "LGBT+" acronym, and I essentially use it to mean "anything other than cisgender and heterosexual". I personally like the word queer because of its linguistic connection to being different, strange, or unconventional. Though I want to normalize queerness in the sense of allowing everyone to lead safe and happy lives free of persecution, I also like the idea that being queer is inherently <u>not</u> normal and not universally accepted. By embracing queerness, we are "queering" our society, standing up for those who are different or "weird", and pushing for greater tolerance, visibility, and authenticity.

I also understand and respect that "queer" was used as a slur for decades, and many LGBT+ people are uncomfortable adopting this identity. I try not to use a "queer" label for individuals unless they've chosen it for themselves. Still, with this understanding and sensitivity, I have found immense value in this identity both personally and politically. While some use "bi" and "queer" interchangeably, I will use queer as an even larger umbrella term than Bi+, because it includes lesbian, gay, and trans people (who may identify as straight), as well as anyone else who chooses to identify as queer without necessarily adopting a more specific label (a growing trend especially among young people, who are resisting any label which could box them in).

RECOGNIZING AND MEASURING INDIVIDUAL BISEXUALITY

In a sense, Bi+ identities are unquantifiable by definition. Bisexuality is about the possibility of anything, and it includes an acceptance of fluidity and change. Still, scales that measure sexual fluidity have become a useful tool both for understanding one's own identity and also for educating and uniting the Bi+ community.

The most well-known of these is the Kinsey Scale, developed by Alfred Kinsey and others, first published in their 1948 study, *Sexual Behavior in the Human Male*. (The same scale was used in their follow-up, *Sexual Behavior in the Human Female*, in 1953.) Introducing the scale, Kinsey, who was bisexual himself, wrote:

> ALFRED KINSEY: Males do not represent two discrete populations, heterosexual and homosexual. The world is not to be divided into sheep and goats. It is a fundamental of taxonomy that nature rarely deals with discrete categories . . . The living world is a continuum in each and every one of its aspects.[2]

To represent this "continuum" or spectrum of sexuality, the Kinsey scale ranges from 0 to 6, with 0 meaning exclusively heterosexual ("hetero" meaning "different", "heterosexual" meaning attracted to a different sex than one's own) and 6 meaning exclusively homosexual ("homo" meaning "same", "homosexual" meaning attracted to the same sex as one's own). The center of the Kinsey scale would be a 3, meaning "equally heterosexual and homosexual" (a slightly outdated way to think about bisexuality, but still useful for this scale). People at a 1 or 2 are predominantly heterosexual but not exclusively, and people at a 4 or 5 are predominantly homosexual but not exclusively. There is also an "X", which falls outside the 0 to 6 scale, for people who have no sexual contacts or desires – this is commonly described as an "asexual" identity.

Kinsey assigned his research subjects their place on the scale based on their reported behaviors. These days, however, the scale is used primarily as a self-identification tool, with no set list of behaviors that determines your placement. You get to choose for yourself based on your own desires, experiences, and how important they feel to your identity.

One of the "drawbacks" of this scale is that is has seven distinct categories and no more, which of course does not reflect the infinite possibilities represented by a spectrum of sexuality, but Kinsey was aware of this. His original scale had 30 different categories representing 30 different case studies, and there was even more diversity among the 8,000+ interviews he conducted. His seven-point scale was an intentional and necessary compromise to be able to quantify and study sexual fluidity scientifically, which had largely been ignored until then. As he wrote at the time:

> ALFRED KINSEY: While emphasizing the continuity of the gradations between exclusively heterosexual and exclusively homosexual histories, it has seemed desirable to develop some sort of classification which could be based on the relative amounts of heterosexual and homosexual experience or response in each history . . . An individual may be assigned a position on this scale, for each period in his life.

Even if a seven-point scale was a bit reductive of the "gradations" along the spectrum, Kinsey knew that developing a simple method of classification would allow bisexuality to be discussed in both scientific communities and in pop culture, and he was right. The Kinsey scale changed the way people think about

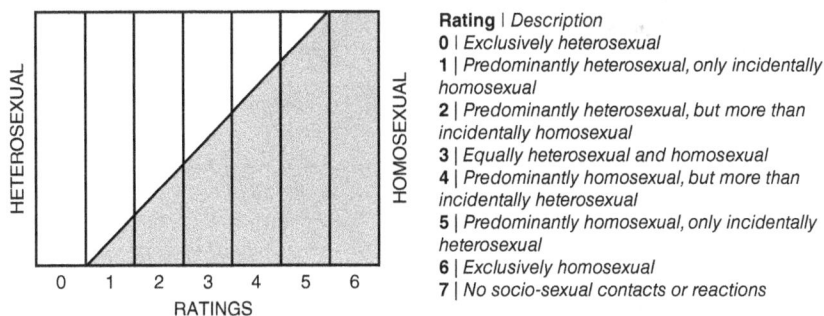

Rating | Description
0 | Exclusively heterosexual
1 | Predominantly heterosexual, only incidentally homosexual
2 | Predominantly heterosexual, but more than incidentally homosexual
3 | Equally heterosexual and homosexual
4 | Predominantly homosexual, but more than incidentally heterosexual
5 | Predominantly homosexual, only incidentally heterosexual
6 | Exclusively homosexual
7 | No socio-sexual contacts or reactions

Fig. 1.1 The Kinsey Scale.

sexuality, and it is still a valuable tool to quickly identify someone's general location on the spectrum.

In 1978 Dr. Fritz Klein, an Australian-born American psychiatrist and sex researcher, published *The Bisexual Option*, a trailblazing book on bisexuality, which included a new and more comprehensive way of quantifying sexuality: the Klein Sexual Orientation Grid. The grid uses a similar seven-point scale (although it goes from 1 to 7 instead of 0 to 6), but it allows for separate measurements on different aspects of sexuality: sexual attraction, sexual behavior, sexual fantasies, emotional preference, social preference, lifestyle preference, and self-identification. It also recognizes that each of these aspects can be fluid over time, so it separates these measurements for one's past, present, and their ideal (i.e. future).

The Klein grid gives a more complete picture than the Kinsey scale, and I love that it includes our "ideal" rather than just our past experiences, which can tap into our internal sexuality which may not have been expressed externally, but it also still has drawbacks and does not quantify all aspects of Bi+ identities. Other scales have been developed since then, such as the "Self Assessment of Sexual Orientation" and the "Multidimensional Scale of Sexuality" – I recommend researching these if you are still trying to figure out where you fit on the spectrum.

The Klein Sexuality Grid

	Variable	Past	Present	Ideal
A	Sexual Attraction			
B	Sexual Behavior			
C	Sexual Fantasies			
D	Emotional Preference			
E	Social Preference			
F	Heterosexual/Homosexual Lifestyle			
G	Self Identification			

For Variables A to E:

1 = Other sex only
2 = Other sex mostly
3 = Other sex somewhat more
4 = Both sexes
5 = Same sex somewhat more
6 = Same sex mostly
7 = Same sex only

For Variables F and G:

1 = Heterosexual only
2 = Heterosexual mostly
3 = Heterosexual somewhat more
4 = Hetero/Gay-Lesbian equally
5 = Gay/Lesbian somewhat more
6 = Gay/Lesbian mostly
7 = Gay/Lesbian only

Fig. 1.2 The Klein Sexual Orientation Grid.

Chart provided by Taylor & Francis Group.

There's one other easily digestible (and cute) way to measure sexuality that also factors in gender identity and expression. While this book is not necessarily focused on gender identity or fluidity, these are still vital aspects of sexuality, because as defined above, bisexuality is about our attractions in relation to our own gender. How can we evaluate attraction to genders "similar to" and "different from" our own without examining our own gender?

With that in mind, meet the "Genderbread Person".

The Genderbread Person clearly separates sexual attraction from romantic attraction, like Robyn Ochs does in her definition of bisexuality. Though it doesn't specifically mention non-binary gender identities, it puts "masculine" and "feminine" on separate scales that start at "zero" and go up on a continuum, allowing for various combinations and conceptions of non-binary identities. It also separates out gender identity, gender expression, and anatomical sex, which helps reframe gender as multi-faceted rather than a biological male/female binary. This is especially useful for Bi+ people, even those who fully identify with the gender they were assigned at birth, in order to sort out how we might express our own gender in queer ways as well as exactly what about another person's gender or sex is attractive to us.

The Genderbread Person does have significant drawbacks – it doesn't separate out nearly as many categories as the Klein Grid or other scales; it is not very scientifically useful because of its sliding, non-quantifiable scales; its creator has been accused of plagiarism; and more – but it's still a decent tool for visualizing the complexities of sexuality and gender. It also doesn't proscribe any label based on "results", which brings up an important point about identity that will frame this book: I believe that everyone gets to choose their own label, and that choice should be respected. The same word can mean different things to different people, and different words can mean the same thing to different people. When someone uses a label to identify themself, it doesn't tell the whole story – it's the beginning of a conversation, not the end – so my next question is usually "What does that mean for you?" A label is a quick way to connect and find each other, but we should never make assumptions based on a label alone.

RECOGNIZING AND MEASURING THE BI+ COMMUNITY

Using the tools above, as well as self-identification (arguably the most important measure), we can get a picture of how many Bi+ people are really out there, and it's more than most people realize – in fact, a majority of the queer community identifies as bisexual.

That may be shocking to some, but it's true: in the most recent Gallup poll on LGBT+ identification (conducted in 2021), 57 percent of the LGBT+ community self-identified as bisexual – compared to 21 percent who identified as

The Genderbread Person v4 *its pronounced METRO̧sexual*

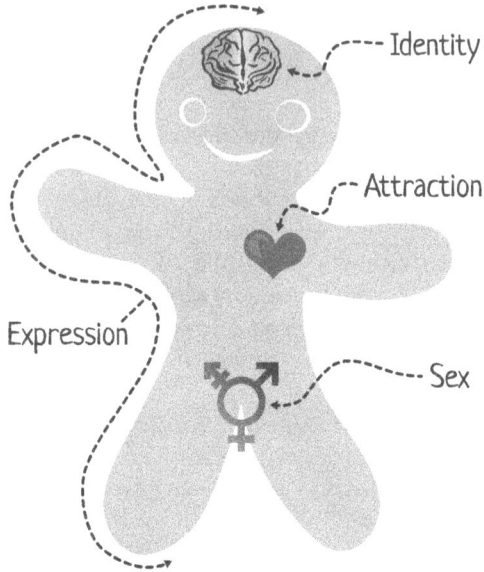

means a lack of what's on the right side

Gender Identity
→ Woman-ness
→ Man-ness

Gender Expression
→ Femininity
→ Masculinity

Anatomical Sex
→ Female-ness
→ Male-ness

Identity ≠ Expression ≠ Sex
Gender ≠ Sexual Orientation

Sex Assigned At Birth
☐ Female ☐ Intersex ☐ Male

Sexually Attracted to... and/or (a/o)
→ Women a/o Feminine a/o Female People
→ Men a/o Masculine a/o Male People

Romantically Attracted to...
→ Women a/o Feminine a/o Female People
→ Men a/o Masculine a/o Male People

Genderbread Person Version 4 created and uncopyrighted 2017 by Sam Killermann   For a bigger bite, read more at www.genderbread.org

Fig. 1.3 The Genderbread Person.

Image provided by Sam Killermann.

gay, 14 percent as lesbian, 10 percent as transgender, and 4 percent as something else.[3] Earlier studies have also shown "bisexual" to be the most common LGBT+ identity.[4]

This also comes at a time when queer identities are increasing overall – and faster than ever. In the same Gallup poll, 7.1 percent of all American adults identified as LGBT+ or something other than heterosexual, up from 5.6 percent in 2020 and <u>way</u> up from 3.5 percent in 2012. These statistics show that the number of queer people (who are willing to identify themselves) more than doubled in just nine years.

Most of that increase comes from younger generations – Millennials (me!) and especially Gen Z. In the same poll, the percentage who identify as LGBT+ was 0.8 percent for Traditionalists (born before 1946), 2.6 percent for Baby Boomers, 4.2 percent for Gen X, 10.5 percent for Millennials, and a whopping 20.8 percent for Gen Z. The number of queer people is essentially doubling with every generation.

Bisexuality is driving this trend. In the same poll, 15 percent of <u>all</u> Gen Z respondents identified as bisexual – nearly 1 out of 6 people – compared to 2.5 percent who identified as gay and 2 percent who identified as lesbian. This means that about 75 percent of queer Gen Z-ers are bisexual.

This staggering increase in sexual fluidity is reflected in other studies and in other countries, as well. In a 2015 YouGov study in the United Kingdom, respondents were asked to rate themselves on the Kinsey Scale, and 19 percent of all adults placed themselves somewhere in the middle of the spectrum (1–5)[5]. That number rose to 43 percent among 18–24-year-olds, with 6 percent identifying as a 6 on the scale (exclusively homosexual) – in other words, nearly <u>half</u> of young people in the UK identified as something other than straight, with the vast majority of those placing themselves somewhere in the middle of the sexuality spectrum.

A YouGov study of American adults in 2018 had a similar result: 20 percent of all adults placed themselves somewhere in the middle of the Kinsey spectrum, climbing to 34 percent among 18–34-year-olds.[6] Interestingly, only 3 percent of those American adults identified specifically as "bisexual", as did 7 percent of 18–34-year-olds – as we'll discuss throughout this book, labels and self-placement on the spectrum don't always "match" the way you'd expect.

There are approximately 260 million adults over 18 in the United States today – if 7.1 percent identify as LGBT+, and 57 percent of that group identifies as bisexual, then there are over 10 million bisexual-identified adults in this country right now. But there are even more people who recognize their sexual fluidity without adopting a bisexual label – if 20 percent of all American adults place themselves in the middle of the Kinsey spectrum, that translates to over 50 million people.

With somewhere between 10 and 50 <u>million</u> Bi+/fluid adults, why is bisexuality so hidden? Why do most of us know more gay and lesbian people than bisexual people? Why do gay and lesbian causes get significantly more resources than dedicated bisexual organizations?

1 in 2 young people not 100% heterosexual

British adults were asked to place themselves on the Kinsey scale, ranging from 0 (completely heterosexual) to 6 (completely homosexual)

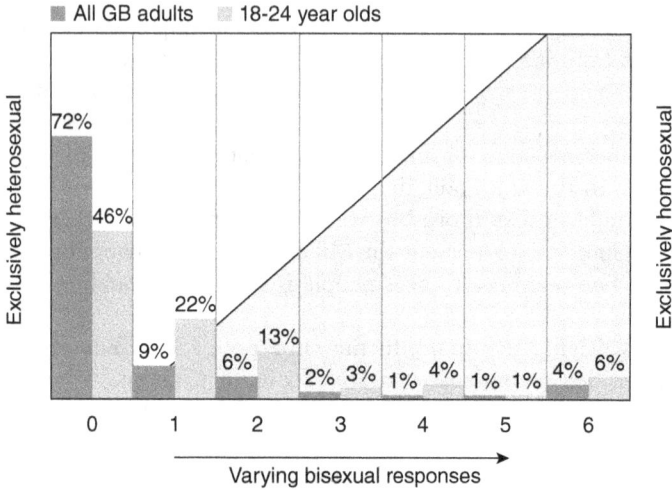

■ All GB adults   18-24 year olds

Exclusively heterosexual

Exclusively homosexual

72%

46%

22%

13%

9%

6%

2%   3%   1%   4%   1%   1%   4%   6%

0   1   2   3   4   5   6

Varying bisexual responses

Fig. 1.4 1 in 2 young people not 100% heterosexual.

Image provided by YouGov.

Over one-third of 18-to-34-year olds are not heterosexual

Please try to place your sexuality on a scale of 0 to 6, where 0 is completely heterosexual and 6 is completely homosexual. %

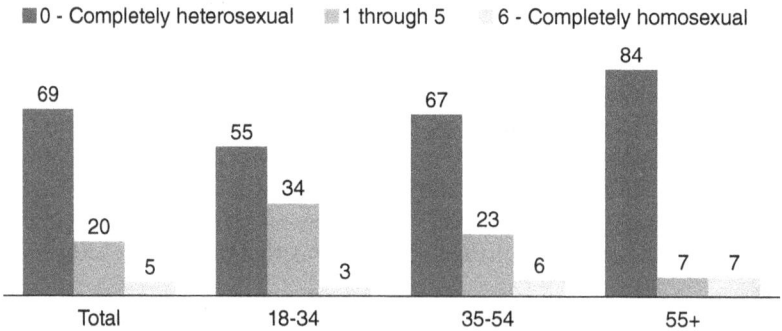

■ 0 - Completely heterosexual   ■ 1 through 5   6 - Completely homosexual

84

69   67

55

34

20   23

5   3   6   7   7

Total   18-34   35-54   55+

Fig. 1.5 Over one-third of 18-to-34-year-olds are not heterosexual.

Image provided by YouGov.

There are many reasons which I'll discuss throughout this book related to shame, stigma, and overall bi-negativity, but I believe a big and often-overlooked reason is that a majority of Bi+ people currently end up in "straight-passing" marriages, and their bisexuality becomes largely invisible. This is by far the most common Bi+ experience currently, but it has barely been represented or understood, and that is why I chose to write this specific book.

THE MARRIED BI+ EXPERIENCE

There are a few reasons why Bi+ people often end up with a partner of a different sex or gender. Perhaps the most obvious reason is homophobia – things are starting to change, but entire generations have grown up with ubiquitous homophobia which many Bi+ people internalize from a young age and which can subconsciously affect one's choice of partner. Growing up in an environment in which gay and lesbian people are discriminated against or even attacked causes many Bi+ people to downplay or compartmentalize their same-sex attractions for safety. In many places, that cultural homophobia persists today (or is even gaining traction), so there are still tangible benefits to being in a relationship that appears straight.

Another reason: statistics. Given that around 90 percent of the population currently identifies as heterosexual, the pool of potential partners for Bi+ people skews heavily toward a different gender from one's own. For example, a Bi+ man could date gay or Bi+ men, who make up about 3–4 percent of the total population combined; non-binary folks, who make up less than 1 percent of the population currently; or straight or Bi+ women, who make up nearly 50 percent of the population (over 90 percent of women). Thus, the odds alone heavily favor opposite-sex pairings, at least for now.

I see one more subtle but important reason. In both of the Kinsey scale studies above, the majority of the "middle" group ends up clustered around 1 and 2 – "mostly straight", so to speak, but not entirely. It's impossible to say if this is naturally occurring or the product of a homophobic, biphobic, heteronormative society that celebrates different-sex pairings and prioritizes biological children, but whatever the reason, people at a 1 or 2 have more sexual or romantic desire for people of a different gender than their own, so they're more likely to end up in a straight-passing marriage.

All of this helps explain why, according to an analysis by the Pew Research Center of data collected by Stanford University in 2017, 88 percent of partnered bisexual people are with someone of a different gender.[7] In that same study, 44 percent of bisexual people said they were attracted only or mostly to the opposite gender, 43 percent were attracted to men and women equally, and only 13 percent were attracted only or mostly to the same gender. These statistics can help us understand why bisexuality is so hidden: outsiders make assumptions based on our choice of partner, so without getting to know someone personally, many bisexual people "appear straight".

As you'll read about more in later chapters, in partnerships like this, many people feel their bisexuality "doesn't matter" or is immaterial to their lives. A 2015 Pew Research Center poll found that only 20 percent of bisexual people said their sexual orientation is "extremely important" to their identity, compared to 48 percent of gay men and 50 percent of lesbian women.[8]

If bisexuality doesn't feel "important" to Bi+ people, they are less likely to come out – and that's exactly what's happening, to an almost unbelievable degree. In the same Pew analysis of 2017 data, only 19 percent of bisexual people said that all or most of the important people in their life are aware of their sexual orientation (i.e. they've "come out") – compared to 75 percent of gay and lesbian people.

This single statistic explains the unfortunate Bi+ landscape so well. We are the vast majority of the queer community, but because we so often end up in straight-passing marriages that downplay the importance of our queerness, only

About nine-in-ten partnered bisexuals are in opposite-sex relationships

% of those who identify as straight, bisexual or gay or lesbian saying they are ...

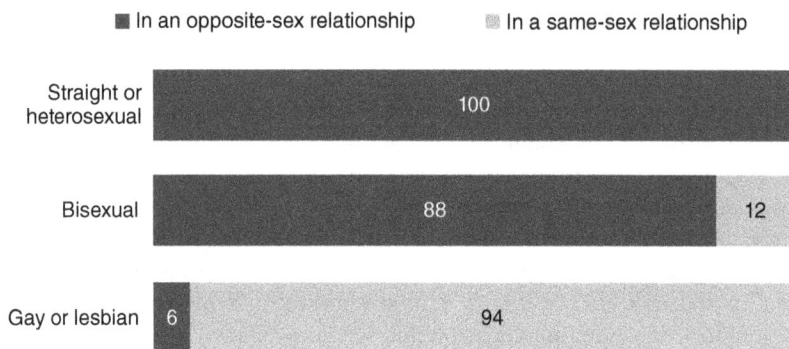

■ In an opposite-sex relationship   ▨ In a same-sex relationship

Straight or heterosexual	100	
Bisexual	88	12
Gay or lesbian	6	94

Note: Includes only those who are currently or have ever been in a relationship or married. Those who are not currently in a relationship or married were asked about their most recent relationship. The question asked only about relationships between people of the same or opposite sex, even though some may be in relationships with people who don't identify as male or female.
Source: How Couples Meet and Stay Together 2017 survey (fresh sample), conducted by Stanford University July 13-Aug. 1, 2017.

PEW RESEARCH CENTER

Fig. 1.6 About nine-in-ten partnered bisexuals are in opposite-sex relationships.

Image provided by Pew Research Center.

About four-in-ten bisexual adults say they are attracted to men and women equally

% of those who identify as straight, bisexual or gay or lesbian saying they are sexually attracted ...

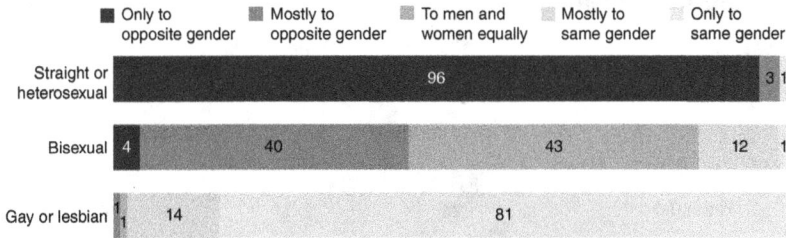

	■ Only to opposite gender	■ Mostly to opposite gender	▨ To men and women equally	▨ Mostly to same gender	▨ Only to same gender
Straight or heterosexual		96			3 1
Bisexual	4	40	43	12	1
Gay or lesbian	1	14	81		

Note: Includes only those who are currently or have ever been in a relationship or married. Share of respondents who didn't offer an answer not shown. The question asked only about attraction to people of the same or opposite gender, even though some may be attracted to people who don't identify as a man or a woman.
Source: How Couples Meet and Stay Together 2017 survey (fresh sample), conducted by Stanford University July 13-Aug. 1, 2017.

PEW RESEARCH CENTER

Fig. 1.7 About four-in-ten bisexual adults say they are attracted to men and women equally.

Image provided by Pew Research Center.

Bisexuals Less Likely to Say Sexual Orientation is Important to Their Identity

Percent who say being LGBT is ... important to their overall identity

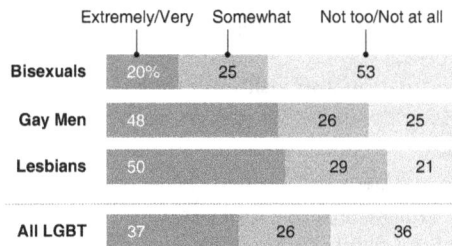

	Extremely/Very	Somewhat	Not too/Not at all
Bisexuals	20%	25	53
Gay Men	48	26	25
Lesbians	50	29	21
All LGBT	37	26	36

Notes: Based on all LGBT (N=1,197). Responses for transgender adults are not broken out due to small sample size but are included in the total for LGBT. Respondents' individual sexual or gender identities were inserted; for example, lesbians were asked how important "being lesbian" is ....

PEW RESEARCH CENTER

Fig. 1.8 Bisexuals less likely to say sexual orientation is important to their identity.

Image provided by Pew Research Center.

Bisexuals are far less likely to be 'out' to the important people in their life

%of those who identify as bisexual or gay or lesbian saying that ____ of the important people in their life are aware of their sexual orientation

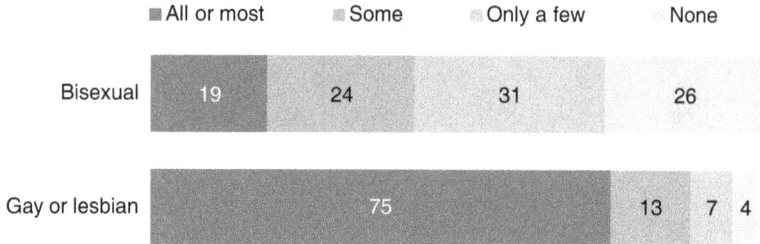

	■ All or most	▨ Some	▧ Only a few	None
Bisexual	19	24	31	26
Gay or lesbian	75		13	7 4

Note: Includes only those who are currently or have ever been in a relationship or married. Share of respondents who didn't offer an answer not shown.
Source: How Couples Meet and Stay Together 2017 survey (fresh sample), conducted by Stanford University July 13-Aug. 1, 2017.

PEW RESEARCH CENTER

Fig. 1.9 Bisexuals are far less likely to be "out" to the important people in their life.

Image provided by Pew Research Center.

about one in five of us come out, creating a vicious cycle of invisibility, repression, shame, and erasure.

That lack of representation and visibility is even worse among Bi+ men. In a 2013 Pew Research Center survey, 28 percent of bisexual people said they were out to "all or most of the important people in their lives" – slightly higher than the 19 percent of bisexual people who said the same in 2017, oddly (perhaps due to random variation) – but when they broke it down by gender, 33 percent of Bi+ women said they were out, while only 12 percent of Bi+ men said they were out.[9]

Let me repeat that and give it its own paragraph, because it's the most important statistic to contextualize the stories in this book: only 12 percent of Bi+ men are out to all or most of the important people in their lives.

In the same Pew survey, 77 percent of gay men said they were out, and 71 percent of lesbian women said they were out, so the biggest discrepancy is among men, perhaps because of added stigma surrounding masculinity and fluidity. It makes sense that Bi+ men are both more likely to be closeted and more likely to end up with women, although either could cause the other: a closeted Bi+ man is more likely to marry a woman (it's pretty hard to date men if you're not out!), and a Bi+ guy with a woman is more likely to remain closeted (and feel that their bisexuality is "not important").

While there may be tangible benefits to remaining closeted in a homophobic society, this "choice" to repress or hide a queer identity takes a huge toll on Bi+ men, especially within straight-passing marriages. We'll explore this in-depth in later chapters, but according to a 2020 study by psychologist Kristen Mark, simply acknowledging a bisexual identity improves sexual and relationship satisfaction of Bi+ couples.[10] If 88 percent of Bi+ men do not acknowledge their bisexuality, a lot of relationships are potentially suffering.

Bisexual men who are married to women are thus one of the largest but most invisible queer groups in this country. Their experience is uniquely challenging and joyful, but it is barely represented and often erased as "not queer enough". I believe that Bi+ people are queer, and even in monogamous, "straight-passing" marriages, their queerness matters – in fact, it is fundamental to their lives. It has a huge effect on their relationships, their careers, their worldviews, and their mental health in complex ways that have rarely been explored critically.

My focus in this book is on Bi+ married men so that they can see their experience represented and feel more comfortable embracing their whole selves, but this book is also for their partners, family, and friends – as well as students, researchers, clinicians with bisexual clients, and allies – so that they can better understand the challenges of this identity and provide meaningful support. Given the hidden prevalence of Bi+ men, nearly everyone can benefit from these stories.

I also believe that precisely because of our hidden prevalence, Bi+ men have enormous potential for progress and change, both for ourselves and for the queer community. We often feel caught "in between" straight and queer culture, but we can use that to our advantage and become bridge-builders. We can help normalize

How Many People Know?

% saying all or most of the important people in their life are aware that they are LGBT

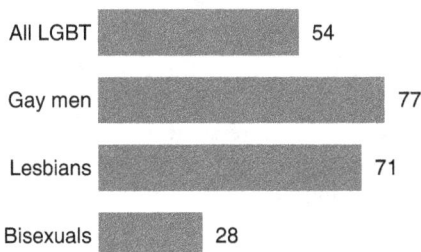

All LGBT	54
Gay men	77
Lesbians	71
Bisexuals	28

Note: Based on all LGBT (N=1,197).

PEW RESEARCH CENTER   LGBT/49

Fig. 1.10 How many people know?

Image provided by Pew Research Center.

queerness within the straight communities that we often inhabit, and we can expand what it means and looks like to be queer at the same time.

MY BISEXUAL JOURNEY

For a long time, I viewed sexuality as binary and didn't see any possibility besides "straight" or "gay". I knew that I liked women and enjoyed sex with women, and that was all the proof I needed to call myself straight. It felt easy and natural to identify this way.

But this "decision" and binary way of thinking caused me to subconsciously repress my attractions toward men. In my late 20s (perhaps because I was reading more about bisexuality and seeing an ever-so-slight increase in Bi+ representation), I became more aware of my same-sex attractions. I started watching gay porn, usually featuring straight-identified guys who for some reason were having sex with each other ("gay-for-pay" and fraternity hazing were my favorite "justifications"). I began noticing guys in real life who I thought were hot, and I had fantasies about exploring sex with men.

Suddenly, it was no longer "easy" to identify as straight – and over time, it was torturous. I felt like I had to lie and censor myself whenever the topic came up. Even though I was aware of my attractions, I thought I'd take them to the grave. I was terrified that if I shared them, everyone would think I was really gay. And in any case, I was pretty sure that I still wanted to marry a woman, so why did anyone need to know what was going on inside my head? I didn't think it mattered. I struggled with this for a few years, and I felt completely alone during that time. My relationships with women often ended quickly, because I couldn't open up to them fully.

When I began exploring intimacy and sex with men, it was enjoyable, but it was also confusing. It felt so familiar and natural, and yet I feared that coming out would completely change my life in ways I didn't want. I didn't think anyone would believe that I was really bisexual.

But eventually, I couldn't live with these contradictions unless I talked about them. When I finally attended a BiRequest meeting, everything changed. I expected to sit in the back and just listen, but soon I was explaining to a room of 40 people exactly why I was there and what I was struggling with. To my surprise, they nodded along, understanding my story.

It's one thing to read about that online or in a book like this, but it was another to feel the energy in that room, to hear other people's stories directly, to put myself out there in front of strangers and get positive feedback. They saw their bisexuality not just as acceptable but something to celebrate and cherish – and I slowly started to believe that, too.

It was a turning point in my conception of sexuality and of myself. I no longer felt so alone or "crazy" – instead, I gained confidence in my identity. I re-entered the dating pool with an open mind, exploring new things and learning about the nuances of my orientation. At first, I thought I was attracted more to men sexually and to women romantically, but even that proved to be fluid, as I soon realized I was capable of emotional and romantic connections with anyone, regardless of gender. Within a few months, I started coming out to friends and family.

I began reading more books and articles about sexual fluidity, learning about the many different ways to be bisexual. I started to connect my progressive politics and worldview with my new understanding of the gender spectrum. But I still had trouble finding other experiences that matched mine. I didn't feel "very queer" at the time – I felt like a "mostly-straight" guy taking a timid step into a new queer world – but what I was reading mostly came from "very queer" scholars and activists, usually women. Even at BiRequest, it took a while to meet other Bi+ guys around my age with similar trajectories. I tried to find a podcast or documentary series about male bisexuality, but nothing worthwhile existed.

A few months into my coming out process, I was featured in an episode of *Slutever* (a shortlived show on Vice TV) about male bisexuality, along with my friend Alex and others from BiRequest. We loved sharing our stories, but in the end, the show only used about five minutes of the 90 we recorded, and we wanted to share the rest – and more! The night that episode aired, Alex and I chatted about starting our own podcast where we could discuss male bisexuality and related issues in depth – and *Two Bi Guys* was born.

Alex and I hosted and produced the first season of ten episodes together. Alex had identified as gay before he realized he was Bi+, so our stories were "opposite" but complementary. Though we arrived at our identities in different ways, we had very similar views on the freedom and expansiveness that bisexuality offers. We chatted with each other, telling our stories, and we also interviewed some prominent bisexual activists, scholars, and artists. The response was overwhelming – our listeners grew with each episode, and we began receiving dozens and soon hundreds of personal messages on social media from people who identified with what we were saying, thanking us for helping them feel less alone.

We paused the podcast when the Covid-19 pandemic hit, and Alex soon got a job working at the Trevor Project, an organization dedicated to improving the mental health of LGBT+ young people and preventing suicide. I resumed the podcast later in 2020, and Alex still makes occasional guest appearances, but he has primarily focused on his work at Trevor. I continued the podcast, and we're now five seasons in with over 200,000 downloads across 50 episodes.

Over time, I noticed that we got the most engagement when we discussed one topic in particular: Bi+ men who are married to women. Our first season finale focused on this experience, and we got more social media messages than ever before.

> "Thank you so much for this podcast, and especially the topic of married bi men. I am one of those men. I'm still learning to navigate all this, it's good to not feel so alone."

"This podcast has become vital to my journey of discovering my sexuality. As a 36 year old bi guy in a opposite sex marriage, I'm needing this conversation more than anything."

"I found *Two Bi Guys* during an especially vulnerable time. I was feeling isolated, alone, and shameful, especially as a father and someone in a straight-presenting marriage. Listening has been such a gift. Thanks for making me feel seen and good about who I am."

"I just wanted to tell you how happy I am to have discovered your podcast. I am married to an awesome woman for 11 years who is totally supportive, understanding, and affirming of my bisexuality. But I have been DYING forever for the kinds of discussions and information you share on your podcast."

I realized that a large portion of our listeners identified this way – which makes sense, based on the statistics I've laid out – and we were one of the only podcasts talking about this hidden experience. So I reached out to some of the men who had contacted us about that episode, and I asked them to share their story with me.

My mom is a (wonderful) teacher and writer, and she's recently done a lot of work on oral histories, so I consulted with her, studied her methods, and conducted oral history interviews with these men. An oral history is different from a journalistic interview or the types of conversations I have on *Two Bi Guys* – it is not about getting answers to specific questions but rather about allowing the subject to reflect, recollect, and share memories that matter most. My job was mostly to listen, allowing for depth, and sometimes to elicit aspects of a story or steer as needed. Over an hour or two on Zoom, I tried to create a safe space for each interviewee to open up about their bisexuality, coming out, getting married, and navigating their relationship. I transcribed and edited the interviews, and this book is the result.

Though I was not married myself when I began this project, marriage and commitment were clearly on my mind. I met my partner Moxie in 2018, and during the pandemic, we started to think about getting married. Though Moxie identified and presented as a man when we met, she came out to me as non-binary within a month of dating, and a year or two later came out as a trans woman and began transitioning medically. Over that time, I found that my romantic, sexual, and emotional feelings for her were not affected by her gender transition – if anything, my feelings deepened, because she was becoming her authentic self.

I knew very few Bi+ men married to women at the time, and none my age. I had no clue what these partnerships looked like. I didn't know what the challenges would be, and I didn't know anyone who had overcome them. I knew on some level that I needed better models for this type of relationship, and I also wanted help navigating non-monogamy.

My relationship developed quickly alongside the men I interviewed: Moxie and I got married in 2021, and we are currently polyamorous, dating and exploring with other partners, too. I needed to hear these stories as much as I wanted to share them with others, and I am grateful for everything they taught me at an important moment in my life.

For me, bisexuality is about more than just sex or dating – it's an entire worldview, one that challenges assumptions and binaries and affects many types of interpersonal relationships. It opens the door to examining other aspects of our lives, like pleasure, kink, relationship structures, and communication, forcing us to question "rules", norms, and authority figures and instead build relationships that work for those involved, from the ground up.

Bisexuality is intersectional, connecting me in tangible ways to other marginalized and oppressed people, affecting my entire political ideology. These connections helped me to understand my own white and male privilege in new ways and recommit to anti-racism and dismantling patriarchy. My bisexuality also allows me to see past the way the world is and "always has been" and imagine entirely new systems and ways of living that challenge the status quo across multiple social hierarchies. I thought I was alone in this worldview for many years, but coming out proved I was not. Now I want to share that discovery with the large number of Bi+ men that I know exist, especially those in straight-passing marriages and those who might not be out yet.

THE NECESSITY AND URGENCY OF THESE STORIES

Because of the unique stigma of male bisexuality, many bisexual men only come out to their wives after marriage, if ever, and because monogamy is the default in our society, many never get a chance to explore their same-sex attractions before tying the knot. Many of these men live in fear and shame. They know few or no other Bi+ men who they can share their feelings and concerns with. If they do come out to their wives, it can be difficult for both of them to navigate without a like-minded community, which is often impossible to find.

These men need to hear each other's stories for support and growth. Queer representation in media is increasing, but the specific dynamics of Bi+ men in relationships with women are still not being fully explored, despite their hidden prevalence. Whatever prompted you to pick up this book, I hope that these personal narratives will answer (or at least help you think about) the following questions.

- ◆ How does sexual fluidity impact straight-appearing marriages and long-term committed relationships?
- ◆ What helps these relationships succeed, and what contributes to them ending? In a community that is rethinking heteronormativity and traditional relationship models, how do we even determine what "success" means?
- ◆ How does coming out before or after marriage affect a relationship as well as the lives of each partner?

◆ How do open, swinger, and poly couples navigate non-monogamy along-side sexual fluidity?

◆ How can Bi+ people better communicate with their partners, and vice versa?

Bisexual people have a unique ability to think outside the box; after all, to recognize one's own sexual fluidity in a culture that is dominated by binary thinking is no easy feat. But to do so within a "traditional", straight-passing marriage – especially if the other partner identifies as straight – can causes unique interpersonal conflicts and internal cognitive dissonance. This book does not contain all the answers, but I believe that learning about how other Bi+ men have navigated these challenges is a helpful start.

AN ORAL HISTORY, STRAIGHT FROM THE SOURCE

This book contains 13 interviews with Bi+ men as well as two of their wives. I conducted the first seven interviews in 2020 and the remaining six in 2022 (with some follow-ups in 2023), after I knew this book would be published. I interviewed them anonymously, changing everyone's name and removing identifying details, so that they would feel completely comfortable sharing personal struggles and sensitive relationship dynamics. I talked to men from all over the country, from diverse backgrounds, with different relationship structures and outcomes. I have framed these interviews and given them context with my own thoughts on queerness and fluidity, as well as some of my life experience as a Bi+ married man.

I was a psychology major in college, and I've always identified as a scientist at heart, curious to research, experiment, and discover how our world works. However, I did not know I was bisexual at the time, so I didn't focus on gender/sexuality studies or queer theory (now I wish I had). Since then, I have pursued a career as a writer and creator (I spent seven years writing for *Law & Order: SVU*, among other TV shows), and I have no postgraduate education in psychology or any related field (my MFA is from NYU in "dramatic writing"). Thus, this book is not an academic text, and it does not present new theories or synthesize any major findings in the field of queer studies. Instead, it offers real people's stories, transcribed and edited, along with my personal observations and experiences. Think of it as an extension of my podcast. Here and there, I'll also explain how certain books I've read and queer scholars I've followed have affected my development and worldview.

Though I studied the scientific method as a psychology student and even conducted some original research, this book is not a formal research study. First, and most importantly, the sample is not random. The interviewees are mostly people who have listened to my podcast and volunteered to participate. In 2020,

I interviewed seven of about a dozen people who volunteered, and when I put out another call for participants in 2022, I got about 150 responses and chose six people whose stories seemed interesting to me and different from each other. Still, these 13 interviews could have similarities simply because of what I was drawn to, or because of what type of people were drawn to my podcast. There are likely many Bi+ experiences that will not be represented here, so overall conclusions about the Bi+ community should not necessarily be drawn based on what is common or uncommon in this book.

While I did attempt to conduct these interviews in a uniform manner, this was not strict or scientific. I asked different people different questions, attempting to uncover the most difficult and dramatic aspects of each story. I did not ask many questions with quantifiable answers that could be compared to each other statistically. The length of each interview was different, and some required follow-ups. I knew where some stories were going based on survey responses, so as an interviewer, I was not "blind" and may have influenced the storytelling with leading questions.

My goal was to provide a safe space for each interviewee to be vulnerable and share their story as openly and clearly as possible. I tried to help shape them dramatically, with a narrative arc, so that readers could immerse themselves in each scenario. When I noticed similarities among stories or with my own experience, I tried to point them out so that Bi+ men and others reading this can find connections in what is often an isolating experience.

While this book is not an academic text nor a scientific study, I hope it can serve as a self-help aid for anyone struggling with this identity or anyone in relationships with or providing support for Bi+ people. I also view this project as part of the Bi+ activist movement: as with my podcast, my goal is to normalize these experiences and expose them to a wider audience so that our community is more visible, better understood, and taken more seriously, and also so that we can better connect with each other in solidarity for political purposes, because as I'll discuss in later chapters, Bi+ people are often left behind to fend for ourselves.

OUT OF MULTIPLE BISEXUALITIES, A COMMON EXPERIENCE

There are infinite ways to be bisexual. It's the most diverse community I've ever been a part of. It is queer, subversive, and marginalized from heteronormative society. It is an identity that forces us to think differently, lean into our "quirks" and non-conforming thought patterns, and accept ourselves and each other with radical empathy.

This book is about all that in theory, but in practice, it's about one large, invisible subgroup: Bi+ men who are married to women. Many of us lead similar, parallel lives without ever realizing it. This is one of the most underrepresented groups in the entire LGBT+ community, which is why I've decided to focus on them in this book.

We live in a heteronormative, binary society that makes coming out as Bi+ uniquely challenging, and because of this, many men who would naturally experience sexually fluidity repress it from a young age to fit in. It's impossible to know how many men like this are really out there, because eventually that repression can take hold and become real. You can't come out (to your wife, friends, or family) if you never fully examine your own sexuality and accept your queer desires.

This book is about men who <u>have</u> accepted their bisexuality, who have at least begun the process of coming out, and who consciously volunteered to share their stories with me. They are all different, and they each reflect the infinite possibilities in a fluid identity – but there are similarities in their stories, because they're all fighting similar battles of erasure, shame, and misunderstanding. I learned that their marriages are uniquely challenging – like all marriages. I learned that there can be jealousy, miscommunication, and yes, cheating – like all marriages. But I also learned that these marriages can work and can be as joyful and meaningful as any other, if not more so; that with the right mix of open-mindedness and honesty, any obstacle can be surmounted; and that sometimes overcoming adversity together creates an even stronger marital bond.

Relationships are really fucking hard, but they're also immeasurably beautiful, sometimes especially when they're hard – a concept that Bi+ people, who have experience with duality and accepting seemingly contradictory ideas, should have a unique ability to understand. As we used to say at my old job …

These are their stories.

NOTES

1.   Ochs, R. *Bisexual.* https://robynochs.com/bisexual

2.   Kinsey, A. C., Pomeroy, W. R., Martin, C. E. (1948). *Sexual Behavior in the Human Male.* W.B. Saunders.

3.   Jones, J. M. (2022). LGBT Identification in U.S. Ticks Up to 7.1 percent. *Gallup.* https://news.gallup.com/poll/389792/lgbt-identification-ticks-up.aspx

4.   Gates, G. J. (2011). How Many People are Lesbian, Gay, Bisexual, and Transgender? *Williams Institute.* https://williamsinstitute.law.ucla.edu/publications/how-many-people-lgbt/

5.   Dahlgreen, W., Shakespeare, A.-E. (2015). 1 in 2 young people say they are not 100% heterosexual. *YouGov.* https://yougov.co.uk/topics/society/articles-reports/2015/08/16/half-young-not-heterosexual

6.   Ballard, J. (2018). More young Americans now identify as bisexual. *YouGov.* https://today.yougov.com/topics/society/articles-reports/2018/06/18/more-young-americans-now-identify-bisexual

7.   Brown, A. (2019). Bisexual adults are far less likely than gay men and lesbians to be "out" to the people in their lives. *Pew Research Center, Washington, D.C.* https://www.pewresearch.org/fact-tank/2019/06/18/bisexual-adults-are-far-less-likely-than-gay-men-and-lesbians-to-be-out-to-the-people-in-their-lives/ Source: How Couples Meet and Stay Together. *Stanford University.* July 13-Aug 1, 2017.

8. Parker, K. (2015). Among LGBT Americans, bisexuals stand out when it comes to identity, acceptance. *Pew Research Center, Washington, D.C.* https://www.pewresearch.org/fact-tank/2015/02/20/among-lgbt-americans-bisexuals-stand-out-when-it-comes-to-identity-acceptance/

9. (2013). A Survey of LGBT Americans. *Pew Research Center, Washington, D.C.* https://www.pewresearch.org/social-trends/2013/06/13/a-survey-of-lgbt-americans/

10. Mark, K. P., Vowels, L. M., Bunting, A. M. (2020). The Impact of Bisexual Identity on Sexual and Relationship Satisfaction of Mixed Sex Couples. *Journal of Bisexuality.* https://www.kristenmark.com/wp-content/uploads/2021/08/Mark_Vowels_Bunting_2020.pdf

2

Gregory and How "Weirdness" Unlocks Queer Possibilities

I was born in 1972 in the South Bronx, in an area called Soundview. Routinely in the top three most dangerous neighborhoods in the Bronx. Lived there most of my life in a New York City housing project until I went to college.

My earliest memories are actually fond. And we were really, really poor. I grew up on public assistance, two blocks from both my grandmothers, four blocks from my great-aunt. My parents met because my grandmothers lived in buildings facing each other. My mom was 20 when I was born. My dad was 19. My mom, she's never worked [since] I was born. My dad is a structural engineer.

From the mid-eighties through really the nineties, it was a pretty rough place. [That had] a lot to do with the crack epidemic. But I was lucky: my family was well known. My parents, my grandma had a lot of respect as elders, so people didn't really mess with us.

Gregory is a Black, bisexual, cisgender man living in New York City. Born in 1972 in the South Bronx, he was 50 years old at the time of our interview in 2022. He describes his race as mixed (Black/white/Asian). He grew up low income and currently identifies as "well off". He describes himself as religiously agnostic.

DOI: 10.4324/9781003385585-2

For this project, I began every interview by asking where and when the interviewee was born, what his childhood was like, and to tell me a bit about his parents. Some people got through all that quickly – they were ready to talk about their sexuality! But Gregory had a lot to say about his parents that provides valuable context for his own self-discovery.

[My parents] did not stay together. Their personalities … you would think decades of therapy would make this question easier to answer [laughs]. My father was somewhat of a mini gangster. When I was young, he had really bad drug problems. He was one of those people who's so talented at what he does that people kept giving him chances, even when he was fucking up royally.

I have keenly felt in a lot of spaces, in high school, at Harvard, that if I mess up, I could lose everything. There's very little room for error for me. But he just got every chance, could do tons of drugs, any number of illegal things, not get caught. Friends of his went to jail, were killed, died of overdoses – he's fine in the end. Went through three marriages. When we have family events, all of these ex-wives come, and I'm like, "How does this guy fucking deserve this?" All of his kids love him, including me, even though he's impossible to get along with.

He's incredibly loving, also. I hug and kiss my dad every time I see him, he tells me he loves me all the time. But sometimes when how he acts doesn't match what he says or what you know he feels, that makes it harder.

We'd do family things together, and he would always take us to this really shitty Chinese restaurant in the Bronx. Finally, I was like, "The food is not good, why do we always come here?" And he's like, "When I was messing around, me and Steve robbed this place at gunpoint and locked everyone in the freezer. I felt guilty about it, so I called the cops to tell them they were in the freezer, from a payphone." Bringing us there years later was like him working off this guilt-ridden cosmic debt. But of course he would never fully admit it. That's my dad.

I find this duality fascinating. It must feel confusing to love someone who is "impossible" to get along with, to see someone succeed when they are obviously fucking up, to receive honest affection from someone who can't be honest about his actions.

But Gregory is aware of all this, and he's accepted it, which I find even more interesting. I think bisexual people must eventually embrace duality and contradiction in order to accept themselves – or, put another way, life experiences that allow us to embrace duality may be a helpful foundation for recognizing our own bisexuality.

My mom and my grandma raised me. I love my mom. It's hard for me to be objective about her, even the way she's difficult and challenging, because she is my heart. We were there for each other when my dad was at his worst.

Raised four boys out of the projects, all went to college. I was really lucky, we grew up in an incredibly affectionate household. And that's why with friends, with partners, with lovers, being affectionate is my default.

I'm mixed race, which is important to a lot of this story. My mom is Black, but my dad is half-Filipino and half-Polish, and being mixed race really set the tone of not understanding where I fit in. I was mostly raised by my mom, so I feel culturally Black, but when you look at me, I'm not Black. My brother, who looks a lot like me, just says, "Oh, I'm Black." But I like to joke that when people meet us, we are of indeterminate racial background. People put on us whatever they think.

Gregory didn't quite fit in and felt he was caught between multiple worlds, long before any awareness of sexuality. Gregory's mixed racial identity likely gave him an early understanding of being "different" – but that wasn't the only thing that made him stand apart.

I was a smaller kid when I was younger. I was really nervous, I didn't want any attention called to me. I never felt particularly tough or masculine in a traditional sense. I was nerdy, I liked to read, I always did really well in school. None of [that was] valued highly in that neighborhood by other kids.

I also went to elementary school out of district. The school districts changed in between my house and my grandmother's house. So I essentially lived with her when I was really young to go to that school. It wasn't a big deal, my mom and dad literally lived two blocks away, right? But each housing project, it's like a different world, a different culture, a different community. And I was straddling between two: Soundview, where my mom and my siblings lived, and Bronxville, where my grandmothers and most of my friends lived.

I had a very small close group of friends. I was never "cool". I had a reputation [as] the smart kid – people knew me because I wound up skipping a grade. I had resisted it for a long time, but my reading level was so high in third grade, they were making me go up to the fourth grade class to read, and that was so embarrassing. I was like "Just skip me, because I can't do this back and forth." And when I got into Harvard, it was like I was a mythological figure, like, "That's the kid who went to Harvard." So I always had attention on me that felt unwanted, that highlighted how I was different.

Gregory described standing out because of his intellect, and he's not the first queer person I've met who seems "too smart to be straight". (Don't tell any straight people I said that.) And okay, maybe comfort with duality doesn't extend to being in two grades at once … but accepting himself as a fourth-grader helped prepare Gregory for similar challenges in the future.

When I was a kid and started coming into my sexual awareness, I knew I was really sexually attracted to women, but I also knew that I was attracted to men. I remember finding some of my dad's [pornography], and it was fairly explicit. And even then, like, you know, looking … I knew you're supposed to like women, right? That's what everything's telling you. But seeing naked guys, seeing erect penises and things like that, I was like, "Wow, that's pretty exciting, as well."

But I was not about to be open about anything else that made me feel more different than I already did. 'Cause at every point in my life I felt like, "You don't quite fit in." There's not one race that you belong to. You're split between two physical neighborhoods. You don't fit into your class, and then you physically go to a different school miles away. Everything was like, I am different.

It was at the same time I started to feel like I didn't wanna sleep with clothes on any more. I was viscerally into nudism. I didn't want to be different. I was a teenager. But I just kept doing things or feeling things or being things that were different.

Though Gregory recognized his multi-gender attractions early, his desire to fit in put him into the closet quickly. This was psychically challenging in the long run, but it may have felt natural in the moment, because he already had experience downplaying other things that made him "different".

It's notable that Gregory first recognized his interest in nudism around the same time. Once we notice our non-conforming gender attractions, we may be more open to seeing other interests that fall outside the norm, like nudism, even if they're totally unrelated to gender or sex (and vice versa – if we have an undeniable interest that crosses the gender spectrum, it can open us up to sexual fluidity). Gregory explained how and why he got into it.

I am incredibly insecure about so many things. My parents were so relaxed about nudity, it was never a shameful thing in the house. As I got older, I realized, "Oh, there are people who do this. This is a thing." First experience was at a beach, and I went swimming. How my body felt, just being free and out in nature … I have to tell you, I hate swimming with bathing suits now.

It's not about sex. It's funny because when I think about meeting up with someone that I may sleep with, I'm so self-conscious about my body and looks. But yesterday I went with two friends to a Korean spa for six hours, didn't think about how I looked once. And there were a lot of good-looking guys there. I've been in a lot of social nudist spaces, and every time it's been a really positive experience. I love how it feels, and I've met some really great people.

We continued talking about Gregory's dating and relationships growing up.

I started dating when I got into middle school. Eighth grade, I got a girlfriend, and we dated for like six years, into our freshman year of college.

I think about how crazy sexually active we were. She's who I lost my virginity to, I had just turned 15.

Once I got into college, having only dated one person, I was like, again, not thinking about any … like, I was never … I acknowledged to myself, oh, you're sexually attracted to men, right? But I never was convinced at that point, like, oh, you could have a relationship with … or even do anything with one, right? I was content to just be a spectator in that area. So I was serially monogamous, in mostly long-term relationships with a series of women that I cared a lot about. I'm still friends with all of them. Two of them, I went to their weddings.

It wasn't until I graduated and moved to San Francisco – duh – to start a theater company, that I actually acted on any attraction that I had to men. It was sort of like edging closer to it. I lived four blocks from Castro, and you could go to this kabuki spa in Japan town and just hang out naked with guys. I did that a lot. That led to very casual things … like I'm gonna get a massage from this guy, but it's gonna have a happy ending. That was probably my first time, like being, you know … I probably had in my mind, "Okay, if nothing happens, I'm gonna be okay. 'Cause I just love massages." But I secretly wanted something to happen. And that sort of opened up, I don't wanna say the floodgates, it didn't go that far. But it really did get me on like, oh, okay. Like this is … I like that. You know?

I've edited every interview in this book for clarity and concision, but I've kept certain passages intact, verbatim, to show how people actually talk about sexuality. Gregory was extremely open and honest throughout our chat, but even he danced around certain ideas and phrases, used euphemisms, and trailed off to avoid explicit descriptions of sex when we started talking about men. In my experience, this is a common theme among Bi+ men, and I can't help but wonder if it's related to how hidden and misunderstood male bisexuality is. Nearly all of us, even those who eventually come out, have spent some time in the bisexual closet, so we learn how to talk about ourselves without being explicit, how to give subtle hints without confirming anything to a potential homophobe or biphobe.

One of the things I love about women is the sense of softness, of gentleness, and intimacy. I had in my head that you couldn't have that with a guy, even though I feel I'm like that as a guy. That's why I'm kinda glad my first sexual experience with a man was getting a happy ending massage because it was actually super nice and sweet and gentle. I was like, "Oh, there's a range of interactions that you can have." It doesn't have to be this thing I had built up in my head, that the only thing you can do is pick up somebody in a bar and they're gonna take you home and throw you over the bed and start fucking you.

I knew that Gregory eventually came out publicly, so I asked how he got over that hump and became comfortable in his own skin. His answer surprised me.

My whole college experience was trying to own the various parts of who I was. You're weird, right? In a lot of ways. And so how can we be good with that? How can we enjoy that? And I swear this is gonna sound crazy, but the way I got to that was because of "Hello Kitty".

The distance in age between me and my youngest siblings [is] about 16 years. When I moved to California, right after I graduated from college, they were kids, so I decided I was gonna write them letters to stay in touch. I was looking for stationery, and there was a three-story Sanrio store, Hello Kitty's parent company. I found all this cool stationery with little stickers and things. I started writing them letters and I kept going back to the store, and I was like, "I really like this stuff. This stuff is really cute." So I started buying a couple things for me. They had these little loyalty punch cards, I was filling them up, and I did not care. I realized, this is a weird thing that I like, but I'm just gonna own this.

It was sort of my gateway weirdness. Like, I'm just gonna workshop this and see what happens, wearing a Hello Kitty T-shirt or having Hello Kitty figures in my room. People thought it was strange. But when I was like, "Yeah, I like this, this is great", people were like, "Oh, okay." And it sort of put in my head like, if you really own it, some people are gonna be weirded out by it, but other people are gonna be okay with it.

I kind of wish I had a "gateway weirdness" like Hello Kitty growing up! I was definitely more into musical theater than the average kid, which could have clued me in, but perhaps my trajectory was different because I didn't fully embrace it – I listened to showtunes constantly, but mostly in my car and only when I was alone. Perhaps if I'd been as brave as Gregory, I would've learned that people were okay with it, but I was so scared they wouldn't be that I hid my "weirdness" until much later.

Telling others about something "weird" can be risky – they may be turned off – but it's also a great filter for authentic friendships and connections. If they're not turned off, that means they actually like the real you, and you can be yourself around them – which has obvious parallels to embracing and sharing a Bi+ identity. For Gregory, "workshopping" his Hello Kitty weirdness and receiving mostly-positive feedback affected multiple areas of his personality.

That period was very pivotal to me. That's when I started going to nude beaches publicly and being like, "You know what? I like to be naked." And then people were like, "Hey, can I come next time you go to the beach?" And I'm like, great. Let's workshop this a little bit, too.

I didn't have a relationship with any guys when I was there, but I did fool around with some people, and it was totally fine and nice. My last girlfriend that I had [in California] knew. When we started dating, I was shifting into monogamous mode, so it almost didn't matter any more in my mind. I sort of erased it. But she knew that I liked guys, I fooled around with some.

I went [to California] to start a theater company. We ran it for six years, but I knew I wasn't gonna continue in theater. It was so much fun, but I was like, this is not a career for me. Then I got a job offer to come back to New York to work at a nonprofit, being the director of college guidance. Something I never knew how to do, but I was like, "Okay, I'll do that. That seems great."

My job was really, really demanding. I loved it. My hours were super busy. I didn't hardly even date during the first few years I was back. I never went out to bars.

Because I always felt weird, I was never a confident person. I never picked someone up. I'm always the person who gets picked up, in every relationship I've had. And strangely in all my jobs, I've never applied for jobs, jobs just have come to me. It's great, but it's bad for making you practice putting yourself out there. I never had to, I just had to be. So if someone's coming to me, they must know I'm a little bit strange, and they like that – and that's really attractive to me.

I was doing college guidance for really smart kids of color. Then my [future] wife started working at my job, and she was working with them on public policy stuff. I was like, "Oh, she's cute." But whatever, outta my mind. I was attracted to her, but of course I was never gonna make the first move.

But she thought I was cute, too. Lucky for both of us, I guess. We were on a retreat in upstate New York with the kids, we were facilitators. Once class was over, a bunch of the facilitators went out to karaoke. Being part Filipino, I cannot resist and sang a couple songs. She knew I was the one from that. And things quickly went from there.

A karaoke meet-cute is just too adorable, but what I really love about Gregory's story is that he found a compatible partner at a time when he really wasn't looking for one. I think this was made possible by his extended period of self-discovery and acceptance. It's a reminder that searching for the "perfect" partner is often stressful and fruitless if we haven't fully examined and embraced ourselves first – and that once we have, an intentional search for a partner can become unnecessary.

I asked about how Gregory's Bi+ identity factored into the relationship.

I definitely considered myself bi at that point. It wasn't a thing I resisted, like when I was in California. But I would tell a very small number of people, like literally two of my very best friends.

As [my wife and I] got to know each other, I told her upfront that I was attracted guys, had been with guys. I forget how that came up. It was like, "Oh well, you know, like … you know … " Like, of course she didn't know – how would she know? I was like, "Yeah." 'Cause I just wanted that to be a thing.

I wasn't sure if Gregory was dancing around the words with me or with her at the time – or maybe both! This conversation definitely didn't sound easy, but it opened the door to greater transparency between them.

> The other thing was that I didn't wanna have kids. It was a visceral feeling, even when I was younger. Part of it has to do with my relationship to my father and how shitty he was. I was like, "I'm OK without that dynamic continuing in my life."
>
> But I chickened out on talking about that. I felt at the time, I'm gonna lead with the less serious stuff. It was somewhat easier to talk about my sexuality, because that's not gonna be material. It's a thing about me, but it's not a thing you need to worry about while we're together. It seemed less high-stakes, right? Like, you're either gonna be fine with that, or you're not. And I had such a great experience with my last girlfriend about it. She was like, "Whatever, I don't care that last week you gave a guy a blowjob. I'll date you." So I think in my mind it seemed different, whereas the baby thing seemed serious.
>
> [My wife] actually brought that up. She was like, "I don't wanna have kids, and if this is a thing … " And then I was really like, in my head, "Oh, so she knows I don't like wearing clothes. She knows I like Hello Kitty. She knows I like guys sometimes. And she doesn't [want] kids? We're gonna get married." That was my literal thought process. And she's cute and nice and smart.

Again, Gregory was able to hold onto multiple conflicting concepts at once: he knew that his bisexuality was important enough to disclose early, but he didn't think it was that serious compared to not wanting kids – or "material", because they planned to be monogamous.

Many people downplay the importance of bisexuality within a monogamous relationship, especially early on. But as I've experienced, and as many men in this book would attest (including Gregory at this point, I suspect), our attractions are part of our identity, and fully sharing that identity with a partner is important, even if those attractions are never acted upon. So while he didn't think it was "material" at the time, coming out to his wife early seems to have been beneficial.

> We dated and were pretty serious, pretty quickly, and we had an amazing level of compatibility sexually right out the gate. It was casual dating for several months and then serious dating and then let's get married. Neither of us were getting any younger.
>
> [My wife] identifies as a straight. She's from New Jersey. She's mixed race, she's half-Black, half-white. How do you describe someone who is like every part of your life? She's smart. She likes to think she's funnier than me. She's pretty funny, just not funnier than me. She is a super caring person, sometimes to a fault. She'll often put other people ahead of herself. I have been trying to get her to do little things to put herself first, like she just spent

two months in Italy living by herself, 'cause she left her job. That was really a big deal for her.

She is a rules follower, and she grew up that way. One time, we accidentally forgot to pay for a toothbrush, and I swear she ran back into the supermarket and I thought she was gonna ask them to arrest her.

Our decision not to have kids was rough because of how it made people think about her as a woman. Anytime we would step out these boxes, it's a challenge for her. Less so for me. We decided not to have a wedding, we eloped, and that was really hard, because all of our siblings had weddings. My mom said to me, "You've never done anything like everybody else, so why would this be different?" Those are the messages I get. But for her, she's really fighting against the status quo, and she feels it.

If embracing and accepting our "differences" early in life makes it easier to do in the future, it stands to reason that always toeing the line, following the rules, and people-pleasing would make it that much more difficult to do things differently later in life. It thus made sense to me that even though neither Gregory nor his wife wanted kids, she struggled with how people might perceive that decision much more than he did.

As we'll explore throughout this book, non-monogamy often comes up for queer couples, although there was a specific reason in Gregory's case, unrelated to his bisexuality.

We've been together for 20 years, and [an open relationship] did not come up as a topic of conversation until five, six-ish years ago. That was because her sexual drive completely changed. Some of that is medical, but there were some other reasons. We really struggled with it, both of us.

There was a point where I thought we just weren't gonna be able to be together any more. And this is someone that I love more than anything. There's zero anybody else I'd want to be with for the rest of my life. But at the same time, I just didn't want like a deluxe roommate, you know?

There was lots of therapy involved, both for me and together, and out of that came, "Well, is this something that could work?" It's not an ideal solution. I feel like it works, but it's a solution that was crafted for me, not for the both of us, and that doesn't always sit well with me. Except for when I'm sleeping with people, in which case it's fine. But when I'm just thinking about it, I'm like, "This is not ideally how I would fix this."

It works as far as it works. Some of it is just in my head. And people have told me, look, if you're communicating and she's okay, let it be okay. Don't be in your head more than you need to be. If the outlines of it are really well delineated and everyone's on the same page and everyone can discuss that . . . but I can't help it.

I see Gregory's story as different from most non-monogamous couples I've met, because I don't even think it's something <u>he</u> necessarily would've wanted. He seemed oriented toward monogamy and never had much trouble in monogamous partnerships – as long as there was some sex and intimacy involved. If it weren't for an unexpected change in their sex life, that likely would have continued.

But Gregory was aware that he couldn't compromise on sex completely. It must've been a hard boundary to re-negotiate, especially since it came up years into their marriage, and I'm impressed with how he supported his wife while also prioritizing his own needs.

> The challenge was that sex is uncomfortable for her, and she just doesn't want it. So we're not looking for other relationships, we're not polyamorous. But at any point, if we wanted to have a sexual relationship, that's fine. It's not a thing where she wants me to come home and tell her the hot stories. No. She just needs to know where I'm gonna be to assure that I'm safe. And really that's it. Theoretically that's reciprocal for both of us, but she's never done it.
>
> I've never come up with a good word that I call these people, but we are clearly just friends and occasionally sleep with each other. Both men and women. Right now, I have a female friend and a male friend, not that I see consistently, but fairly regularly.
>
> I just went a couple weeks ago on a date with my female friend and her husband. They're open. He's straight, which was the challenge. I was like, this would be so much better if you weren't straight. He was a little freaked out [laughs]. But he was very open to new experiences and willing to see where his comfort would take him. I was hyper aware, like, "Oh man, am I gonna touch his butt too long? Is he gonna freak out?"

Gregory seemed very comfortable talking about his open relationship – but that doesn't necessarily apply to his wife.

> If I said at a party, "We're in an open relationship", she would die. Like, die. I talk about it pretty freely when I meet people. She's a very private person. My Instagram, I have tons of pictures, but my friend was like, "I've never seen pictures of your wife." I was like, "That is because my wife forbids pictures of her on my Instagram. You'll never see one."
>
> I think we're in a pretty good place now. I'd be totally fine with closing up again, and I always hold out hope that we can do that. But I honestly cannot go without having sex, like, at all. So …

He shrugged, ending the thought, and once again I was in awe of his self-awareness and bravery. I've seen many others compromise their own needs to avoid conflict (and I've done it myself). To build the dynamic he needed, Gregory had to know that the relationship might end, but it didn't, and now – by necessity and by taking risks – he gets to be even more open and authentic with his wife.

> I would never tell this to anyone else, but I would've wanted to be more open and out earlier. For myself. I could have had a lot more fun for so many

more years. That's really the only reason [laughs]. I think of a lot of "what could have been".

I never [came out] to my parents. I hate having my parents in my sex life, at all. [I tell] mostly new people I meet. A lot of people from my past don't really know, and it's like, "Why am I bringing this up to you after you've known me for 15 years?" I guess it's not totally immaterial because I do occasionally sleep around with guys, but I'm not looking for opportunities to invite people into my sex life.

I think many Bi+ men struggle with how "important" our sexuality is in different spheres of our lives, and there's no easy answer: it's always on a spectrum, and it can change over time. Yes, it's about sex, but it can also be about much more, and I believe that coming out as Bi+ is an invitation into more than just your sex life, even if that's what many people assume.

But I understand where Gregory is coming from, and it felt like he was grappling with these issues and putting things together as we spoke. By the end of our interview, he seemed to have a more nuanced expression of his fluidity, and his final thoughts represent another acceptance of duality – his bisexuality is both important and it doesn't have to be, and how much he incorporates it into his life at each stage is up to him.

There's always that weird thing of being a bi guy in a male–female marriage. It's easy to be what the default is. "Bi" doesn't have to be part of your identity any more if you don't want it to be. It really doesn't. Fortunately for me, I'm able to have sexual partners who are men, so it does matter, and I think that's part of the reason why I felt more comfortable going to [a bi group meeting] and looking for that community and feeling like, "Hey, this is actually not unimportant." Is it the defining thing? No. But it's a thing that I like about me. It's one of those things I wanna bring in.

3

Rich on Confronting Internalized Homophobia and Bisexual Parenting

I live in the LA County area, and I grew up here also. I was born in 1980. I have a younger brother and younger sister, both of them straight, as far as I know. My parents are still together. They just celebrated their 42nd wedding anniversary last week. They celebrated with Covid.

My grandparents had a lot of money; my parents, not so much at all. I think they only got by through help from my grandfather. My dad didn't finish high school. He was like a stoner, beatnik kind of guy when he was younger, and my mom, also. They've totally changed. They've become super conservative over the years. I have a good my relationship with my brother and sister, we're still close, and I still have a halfway decent relationship with my parents.

Rich is a white, bisexual/pansexual, cisgender man with some gender fluidity, as he described. He was born in 1980 in Los Angeles (where he currently resides), and he was 40 years old at the time of our interview in 2020. He described his religion currently as "Omnism", which is a respect or belief in all religions without claiming any single one. He grew up and still considers himself to be working-class.

Rich was excited to participate in this project and jovial during our interview – which he joined from his car, because doing so in his home, with four kids

DOI: 10.4324/9781003385585-3

running around, would've been too distracting. Though he's embraced his bisexuality and was eager to share what he's learned, it wasn't so easy to figure out when he was growing up in a rather chaotic environment.

> I didn't know this until I was a little older, they hid it, but my dad started to develop anxiety disorders. I remember him being carried out of the house on a stretcher in the middle of the night when I was a kid, because he was having a panic attack. It seemed so much bigger than that at the time.
>
> My dad grew up in a super abusive house. His parents were incredibly abusive. He didn't pass that on though, at all. His siblings definitely did. They were violent with their kids. My dad somehow stopped that cycle, but he's never dealt with it. That's always been a major part of our family, my dad's untreated anxiety and trauma. He drank heavily through most of my childhood. But we had a generally good relationship. He coached my baseball teams, and he took me to group camping things. He definitely was very involved.
>
> My grandparents raised us a lot because of my parents working. And that shit is a whole 'nother fucking situation. My grandfather was a radiologist and my grandma was a housewife. Their son, my uncle, was mentally ill, but I don't think they ever treated it, so he never left their home. He still lives with my grandmother. He's been a menace in this family. I've tried to keep my door open to him over the years. Most of the family has shut the door on him.

Though Rich's dad did a good job of breaking a cycle of physical abuse, his untreated anxiety seems to have affected the family in less visible ways. Rich's experience navigating that likely attuned him to other people's mental health struggles and may have made him more curious about his own psyche and identity.

On top of that, at least some of the chaos and confusion in his family may have been tied directly to sexuality – and the shame and anxiety associated with suppressing it.

> [My uncle] is just incredibly hate-filled, racist. I wonder if he's closeted himself. He's extremely homophobic. It's one of his defining life skills – he's really good at being homophobic. My aunt, his sister, is lesbian and has probably the longest-term, healthiest relationship in my family. Her and her partner have been together for longer than I've been alive. But his treatment of her was always atrocious. He's been another male figure in my life that has not been positive.
>
> My grandmother on my dad's side was very fundamentalist. With her religion, [there were] groups that she thought were ruining everything, like immigrants or gay people. She would buy me these evangelical, apocalyptic books. I never really bought into it, but looking back, it definitely fucked with me. I had a war going on inside myself. Do I want those to be the

voices in my head telling me who I am, or other voices that were more positive? And luckily the positive ones won out.

Again, we see duality in Rich's life and family – extreme homophobia right alongside a healthy, long-term queer relationship. This may help explain why Rich was so internally conflicted (as he'll describe below), mirroring the external conflict among his aunt, uncle, and grandmother.

Despite that homophobia and religious fundamentalism, Rich was exploring his sexuality from an early age, even though he didn't know what it all meant at the time.

I was making out and doing things with people pretty young, probably like fifth grade. I was 11. We had this group and we had one guy who didn't participate – I look back and feel really sad for him – but we called him our "coach", and he would go, "[Jessica], [Rich], you guys, bathroom, now." He'd designate these make-out partners. There were like four girls and four guys. We never did guy–guy, girl–girl, but we switched off and made out with each other.

I remember that was when I was fully sexually attracted to someone. There was a girl, I would just think about her . . . I would call her out of class, this was maybe sixth, seventh grade, and we'd go into a bathroom and make out. I was actually suspended from school, I got caught getting a blow job from her. The PE teacher walked in and she was on her knees, and I took off. I thought she was going to take off with me, but she got stuck back. She was somebody who I just … I was obsessed. I think that was the first orgasm I had, before I even did anything with her, just thinking about her at home to the point where I didn't even have to touch myself.

I was probably 15 or 16 when I started to realize that I was not only attracted to girls. I was in fourth period art class – [Melissa] and [Anita] sat next to me, and this guy, [James], who was openly gay, sat across from me. He was fucking legendary. He would wear dresses to school and short shorts with Mary Jane shoes, stockings and shit. I was so jealous of this guy, 'cause I didn't have the guts, but I was so attracted to him, and that was when I started to realize I was not straight. I would go home from school and masturbate thinking about him and [Melissa] and [Anita], all of us. For him, it was just completely undeniable. It was the type of thing that I'd already experienced with particular girls, when I would be around them and the blood would just start flowing to, you know … He'd be in my presence and I'd start to get really excited. It was undeniable.

I identify strongly with Rich's use of the word "undeniable". In my experience and for many Bi+ men I've met, we spend a lot of time questioning our attractions and trying to deny them if possible. "Am I really attracted to men?" Life might be easier if not! At times I've obsessed even more over the other pressing question: "Am I really attracted to women?" Many of us play mind games and run thought experiments for years to figure it out.

But then an "undeniable" person or situation comes along, and it can be extremely clarifying (even if initially frightening). I have had undeniably arousing experiences with both men and women, and those helped me tremendously in accepting my bisexuality. Though no one should have to "prove" their orientation, for me, the perceived "proof" did calm my anxiety. Even today, perhaps because attractions are fluid, I sometimes doubt myself, and thinking back to those undeniable experiences and partners gives me confidence in my identity.

Soon, Rich was exploring with guys while remaining closeted and not knowing what to call it, if anything. Interestingly, he ended up in a situation that mirrored his family upbringing when he explored with guys who were homophobic themselves.

> There was another guy who was like my best friend through high school. Me and this guy would get our dicks out all the time and be doing all sorts of stuff ... Looking back, I had a different relationship with him than I had with anybody else. And as I started to realize how I was attracted to certain types of things, it got more intense. We would hang out after school every day. The first thing we would do is take our pants off. And he was deeply homophobic, like we'd jerk off together and then it would be homophobic fucking slurs for the rest of the afternoon. My friendship with him was very confusing.
>
> Through him, I fell in with a crowd that was very homophobic, so I was completely closeted through high school, like completely. I was terrified. We got into some hard drugs for a while, which led certain people that were close to me to get into racist skinhead culture. Not me. I remember one guy shooting at a Black kid because the Black kid was on a skateboard and he thought a skateboard should only be ridden by white people. I mean the level of stupidity ... but I was terrified. I thought I could literally be killed if I ever revealed any of this stuff to these people. I was so in the closet, and like I said, the guy in my art class was so out, and I was so jealous of that. I so admired him to be able to do that.

Rich's crush reminds me of an early crush I had in high school on a guy – which I didn't even realize was a crush until years later. I was jealous of his good looks and athletic ability (he played soccer, so dreamy ...), and I was always awkward around him, hoping to impress him. I didn't realize that in addition to wanting to be him, I wanted to be with him – a common refrain I've heard from queer people. We often look up to people of the same gender as role-models before we realize we could be attracted to them, too.

While remaining closeted for safety, Rich was still able to do a lot of self-examination and processing to better understand his undeniably sexual fluidity. He even learned from his attempts to deny it.

For a long time, I knew I wasn't straight. I was aware of it. It was intense. It wasn't something that passed through my head – it was ongoing, recurring. But I had these little lines I wouldn't cross. I would fully be fantasizing about [James], but when I was going to come, I would make sure that I shifted my focus toward women. I did weird things like that for a while [laughs]. It's funny, I'd think, "It's okay because I came thinking about the woman." I didn't have to fully take responsibility, I didn't have to reckon with this right now and find a label for myself.

I remember watching movies and different things came up and I'd go, "Oh boy. Okay. Not straight." This one embarrasses me, but I remember seeing *The Birdcage* and being super attracted to Hank Azaria. I mean, Jesus Christ. That guy totally was part of my sexual awakening.

I was aware of the idea of bisexuality, but I didn't know a single person who identified as bisexual. My aunt was a lesbian, I knew her and I respected her, but I knew I wasn't gay. A bunch of people that I admired – artists, musicians, writers – <u>now</u> I know they're bi. I didn't at the time. I thought Freddie Mercury was gay until last year. So I just did not see examples of this type of sexual orientation.

I definitely did what I would describe as self-conversion therapy. I tried techniques to deprive myself of those thoughts, like I'm going to go a week without thinking about this type of thing. And it was horrendous. It was horrible. It was ridiculous. That went on for a while.

I was way closeted, but I was messing around with my best friend and another couple guys in that group, jerking off together regularly and all these kinds of things. It was definitely queer, homoerotic. Generally it wasn't talked about. It just sort of happened and then nobody ever would mention it.

For years, Rich lived with these competing experiences: intense homophobia and secret homoeroticism. Perhaps he was able to compartmentalize <u>because</u> of his bisexuality, because he knew his same-sex attraction wasn't "everything" – which can make the Bi+ experience uniquely confusing. Without Bi+ role models, he wasn't sure what to make of his multi-spectrum attraction, and without a clear identity or story to tell about his sexuality, he continued to hide it.

I don't think it's a coincidence that Rich finally had an awakening soon after he severed ties with his homophobic friend group.

I wanted to be out. I wanted to be open. But I didn't say anything. I just didn't know how to talk about it. Especially with these guys who terrified me, you know? But I finally got to the point where I was so dopesick and all this kind of stuff in my late teens that I basically had to sever ties with that whole group.

I discovered Jack Kerouac's stuff … I read a biography about him that he identified as straight and he was very homophobic actually, even though Allen Ginsburg is his fucking best friend, and he was having sex with

Allen and his other guy friends all the time, but he had this internalized homophobia that he was never able to fully be okay with. But just the fact that I found somebody whose work resonated with me so much and touched me on all these other levels [and who] was living and behaving that way ... it's strange, but this really wounded, closeted guy was comforting for me to discover. It really was.

Meeting or learning about someone who is "like you", whose views and experiences you connect with, can be deeply moving and transformational, even (or especially) if that person is flawed or struggling.

In my late teens, I started to read Gore Vidal, his sexual orientation stuff. He's claimed that he's fucked Fred Astaire, he's fucked Jack Kerouac. Somebody asked him in an interview, "What do you identify as, gay?" And he was like, "Fuck no, I'm not going to put that label on myself." I think in hindsight, it was huge for me to find somebody who said, "Yeah, I sleep with men and women." His attitude was: everyone's fucking bisexual.

Then reading the Kinsey studies, it's a sliding scale, you don't have to define yourself, I kind of bought into his idea that everyone's bisexual or everybody has the capacity. So I started to come out to people in my late teens, early twenties. When I would come out, I didn't really call myself bisexual other than to say that everyone's bisexual, and so am I.

Looking back, I feel like the Gore Vidal attitude doesn't give people space to define themselves. I ended up having a problem with that. If somebody tells me they're straight, like my wife is straight, I'm not going to endlessly argue with her, like, "No, look, in the right circumstances ...". But discovering that early on was sort of how I saw my sexuality and how I would come out to people.

I went through the same evolution. The idea that "everyone is bisexual" really appealed to me early on, and it helped me get comfortable with my own sexual fluidity. While I still believe that sexuality is a spectrum and that everyone has the capacity for fluidity, I agree with Rich that it's reductive to say "everyone is bisexual" and much more useful to let people choose a Bi+ label themselves – or not. If everyone is bisexual, it erases the important and difficult process of adopting that label in a society that values binaries and hierarchies, and given the relative invisibility of bisexuality, that process needs to be highlighted and celebrated right now rather than bisexuality becoming a new default.

As he gained a better understanding of his fluidity, Rich realized his expression was different based on gender: he mostly had casual sexual encounters with men, while he dated women.

I'd have girlfriends here and there, and I'd mess around with guys. I happened to meet this woman who was equally fucked up as I was, maybe more, who was also bi, who had just gotten out of a mental hospital for a suicide attempt. We were so fucked up, it was perfect for each other. I was with her for two years in my early 20s. We basically nursed each other back to health, emotionally.

One thing I do regret is that I never had a relationship with a guy. I didn't have the guts. I didn't understand myself as much as I do now. It was mainly going to a bar, meeting a guy, fucking around, and then never seeing him again. Which was fun as hell. It was fucking great. But I do regret that I never pursued any sort of romantic relationships with guys. That's one regret.

This is a common regret I've heard from Bi+ married men, and you'll hear it in multiple stories in this book. But Rich didn't have much time to explore that, as he met his future wife pretty quickly after his bisexual awakening.

I've worked at the same shop on and off for almost two decades. I didn't finish college – I didn't want the debt. So I was a musician, I was just being a fucking hippie, playing music around town, and started seeing my wife when I was 23. We met while we were working at the shop together. She asked me out, and then we just kept going out.

We ended up being together for six years, and it started to make sense to both of us that we could do this for a long time. It's kind of a blur, but we ended up talking about getting married and what that would look like, kids or no kids, all the boxes you can check. We got married when I was 29, she was 27. Had our first kid two years after we got married.

I was pretty skeptical of marriage. I still am, really. It's insane if you think about it, like, "Oh, me and this other person are going to be together forever and we're going to be the only people that we ever sleep with again." It's a terrible idea. I didn't really picture myself with anybody. And seeing my parents' marriage, do I really want to fucking put myself in that situation? I was pretty skeptical.

But somehow with this woman, it seemed like a thing to do. And it works – I'm happily married. I mean, it's a challenge, for sure. We have four fucking kids, so it's not a picnic. But somehow I ended up deciding that I would do this with her, and we've been married now for 11 years. I've been with her for 17 years.

I asked if and when Rich came out as bisexual to his wife.

I told her really early on. I feel like that's important, 'cause it had happened before where I started to get serious with somebody, and then they found out, and then it's a big deal, you know? So I told her early on, but I don't think I was using the label "bi". I was sort of like, "Kinsey did these studies … ". I had this whole lecture. I hadn't decided on using that label as much as I have since then.

When I started to come out (in my early 30s), it was my number one topic of conversation for about a year. I wanted to tell everyone. Perhaps because Rich was finally understanding his sexuality not long before meeting his wife, he came out to her quickly – but like other men in this book, he didn't own it as clearly and confidently as he does today, which may be why it became an ongoing and evolving conversation.

[My wife] struggled with it a little bit at first, but she didn't make a big deal about it. She didn't try to jump ship. She would say, "That's something I'm struggling with", and I'd asked her to explain it to me, and she never was able to. "It's just something I'm not quite there with", you know? And then as time went by, she's fucking great about it. She's amazing.

I think she may have been worried that other people would think she's married to some closeted gay guy. That's a misunderstanding of bisexuality. I try to imagine what it's like to be married to a bisexual person and have to hear that shit. As a bi person, I feel like I can more easily deal with it because I know myself. I know I'm not just a closeted gay guy. But if you're married to me, it's harder to know that for sure. And I think she's become more, in all ways, wanting to be herself also, so what's come along with that is like, "Fuck that, I love my husband. I'm not going to be afraid of what people might think."

Rich said he was skeptical of marriage and of only having sex with one person for the rest of his life, so when I asked him about monogamy, I had certain expectations – but his answer surprised me.

We are monogamous. I've been monogamous for 17 goddamn years, basically. I wouldn't have believed that myself. And I'm happy doing that. It's not like I have to do certain things in our sex life to touch on my bisexual side. I don't have things that she can't satisfy, that I need to go out of my way. And thankfully, we live in a time where we have access to all kinds of toys that can make things more fun and interesting.

Toys are definitely a helpful tool to have new and diverse experiences in the bedroom with the same partner – I highly recommend them. We can't know for sure, but I also wonder if Rich feels less desire to explore outside his marriage because he'd already had the chance to explore his sexual fluidity before he met his wife. Many men who didn't get that chance often feel a greater need to explore later in life (myself included).

In any case, Rich is happy with their decision to be monogamous. That doesn't mean he's not attracted to other people – he is – but he's able to talk about that with his wife, and that openness is fulfilling in itself.

I don't know if it's a hormonal thing, and it's been this way my whole life, but I go through periods where I'm more attracted to men, my fantasies are more about men, I see men and I feel more attracted to them, and then I go back to the opposite the next week. Recently I had a real extreme version of that, where it was the gayest week of my life, and then the next week it was the exact opposite. I remember I was at work and all the moms coming in with their yoga pants on, I was going to lose my fucking mind. And men were not doing anything for me. So I go through things like that, which I guess may have an impact on our sex life. She's more willing to talk about that kind of stuff with me in the last five years than she would have been previously.

Rich and his wife ended up having four children, and Rich's experience navigating bisexuality has certainly helped him as a parent. I asked if he always knew he wanted kids.

I definitely didn't. I think she might've always wanted that for herself, and thank God she dragged me into it with her. I had to hear her out. I wasn't in favor of it, but I wasn't opposed to it. She convinced me to keep it open as an option before we got married, and then very quickly into our marriage, we decided to go for it.

I won't have any hesitation to talk about my own sexuality with my kids, when the time comes. It just hasn't really come up with any of them yet. The oldest is nine, and the youngest is two. I'm happy that I can be able to do that, 'cause it would've saved me years of fucking self-hatred and self-conversion therapy and all sorts of shit if I had anybody around who was able to explain [bisexuality] to me.

My son, he's five, he's still wearing princess dresses all day, and he's into lots of "girl" toys as well as "boy" toys. My wife and I are both trying to let him figure out what he likes, not tell him "No, because of your chromosomes, this is [the way you need to be]." Just let him discover how he lives his gender.

When I was growing up, I heard so many different messages from adults in my life about my sexuality, and none of them were affirming or helpful. I heard from some of them that anything non-heterosexual was unhealthy or bad or wrong or even a serious sin against the creator of the universe. I heard that some people are gay and straight but that being bisexual is not a real thing and that I must be confused. I heard that however I might actually experience sexual attraction, I should just keep it to myself and play along with what society expects.

As a parent myself now, I'm glad I have the understanding and acceptance of my sexuality that I have today. Whatever mistakes I'll make raising my kids, at least I know I won't be one of those adult voices sowing confusion and self-hatred. I'm happy I can be an understanding, supportive presence when it comes to these things. To paraphrase one of my favorite bisexual writers and activists, Misty Gedlinske: If one of the kids ever says to me at the dinner table, "Dad, I'm bi (or queer or gay or non-binary or trans or whatever), please pass the peas", I want them to know that the shocking part of that statement is their willingness to eat a green vegetable.

When Rich first told his wife about his sexual history, he wasn't as confident in his Bi+ identity as he is now. So what changed? According to Rich, finding Bi+ community outside his marriage was crucial.

> I started to encounter out bi people, and it was the best thing ever. I just started hanging out with this other bi guy. Seeing somebody who was clearly defining themselves as bi, there was no explanation, Kinsey never got brought up – that [had an] effect on me. It was incredibly positive to see that. So I started to define myself as bi. It was very healing, too. Little knots in myself sorta got undone. Even though I had not been saying I was straight, I wasn't being as clear. I'd been holding back on myself in lots of ways. Even seeing an attractive guy during the day, I would put it in a different box in my brain than I do now.

Now that he's accepted and embraced his bisexuality, Rich looks back on his experiences with a new perspective – and a greater understanding of biphobia, often invisible to the untrained eye.

> There's real reasons it's been harder for bisexuals. It's hard to be visible. Look at the numbers of mental health issues and even suicide. The bisexual suicide rate is fucking unbelievable. That's one of the biggest reasons why I'm like, "Yeah, I could just disappear into my straight marriage, but Goddamn it, we need to be visible." We need to be better at affirming other bisexual people.
>
> It's so unhealthy to suppress this. It's so fucking bad for you. And I feel like, not that I advise cheating, but [maybe] you need to explore this, you know? Maybe you don't, some guys don't, but it seems like something that needs to be addressed, 'cause it's so bad to sit on it and suppress it. It's a terrible situation for everybody. It may not seem like that big of a deal, but it can be, man. I'll sit there watching a movie with my wife and I'll say, "Oh my God, that guy's hot," and she'll agree or disagree. But having those thoughts and having to bat them down, it's going to take a toll. Getting to a place that you're open about it with your spouse has got to be necessary to be healthy.

I completely agree with Rich. Some men may need to "explore", especially those who feel they "missed their chance" before marriage, but ultimately, most men I interviewed consider honesty and openness with their partner to be much more important than actually opening up and having sex with other people.

Suppressing sexual desire is difficult, I don't want to minimize that, and suppressing a specific fantasy forever may not be healthy – that's something you have to decide for yourself. Still, we can't always act on every desire we have, especially in relationships, no matter how queer or polyamorous they are. We must learn to cope with that and control our behavior, for our own sake or for others'. But suppressing thoughts that are totally normal and valid? Censoring our speech with our spouse because we're afraid of judgment? That's infinitely harder in my opinion, and it happens constantly if you're not out.

The couples in this book that thrive are the ones who can be completely open and honest without fear of abandonment, even if they make compromises and agreements surrounding their behavior. To get there, many couples approach the brink of separation, and the ones who get through it seem to value being their authentic selves within a relationship more than the safety of the relationship itself. This can be incredibly scary, but for most people I've met who cross that threshold – even those who end up separating – it's worth it. By making yourself vulnerable, by allowing your partner to see the real you, whatever the consequences, you open up the possibility of an even deeper, more authentic, and more loving partnership – like Rich's.

4

Quentin on Religious Purity Culture and Negotiating Monogamy

I was born in 1973. I grew up in a farming community in Iowa up until the age of ten. My dad worked in a hospital, and I was just about the only kid in my whole community that wasn't a farmer's kid. I was an outsider because of that. All my friends would argue over whose dad was the strongest and which tractor was the best tractor. That wasn't really my scene.

I also grew up in a very conservative Christian subculture. My grandfather was Amish – he left when he was 18, but he stayed within that tradition, so he became Mennonite, and I grew up in the Mennonite tradition. My parents were missionary volunteers, so we didn't make much money. I was a "bad" missionary kid, and I ended up shoplifting and stealing a lot. If you're going to hell anyways, you might as well enjoy life.

I never fit in with the typical masculine ideal. I was creative, I loved drawing, painting. I would hang out with my girl cousins while my boy cousins would play Matchbox cars and hide and seek. I was a chubby kid, and I had very large breasts, and I thought it was the worst thing ever. People would tease me about it, tell me I need a bra. I had so much shame around that. I would read all sorts of books on how to be a man, a Christian man, but it didn't take the way it could have. Thank goodness.

At the age of ten, [because] my parents decided to be missionaries, we ended up in Northwestern Ontario, [and I went to] a residential high school

DOI: 10.4324/9781003385585-4

for Native Americans. Until I was 18, I was one of the only white kids. I overly identified with my Native American peers and wanted to dye my hair black, [stuff] like that. But on the other hand, I tried to fit in with the missionary culture as well, to get the benefits of both. As a kid, you don't really care, you'll grasp onto whatever.

Quentin is a white, bisexual/queer, cisgender man living in Ohio. He was born in 1973 and was 47 at the time of our first interview in 2020 and 49 during two follow-up interviews in 2023. He grew up in a middle-class farming community in Iowa and now describes himself as lower-middle to middle class. He was raised in the Mennonite tradition and describes his religion currently as Christian/Mennonite/Universalist/Agnostic.

Quentin was the first person I interviewed for this project, and on a personal level, I was glad that I started with him. Though he came from a completely different background – I grew up in an upper-middle-class Jewish household in Westchester, New York – I could already connect deeply with his feelings of not quite fitting in as a child.

I always loved traditionally masculine things – from sports and video games to Teenage Mutant Ninja Turtles – but I also liked "feminine" things from a young age, like arts and crafts, ballet, and the color pink. As a teenager, I had a curiosity about both girls and boys that I didn't quite understand and certainly couldn't name, but I knew I felt "different". As Quentin described his first awareness of his bisexuality, I saw more and more similarities.

I remember at a very young age, about ten, being attracted to boys and girls. But in the Mennonite culture, I didn't know anybody who was queer. It wasn't talked about. When I did learn what gay was from a cousin, I thought that was the only choice: either you're gay or you're straight. It was a very black-and-white culture. You either are in or you're out, you're saved or you're not, you're going to hell or you're going to heaven.

Years later, at the Mennonite Bible college, there was no acknowledgment that there was such a thing as guys liking guys. It was an abomination. But on the other hand, it was an extremely homoerotic atmosphere because you'd have open showers, [naked guys] in the dorm rooms, soap fights in the shower. You'd be like, "Whoa!" And then you'd have these same guys sitting down, praying together, and talking about some girl who was showing too much leg or something. It was just this mind-fuck for me.

Finally I went to speak with the principal at the Bible college. This is the first time I had talked with anybody [about it]. I told him I'm attracted to guys, and he ignored me. He didn't know what to do with it. He literally changed the topic, and then I knew, "That must be the ultimate taboo." I zoned out. I had held him so high, and he didn't have an answer.

I had a lot of shame about who I was. There's this theological concept of your age of accountability, where if a kid dies before he can make a rational decision, then he doesn't go to hell, he goes straight to heaven. So I actually contemplated suicide at age nine, super young, because I knew I didn't fit, and I didn't know how to explain it. There was a point later, when I was 16 or 17, where I was so depressed I had a noose hanging from a tree out in the woods. I feel sad for that kid.

When I became more aware of my sexuality, I just thought I was gay, even though I had crushes on girls, as well. I didn't know what to make of it. There was a whole purity culture, that you keep girls pure at all costs. With guys, there was less of a standard. So I did end up having my first sexual experiences with other missionary kids – guys – and it was basically mutual masturbation. For me, that was this forbidden, I'm-definitely-going-to-hell-now type of experience. I didn't talk to anybody about it until way later.

Like Rich and Quentin, many Bi+ men I've talked to had similar teenage experiences. Some were explicitly sexual, like masturbation – although their teen-age minds may not have classified it as "sexual" at the time. Many memories are just homoerotic, like group showers, horseplay in changing rooms, or intimacy at a sleepover.

I have similar homoerotic memories that felt "charged", activating both anxiety and arousal in me, though I was confused by them at the time. I also felt "charged" moments with girls, and they are similarly memorable but much less confusing – because they fit a familiar narrative, I felt comfortable talking about these moments as I experienced them. I didn't have to hide anything, so I didn't feel as confused. I did feel I had to hide my thoughts about boys; I even hid them from myself and minimized them to the point that I didn't think they mattered at all.

Quentin made a similar choice, but over time, that repression took a huge toll. He was still trying to sort it all out when he met his wife doing missionary work in South Asia.

I was leading teams of Mennonite kids to South Asia, and my wife-to-be came on one of those teams. I knew her family, but I really got to know her over there, and I fell for her.

I asked her if she wanted to date, and she was over the moon. In the purity culture we lived in, I talked with her father first, and then he gave his permission, and then she was all in. On our first real date, I asked her to marry me [laughs]. I had known her quite well, but yeah. I really wanted to be a dad, that was big on my list.

I still hadn't told her anything about my attraction to men. I thought, marriage is probably gonna take care of that, 'cause I am attracted to her. [But] I felt like she needed to know before we got married, [so] I told her. She tells me now that I framed it as something that was in the past and that was no longer an issue. I wanted that to be true, so I could have easily framed it that way. She put it out of her mind – she actually forgot about it. For me it was a continuing reality, but I had so much shame about it that I wasn't gonna bring it up [again].

Most people want to know everything important about their partner before they get married, and Quentin's bisexuality impacted his childhood and personality in meaningful ways. But his story shows that the decision to come out is not so binary. Communicating the feelings surrounding bisexuality can be uniquely challenging because they exist in such a gray area, and since most definitions include an acceptance of fluidity, when we're experiencing these fluctuations and haven't yet made sense of them, it can be difficult to understand what they really mean, let alone to share that with others – even, maybe especially, if marriage is on the horizon.

For Quentin, coming out once was not enough, but it would take a while for him to work up the nerve to bring it up again. After all, they got engaged on their first date, so there was a lot they needed to explore together.

With my wife, because of the whole purity thing, we didn't kiss before marriage. We barely held hands. We were just very pure. That's not how we're raising our kids, let's put it that way.

[Sex] began on our wedding night. I wish that we had learned how to foreplay and all this other stuff. At the beginning, it was very rudimentary, very biological science class. We were both virgins. Technical virgins, I should say [laughs]. My therapist jokes about what I call sex – I had this strict line: in my mind, sex was penetration.

Quentin might have kept ignoring his same-sex desires were it not for his missionary work in South Asia, where the culture helped him recognize and process his own feelings.

In South Asia, men my age were very open with showing affection. They'll hold hands and drink tea together. For me, it was refreshing for there not to be a big, sexual attachment to it, because I'm a very affectionate person. It was a bit odd at first to be sitting beside somebody and they grab your thigh, but over time, that's one thing about the culture that I really appreciated.

They have a purity culture aspect as well, where they need to keep the girls pure. They would actually prefer that their boys be having sex with each other rather than spoil one of the girls. So it was under the table. Here, there's marriage between men. That's not an institution there at all. So they'll follow their cultural norms, they'll get married, they'll do what they need to do. If there is a love-type relationship, it'll end up looking like just a good guy friend. People know, but they don't know. It is what it is.

I frequently would be walking through the park in the evening and a guy would walk up to me, and it would be in very broken English, "Do you want a homo sex?" or something like that. Sometimes it's under the guise of a "special" massage. I went to [a barber], and they're telling the barber's assistant, "Help him with his, whatever … " and then they'd go and give me a hand job [laughs]. So it was definitely available.

There was one time when I was single [and] staying in a rural village, and they had me share a bed with one of the men at the house. And we, um, we didn't … penetrative sex didn't happen [laughs]. But we, uh, definitely pleasured each other. It was a cold night and … for me, I felt so much, a combination of shame and also a release, like, "This is part of me that hasn't been awakened." I carried so much shame about that for a long time, because here I was, this missionary, and this guy that I was supposed to be bringing to heaven, I'm sending him straight to hell.

Through my time in South Asia, I recognized this whole tension I had with needing to hide a part of myself, not only with most people around me, but with my wife as well. It just wasn't healthy. I found myself more and more living in a fantasy-type world, where my real life and what my fantasy was were so far apart that I couldn't reconcile them.

Quentin and his wife got married while living in South Asia, and their first two kids were born there before they moved back to the US. Throughout that time, the tension from hiding a part of himself eventually became unsustainable, and its impact on his marriage became intertwined with his wife's own struggles.

My wife was dealing with depression. She didn't know what was going on with me. [So we went] to a counseling center, and I came out to her again. I was still framing it as unwanted same-sex attraction, and she was blown away. She had no idea. She felt like, "Is our whole marriage a sham?" Her thoughts immediately went to "He's probably actually gay." For me, that was really difficult.

My wife's brother came out as gay, and he ended up divorcing his wife, so her fear right away was that it's going to be like my brother, and I'm going to have to figure out a new life. She really wants the best for me, so she's like, "If you really are gay, I want to know now, and then you can just go. I want that for you. I don't want that for me, but I don't want to be with you [if] you're miserable."

Quentin did some soul searching and assured his wife that he still loved her and wanted to be together, but after years of omitting this important aspect of his identity, it was (understandably) difficult for his wife to trust him.

I had processed a lot, and when I finally was comfortable telling her, that's when she fell apart. She had her own stuff, and it pushed on a lot of her own wounds. Throughout this whole time, I never felt any decrease of attraction to her in any way, but I also didn't feel a decrease in attraction to men, either.

My wife and I share 20-some years of history, we share a very good friendship, and then we share intimacy and sexuality. So there's this whole package that is so precious to me whenever I contemplate other attractions. That's always been the tension. I'm very open with [my wife], which drives her crazy sometimes. She has to balance the idea that she can't meet every need of mine. She feels like that's what a life partner should be able to do.

Quentin and his wife continued seeing a counselor, tried to be more open with each other, and talked through their insecurities. Even though there was still tension, the work they put in made a difference in their marriage, and eventually Quentin's sexuality faded as a pressing issue.

For a while, Quentin was still not out to anyone besides his wife – who became much more comfortable with his queerness over time – until a tragic event prompted a re-examination.

I had a Mennonite friend who had come out to me. He was a beautiful guy. But he ended up committing suicide, and it was devastating to me. I found out later that he hadn't come out to anybody except for me. I put feelers out among his relatives … they didn't know anything.

[Then] my wife said, "Why are you still closeted?" Because in some ways it puts her in the closet as well – she doesn't feel like she can share this big part of her life with her friends. There was really no reason. So I came out – good old Facebook – and freaked out the whole Mennonite community. But I know there's other queer Mennonite kids out there … that was a big motivation for me coming out.

[My wife] became very much an advocate for the LGBTQ community, even more than I did. I didn't want to be a representative for anything or anybody. I just wanted to be. It felt very affirming, actually. Then she started doing all sorts of reading on the bi experience. What do open marriages look like? How do different bi people live out their bi-ness? At one point she was like, "I don't think I can share you." So that's her expectation. And it's my reality because I love her. If she would be open to an open relationship, I wouldn't write it off. It's an ongoing conversation.

Though Quentin's wife feared becoming a "beard" like her sister-in-law, over time she was able to trust that he truly loved her and wasn't "really gay". We're all capable of repression and compartmentalization, but love is hard to fake, and it's real and valid even when it's complicated or imperfect. It's so important for partners to trust Bi+ men about their own experiences and attractions, even if they are fluid or exist in a gray area.

I didn't want to raise boys, 'cause I wasn't confident about my own masculine self. I now have three boys, so … [laughs]. Go figure. It's funny, 'cause they're all into sports. My youngest son, before I came out, we watched a Netflix show about some gay Catholic kid. After we finished, I said, "I felt a lot like that as a kid myself." I told him a little of my story. He's an emotional kid, and he got tears in his eyes and he's like, "Oh dad, I'm so sorry. I love you." He gave me a big hug. He's the one that was the most verbally homophobic as a kid, but he was the most affirming and accepting. [My kids] have queer friends and trans peers, so it's a different world than I grew up in. I'm glad for that.

What has really been helpful for me is that I've really pushed myself into queer spaces. I like when I get together with another gay or bi guy or go to Pride or whatever. It's so affirming, even though I'm in a hetero relationship, I feel like I need those spaces, and there's a part of me that gets life [from them].

Even though Quentin had accepted monogamy at the time of our first interview, he still mourned the loss of unexplored desires.

One of my close friends, he got engaged about the same time as we did, so we started spending time together, talking about our relationships. Looking back, I fell for him. Like seriously. This guy and I were very non-sexually physical, like we'd have our arms around each other. We would pray together, which was this way of sharing secrets and exposing ourselves. That created a weird intimacy.

Eventually he faded out of my life. I think he knew what had been going on in my mind. But not a word. I feel like if there had not been any type of mutual, anything, on his part, I don't think he would have just cut it off like that. So that's painful, 'cause it was a beautiful, beautiful thing. Yeah, wow. I haven't really totally processed that one [long silence]. I'm just sad. To have something that beautiful be forbidden, and for it to cause so much fear in him that … [tearing up]. Wow, okay. I didn't know I was gonna go there.

Quentin's story is complicated, and it's tempting to judge it as an outsider. Would he have ended up with his wife if he had come out sooner? Would non-monogamy help him heal from the trauma of repressing his identity for so long? Are he and his wife a "perfect" match – and is that concept even a real thing? But bisexuality is all about embracing this complexity and resisting the pressure to conform to traditional relationship models. It's about building partnerships from the ground up that work specifically for the people involved.

I kept in touch with Quentin for the past few years, and we've connected on a personal level and become friends (plus, he's a big fan of *Two Bi Guys*, and I do love positive reinforcement!). As I was finalizing this book, he told me that things in his marriage were in flux, so I spoke to him again in 2023 and asked how things were going with his wife.

How we're moving forward as far as our relationship is very interesting. Over the pandemic, I felt a greater need to explore. I knew it was kind of a deal-breaker for her, so it wasn't something I brought up. There was a lot of fear.

I don't know if I actually made a decision, like I'm gonna explore. It's just, as opportunities presented themselves, I didn't say no. And what it did for me was really confirm my bisexuality, for one thing. It was also healing, which was surprising to me, because I have all these religious messages of "this is wrong" and "who you are as a person is wrong". As I interacted with these men, that shame was just let go. I don't have shame about who I am. I don't know how I would've reached that without doing this, even though it was shitty.

What I see as "sinful" is that I didn't keep my agreements with [my wife], and that's where I feel actual guilt. But the idea that because I am attracted to non-females that somehow I'm sinful or I'm broken – that's all gone. That was gone in my head before, but it had not reached my body. I still felt dirty, like there was something messed up with me.

I sensed that Quentin was still very conflicted, as I think anyone in his situation would be: he finally had the experiences he truly needed to understand himself and heal, but he could only get there by betraying his commitments – or to put it bluntly, cheating on his wife, which he realized was "shitty" and hurt the person he loved most.

The result of dropping all that shame, I realized [it] was taking up a huge mind space or heart space that didn't allow me to really feel these other emotions, even guilt. I was like, "Why don't I feel more guilty about this?", because I am breaking an agreement, and I do really care about [my wife]. Once that shame was gone, I was like, "Crap. In order to be in integrity, I'm gonna need to talk with her."

That [was a] really heartbreaking decision, because I was getting to a place of health and wholeness within myself, and then I had to take the step to disclose that to her, which I knew would be devastating. And was. And still is.

I disclosed it, and then over the next few days she had more and more questions about who it was. Then I got tested, just to make sure that everything was fine. Obviously, that's when we stopped having sex [four months ago]. So. That's a long time with no sex, for me.

We've been apart for about two months. Even before I disclosed anything, she had planned to spend some time in the south, so it was convenient to have this time apart. She comes back next week. There's some trepidation, like how do we navigate this together? We're not making any quick decisions.

The exact thing both Quentin and his wife feared for most of their relationship was happening, and while it was devastating and terrifying, it also forced them to communicate in ways they hadn't before.

Since I've disclosed, we've actually had more intimate conversations than ever – minus sex, which I realize now can get in the way. Her fear was that she would be hurt, but that's also my fear, that I would hurt her. We're both realizing that our marriage as we knew it is over, and so we're creating something completely new.

My personal journey has been about getting into my body, and I have done some strange things – like ecstatic dance. I find myself in tears, connecting with other people on this soul level. I'm letting myself go where my body tells me, other than sex. But even that, I've had some amazing solo sexual journeys, getting to know my body in ways more than just moving toward ejaculation.

I think that information will be good for me to put into words my needs and my desires. What do I want? What do I wanna try? She has some hesitation about that. For me, it's about a conversation. I know not all my fantasies are actually [essential] … you explore it once and you're like, "Nah, that doesn't really work for me." But I do sense in my gut that we're moving towards each other and not away from each other.

It's interesting that even at a moment when Quentin was apart from his wife for two months to process infidelity, he felt they were getting closer, not further apart, and it shows the value of emotional intimacy, vulnerability, and honesty. Those are the things that help us feel close to a person, even when damage has been done or when we're physically apart. This helped them both realize that their love for each other could endure, even if the shape of their relationship changed.

One of my fears with our counselors is that they'll ask probing questions, and we'll be like, "This marriage isn't gonna work." But even if that's what happens, we're gonna be okay. We'll still be there for each other. We still have this soul connection that won't change, and we're still the parents of our kids. That's a really sad thought, but it's not a depressing thought. It's no longer this spiral down to "What am I gonna do if I don't have her? Who am I if I don't have her?" I'm embracing who I am in new ways that I thought I would've done a lot sooner in life. But that's life.

I didn't realize how important it was to find space to love myself. For me it was always about sacrifice and loving your partner, so I neglected to really love myself. That's included therapy. It's also opened up more of me to love. I've had body image issues, but now it's like, "Eh, it is what it is." I realized through my interactions that what people were attracted to in me was not that perfect body or anything. There was something about who I was as a person.

I am very grateful to have a spouse who, even though she's straight, is very willing to flex in order to develop empathy for my situation while honoring her own journey, not losing herself. For me, that makes me love her that much more.

Finding people that hold space and listen without judgment may be difficult, but for me that has been so valuable. I have one friend I meet with every Sunday morning, non-fail, and that has been a lifesaver. It's been that oasis where I can be completely myself. And developing queer community has been really valuable. I feel seen in ways that I don't feel seen in hetero community.

The more Quentin and I kept in touch during this project, the more I could sense that his acceptance of himself was deepening. He was appreciative of his journey and his marriage, no matter what happened. Still, he was conflicted. I think that on some level he understood that he would prefer to be ethically non-monogamous moving forward but also that this might be too difficult for his wife, and he was prepared to be monogamous in order to maintain the relationship. I suspect, though, that his wife realized this was a compromise, and while she wanted to maintain her own authenticity and integrity, she also didn't want to put Quentin back in the position he had been in for so many years, especially now that she knew the full story.

So a couple months after our follow-up interview, I got another email from Quentin – he and his wife had decided to separate. It was a difficult time, but they were both content with the decision, and they were ready to talk about it. They were also about to go on a business trip near where I live, so we finally met in person and had lunch together.

They seemed incredibly loving and friendly for a couple who had just decided to split up. It was an oddly joyous experience to meet them together, and a perfect bookend to this project – after three years of wondering if they would deepen their relationship or end it, I realized that ultimately, they were doing both, and they were honoring their authentic selves and each other.

A few days later, I conducted a final follow-up interview with Quentin. It was full of grief and joy, heartache and understanding, uncertainty and acceptance – all at once.

There was a part of me that had this desire for our marriage to work, and there was a part of me that wondered how both of us could live out who we were and still for it to work.

I went to a men's retreat the weekend after she got back, and the morning I got home, we had coffee, and I said, "I was hoping this weekend would give me more clarity about our situation, but it didn't. What about you?" And she said, "Well, I didn't really wanna talk about that right now, but I actually did [get clarity]." It wasn't a mental thing as much as she just felt it in her body that this is right … that we part ways as a married couple.

I was doing a lot of grieving right out the gate. As soon as she said she had come to a decision, I knew what that decision was. I felt it in my gut. But I had been in denial. During her time away, she had a lot of time to process, there was a lot of grieving, and also looking at growing up in a very patriarchal culture and realizing her strength as a woman and that she didn't need me as the man in order for her to have an identity. I think that was a big part of it, realizing "I'm not just giving [Quentin] his freedom knowing that it's better for him, but it's actually better for both of us." That was a good transformation for me to see in her, knowing that she was going to be okay, that she was actually feeling empowered and ready to move forward.

So that's where we're at now, and we're in the process of looking at mediation in order to get a dissolution of our marriage. We wanted to obviously tell our kids. They weren't really expecting that. It was a shock for all of them. The youngest was hoping things would work out. He was like, "You guys were doing so well together." We do communicate well together, and we get along well together, so it seemed like things were moving in the direction of working out.

After meeting Quentin and his wife, I can understand what their kids meant – they were very affectionate towards each other, understanding, communicating well, and seemed to have no ill-will toward each other. I think that after navigating Quentin's Bi+ identity and desire for non-monogamy, their relationship was deeper than ever before, even if it was no longer romantic or sexual.

Because we're good friends, it's hard to imagine what our relationship will look like afterwards. We do get along very well, but we have trouble advocating for ourselves, and it's something we really need to do in this process. We truly want what's best for each other. But we were our primary support system for each other, and now we can't be that, and it makes the separation process difficult.

We had 25 years of marriage, and that's coming to an end, [but] we don't see our marriage as a failure. We see it as a success, and we see those 25 years as something we would re-live if we had it to do over again.

There are ways that we've betrayed ourselves, either in order to maintain the marriage, which we thought was the thing to maintain – within the tradition we were raised, that is what you do, at all costs – or to maintain our friendship and our way of life. We tried to push ourselves into the mold. So now as we are looking at separating, we are realizing that there are different possibilities that may be more in line with who we are and what our values are.

For me, it's very exciting, and [that] has to do with a chance to explore my sexuality in a way that I never did as an adolescent. I never even explored that with women, really, because [my wife] was the first woman I've ever slept with, after we were married. Purity culture drove our whole marriage narrative.

Even though they are separating, the way Quentin talked about himself and his values reminded me of polyamorous communities I'm part of, which focus on communicating your own needs and forming relationship structures that fit you best, even if they are outside the traditional mold. Once Quentin and his wife stopped pushing themselves into that mold, new possibilities have opened up.

His wife has also been able to forgive him authentically, which has helped them both move forward.

The infidelity is a regret of mine, but it also feels necessary to disrupt things in order for us to take this deep dive into who we are and who we could possibly be moving forward. She's even said that to me. Early on she was like, "I don't know how I could ever forgive you for doing this to me." That weighed so heavily on me, to know the impact that my actions had on her.

We were hanging out one evening, and I said, "A while back, you mentioned that you don't know if you could ever forgive me for cheating on you", and almost before I finished the sentence, she was like, "Oh, I have forgiven you, completely. I don't know how it happened, I don't know why it's not a bigger deal than it is, but I'm not holding anything against you, and I'm excited for your future." There were some tears. I didn't want her to carry that, and I would've carried that, as well.

I am so glad that I got to a place where I disclosed to her [and took] responsibility for my own actions. It's very important to me that I operate out of my values and that I have integrity. I think that's the reason we're separating, because we both have integrity with ourselves, and we realize we may not be able to do that together in a marriage. I think with how nice we both are, it would've taken something really big to shake us up. For both of us, it's kind of unimaginable that we are where we are, and that we're okay.

Given that what's happening is not exactly what Quentin wanted when we first spoke, I asked how he feels about the whole journey. Is he happy he came out? Does he have regrets? Quentin seemed very clear.

Coming out for me was just incredible. Some people may have seen it as this slippery slope that eventually divorce was inevitable, but I don't think that was the case. What coming out as bi did for me was it got me connected with a community of like-minded people that actually reflected my experience. Before that, I had a lot of depression. Shame was so much a part of who I was. I had no idea that there were other people like me, so I tried to fix myself, not realizing that I was trying to tamp down something that was beautiful, that was good.

Once I got into community with other bi men especially, I saw myself reflected. And coming out brought up a lot of really good conversations with my wife. I felt seen by her in ways that I didn't [before].

While there was grieving and sadness when they decided to divorce, I also find so much beauty in their story. Quentin realized that his bisexuality was not only acceptable, but something "good" and "beautiful". His wife was able to imagine new possibilities for herself and develop an identity outside of her relationship. As she said to me, "marriage is no longer the container for our love" – but there is still deep love, affection, and respect between them. Neither of them regrets their marriage or their kids together, and they are both content with their decision to divorce and excited for what lies ahead.

Quentin had one final thought for others reading his story.

I know a lot of men are still closeted. They're just dealing with a lot of shame, and depression is part of that. Anxiety, the fear of getting caught, losing everything. The impact that all those closeted men dealing with this stuff has on society as a whole – you can't even imagine. And people in these situations, they're fathers. They're raising families. It's hard to do that well if you're squashing a part of yourself.

5

A Universal Capacity for Queerness

As an undergrad psychology major, I took one class on sexuality and natural selection, where I was taught that same-sex attraction is most likely a superfluous side effect of evolution, like the male nipple. I thus internalized the idea that sex which leads to procreation is natural and innate, while sex with a same-sex partner is not. I believed that some people preferred gay sex, but I didn't have a good answer as to why, from an evolutionary perspective – and I couldn't imagine what it felt like.

I was surprised to find out that it felt almost exactly the same – especially after years of imagining that it would be completely different. (Though some Bi+ people do feel different being with different genders – another perfectly valid experience of bisexuality.)

Once I believed for myself that my same-sex experiences were not categorically different and didn't negate or erase my different-sex attractions, I began to think of gay and lesbian people not as categorically different from me at all, but rather at a different point on a spectrum. I started to re-examine those lessons on evolution, wondering if same-sex attractions were really "superfluous" and didn't aid in species survival – or if that was another myth.

My own experience also contradicted something else I had been taught: that sex drive is a finite resource that is depleted with use. When I began having sex with men, it increased my desire to have sex with women (and anyone, really), rather than replacing or depleting it. (I also learned first-hand that my male nipples

DOI: 10.4324/9781003385585-5

were not, in fact, superfluous.) I felt sexier, more liberated, and more aroused by various types of people, and I began to wonder if at a certain stage in evolution, same-sex attractions are beneficial to the survival of a species, too.

As I ruminated on this, I met a lovely guy named "Jay" – the first man I ever dated. When he told me about his theory that everyone is born with a "capacity for queerness", everything began to click for me. Maybe it's not that we're born straight or gay, but rather that we're born with the capacity for anything ("nature"), and our circumstances and responses help determine our identities ("nurture").

Why not? This model certainly fits with other psychological principles I had studied. We're all born with the capacity to be healthy eating any type of diet (for example, adopted children are not genetically predisposed to certain regional cuisines), but once we get into a routine, our bodies adjust and get used to it. We're all born with the capacity to learn any language, even though most people end up choosing one or two. Why couldn't sexual preferences be the same? Wouldn't it actually benefit our species to have the capacity to form lasting, intimate partnerships with anyone, regardless of gender?

I started to see the entire world as potentially "fluid", even if most people had been conditioned and settled into a straight identity. Many of the men I interviewed for this book had similar feelings – like Rich, who read Gore Vidal and started to see everyone as bisexual or at least having that capacity. I've also met countless Bi+ men in real life who came out in a similar way: it wasn't so much about their own identity as it was about their worldview of everyone else – something to the effect of "We're *all* on a spectrum."

I began to wonder: what if fluidity is actually more common than rigid heterosexuality, but our society represses it in most people? What if there is vast Bi+ potential out there in the world, waiting to be unlocked? I couldn't yet "prove" it to myself, but I finally understood it was possible, and this was the world I wanted to help create.

My Bi+ identity began to merge with this worldview, becoming one and the same. An acceptance of my own "capacity for queerness" is why I call myself bisexual.

WE'RE NOT THE ONLY ONES

If humans have reached an evolutionary stage where sexual fluidity benefits the species, surely we'd expect to see this in other animals, as well. We can't be the only ones, right?

In fact, we're not – not by a long shot. Though we can't ask them about their identities, studies repeatedly show that various animals – from insects to fish, birds to mammals – exhibit bisexual behavior and engage in non-reproductive sex. I recently became obsessed with a book called *Queer Ducks* by Eliot Schrefer which posits that this may actually be the norm in the animal kingdom, not the exception. Very little research has focused on sexual fluidity and polyamory in animals until recently, but the more they're studying it, the more they're finding it. Schrefer lists a few reasons why this might be evolutionarily advantageous:

> Polyamory – the bonding of three or more animals, instead of the conventional two – can expand the effective pool of parents, increasing the survivability of offspring. There's also a theory known as "bisexual advantage," coming from data showing that fluid sexuality increases reproduction chances across a population, making bisexuality an "evolutionary optimum."[1]

Bonobos, our closest animal relatives, are one of the most striking examples of these theories. Studies show that almost 75 percent of bonobo sex is non-reproductive and that almost all bonobos engage in sexual activity with both sexes – in fact, homosexual encounters are more common than heterosexual ones. Researchers believe that bonobos use sex to resolve conflicts, often with same-sex partners. Bonobos are rarely monogamous, and they often have sex with so many partners that they can't be sure of paternity, so they all help take care of each other's kids.

Other animals, like dolphins, often form temporary same-sex sexual partnerships, which researchers believe may establish life-long bonds, before they mature and mate to reproduce. This could explain another benefit to fluid sexuality in humanity, beyond raising children: our species thrives when we work collectively, and sex helps us form close bonds. Why should that be limited to opposite-sex pairings? And why should we only have to choose *one* such bond that includes sex?

EVOLUTIONARILY ADVANTAGEOUS

Many evolutionary theorists (and some of my more annoying straight acquaintances) seem to cling to the principles I was taught in college – behaviors that aren't "evolutionarily advantageous" will naturally die out, unless they are byproducts of extremely advantageous behaviors that outweigh the costs, or if they lead to inadvertent advantages.

These people often try to explain away homosexuality as a byproduct. At best, the argument goes something like this: the urge to achieve orgasm, an instinct which sustains most species by leading to reproduction, can spill over into non-reproductive activities. Thus, the biological impulse to have sex benefits the species overall even if some people are engaged in "useless" same-sex activity. I'm not sure this is actually at odds with a queer evolutionary theory – but I believe we need to look at the question from a different, queer perspective.

I found that perspective talking to Dr. Jane Ward, a scholar and professor of gender and sexuality studies and author of *Not Gay: Sex Between Straight White Men* and *The Tragedy of Heterosexuality*, on my podcast, *Two Bi Guys*.

ME: I was taught that [queerness] was a byproduct, like an accident or a mistake, but you're basically saying everyone has the capacity for queerness when they are born.

DR. JANE WARD: Right. When you think about it, why wouldn't we? Why wouldn't we have the capacity to be interested in the bodies of every kind of person? Now, some people will say, "Well, we wouldn't, because it's not evolutionarily advantageous, because we're all supposed to reproduce." But if you look back again through human history, we have no end of evidence that people engaged in a lot of sex practices that did not lead to procreation: oral sex, masturbation, so forth. Human sexuality is far more complex than that reproduction argument.

Even looking only at recent human history, there are many examples of bisexual behavior flourishing in tolerant cultures, like the ancient Greeks'. This did not lead to less procreation – in fact, most of the men who had sex with each other were also procreating with women, sometimes more so than other men.

I did learn in college that evolutionary advantages come not just from behavior which produces offspring but also from behavior which allows that offspring to reach reproductive age itself. If that's true, then modern-day queerness has clear societal advantages. Not every queer parent can reproduce with their partner, but they can adopt or care for another child in need – of which there are many – which helps to sustain our species. And if we can form stronger, more cooperative bonds with anyone, regardless of gender, that helps sustain us all. That's why I no longer view queerness as a byproduct, but rather as a direct benefit to our collective survival.

THE TRAGEDY OF HETEROSEXUALITY

If humans are "born with" this capacity for queerness and then grow up in a restrictive environment (most of us, unfortunately), what happens to that queer potential? I asked Dr. Ward about this on *Two Bi Guys*:

DR. JANE WARD: Freud believed that when we're born as infants, we don't actually have a sexual orientation at that time. Instead, we're "polymorphously perverse". We have the capacity to feel pleasure in response to so many different stimuli: bodily human touch, but also dipping our finger in peanut butter, and the fur of our kitty cat.

What happens is that as we get older, we get socialized to direct desire toward what Freud called a "proper object", and culturally we believe that we're supposed to desire human beings, and we're supposed to desire people who are of the opposite sex, because we live under heteronormativity.

Parents start to orient children that way very early on, and what Freud argued, and I share this view, is that something has to happen to all those other desires – that beautiful, delicious, diverse range of desires that we have the capacity to experience. They basically get suppressed. That includes homosexual desires. And what I came to believe, looking at how common it is for straight people to engage in homosexual sex practices, is that that part of ourselves never fully goes away.

If this is the case, currently-out Bi+ men are the tip of the iceberg, and we could be at a turning point. What if most people are somewhere in the middle of the spectrum, and only smaller minorities exist on either end? It's certainly possible (and the statistics are moving in this direction), but if we're going to find out, people need to see just how big the rest of that iceberg is. Increasing the visibility of Bi+ men and especially those who are married to women could have a huge impact on combating homophobia and biphobia in a mostly-straight society – we can be the bridge that unites these worlds, if we're willing to put ourselves out there.

INVISIBILITY BY "PASSING"

In order to increase visibility, we must dive deeper into why this group is so hidden. As discussed, about 88 percent of partnered bisexual people are with someone of a different gender, and most are also monogamous (79 percent in a 2020 study[2]). If the vast majority of Bi+ men end up in monogamous relationships with women, many might wonder why their orientation matters – they may see no reason to express their fluid attractions if they don't plan on acting on them.

Multiple men in this book describe their bisexuality as extremely important and consuming when they were younger and figuring things out, but once they're married and monogamous, they describe it as fading into the background. Gregory, for example, talked about his sexuality being "immaterial" after marriage – until they decided to explore non-monogamy, at which point his fluidity became "relevant" again.

Pair this with a persistently homophobic and biphobic society, and you can see why many Bi+ men keep it to themselves. Expressing same-sex desire can lead to being shamed, ostracized, or directly persecuted. In certain environments, it can put friendships, jobs, and participation in support communities (like religious communities) in jeopardy. Coming out as Bi+ in particular can lead to judgment that you are confused, hypersexual, indecisive, or really gay but unable to admit it – which can affect both spouses. And in worst-case scenarios, your spouse my buy into these biphobic stereotypes, so coming out may risk the relationship itself.

Thus, there is a natural impulse for Bi+ men to "pass" for straight and avoid all of these negative consequences, which can feel "easy" within a male-female relationship – you don't really have to do or say anything. "Straight" is the default, and most people will assume it unless you say otherwise. Why correct that assumption if you perceive it to be irrelevant and potentially harmful?

MORE THAN JUST SEX

Obviously, I'm writing this book because I believe it is relevant, even in monogamous relationships, because I see bisexuality as a vital part of our identities and how we view the world, not just a word that describes who we want to have sex with. I've also seen and experienced the harmful effects of repressing queerness to fit in, which must be compared to the potential harm of disclosing.

Even if a Bi+ awakening starts with sexual thoughts or activities (as mine did), these feelings of arousal, connection, and touch are foundational to our existence and experience of pleasure as human beings, and they affect various types of intimacy, not just sex, and various types of relationships, not just romantic or sexual ones.

In my experience, it can be hard to convince straight people of this. Straightness is essentially a "default" orientation in our society, so anyone who has not closely examined their sexuality or relationship structure preferences will probably land there. (Some straight people have done a close examination and concluded they are straight, but I've found that to be less common, whereas almost every queer person has had to examine themselves to arrive at their queer identity.) Without closely examining your preferences, they are easier to compartmentalize, but the more I've learned about my desires and interests, the more connected they feel to other parts of my personality, my upbringing, and my beliefs in other areas of life.

Our heteronormative culture is also extremely puritanical – sex, touch, nudity, and pleasure in general are constantly reinforced as taboo. But we should be able to talk about these feelings and desires openly and from a young age, as soon as they appear. We should be able to experiment and find out what we like, without shame. When we're taught to connect pleasure with sin, we cut off so many potential avenues of exploration beyond sex itself. Bisexuality and queerness allow us to tap into that potential and prioritize pleasure, connection, self-care, and mutual-aid (rather than achievement, competition, secrecy, or personal ownership, which I believe are idealized by puritanical heteronormativity), and this can change the way we think about everything.

Thus, I view bisexuality as an expansive worldview, often predicated on open-mindedness and seeing possibilities in the world that don't yet exist. It's a rejection of the binary in various areas of life, and it involves an ability to see shades of gray and the spectrum of diversity around us. It's about rethinking expectations that often come with labels and categories. It's an ability to hold two conflicting thoughts at once and get comfortable with both being true and valid. While it does affect our openness to partners of multiple genders, it also affects how we approach family relationships, friendships, professional relationships, marriages, and everything in between – often blurring the lines and distinctions among them.

Imagine not just repressing your most basic, primal sexual thoughts and urges, but also repressing your entire worldview. Imagine finally finding a community of like-minded people and a word that has been used for decades to describe their identity – "bisexual" – and still feeling unable to use that word freely. This is the experience for a majority of Bi+ people today.

Keeping all this hidden perpetuates a destructive and unnecessary cycle – though "passing" has benefits and can keep people safe, it is incredibly hard to constantly censor yourself, and it takes a psychic toll. It may seem like the "easy", default choice in a straight-appearing marriage, but when you can't share such a fundamental part of your identity – something you think about daily – you could end up feeling isolated and alone.

Many of the men I interviewed have felt this way. But the ultimate irony is that for most Bi+ people who eventually come out, their bisexuality transforms from a liability into an asset. I often talk about my queerness being a "gift", one that has enhanced my life in immeasurable ways, despite the initial hump of terror and insecurity I had to get over.

When I identified as straight, it was easy to underestimate the damage of repressing part of myself. Only after coming out did I realize how great it felt to be free – free to be able to say out loud any thought that popped into my head; free to openly express my feelings, helping me get in touch with them myself; free from dealing with it all alone. It was truly life-changing.

NEGATIVE PHYSICAL AND MENTAL HEALTH DISPARITIES

In a perfect world, I believe that being Bi+ or fluid should lead to better over-all health – the freedom, self-examination, and open-mindedness that I've seen among out Bi+ people often translates to better mental health and a focus on taking care of oneself physically and emotionally.

Unfortunately, this is not the world we live in now. The vast majority of Bi+ people are not out, so they suffer from the effects of that repression and invisibility. On top of that, homophobia and biphobia contribute to stigma and minority stress, which affects all Bi+ people, even those who are out, so the positive benefits of embracing this identity are tempered by real-world "bi-negativity". This is why research shows that Bi+ people have significantly worse physical and mental health outcomes – and even though this has been true for years, the Bi+ community still receives a tiny fraction of the resources dedicated to LGBT+ issues.

Let's start with physical health. A 2018 study found that sexual minorities (aka queer or LGBT+ people) were at increased risk of negative physical health conditions compared to heterosexual people, and also that "individuals with bisexual identity, attractions, and/or behavior were at increased risk for more physical health conditions than other sexual minority groups", including high cholesterol, high blood pressure, obesity, gastrointestinal problems, arthritis, and cardiovascular disease.[3]

There are many reasons for this. A 2018 analysis by the Center for American Progress found that 24 percent of Bi+ men had income below the poverty line, compared to 6 percent of straight men and 12 percent of gay men, which can have various health impacts.[4] (Bi+ women were at 21 percent, compared to 14 percent of straight women and 13 percent of lesbian women, although these differences were not statistically significant.) The health disparity is also partially related to Bi+ people being less likely to come out to their doctor and seek appropriate medical care. In a 2012 study by the Williams Institute, 39 percent of bisexual men and 33 percent of bisexual women reported never disclosing their sexuality to any doctor, compared to 13 percent of gay men and 10 percent of lesbian women.[5] Many studies and anecdotes reveal biphobic attitudes from doctors (including my own, who used to repeatedly ask if I was "still bisexual" at every visit), which can lead Bi+ people to avoid or delay healthcare visits, even visits that have nothing to do with sexual health.

When asked to self-report on their own health, both Bi+ men and women reported more days per month of "poor" physical health and mental health than gay, lesbian, and straight people (although the comparison was only statistically significant for mental health). Bi+ people also reported that their poor physical health "inhibited usual activities" to a higher degree than gay, lesbian, and straight people (although the comparison was only statistically significant for Bi+ women).

In my experience, I found that repressing my bisexuality got me "comfortable" repressing other things I didn't want to deal with, like physical health conditions. I got used to them, minimized them, told myself I was tough enough to handle them – all things I had learned to do subconsciously with my sexuality. Though these studies don't make this causational leap, other men I interviewed had similar experiences.

At the same time, struggles with sexuality can take up a ton of mental energy, and there may be little left in the tank to properly take care of oneself. These internal conflicts can also lead to using drugs to cope, which can have negative health impacts. Rich, for example, got involved with drugs that sapped his health right at the peak of his confusion and self-loathing about sexuality, and other men in subsequent chapters have had similar self-sabotaging experiences.

Bi+ women report poorer health outcomes than their monosexual peers

	Women			Men		
	Bi+ women	Lesbians	Straight Women	Bi+ men	Gay men	Straight men
Number of days of poor physical health in the past 30 days	5.5	4.8	3.4	8.3	3.7	3.5
Poor physical health inhibited usual activities	66%	43%*	36%*	44%	35%	34%
Number of days of poor mental health in the past 30 days	10.0	4.5*	3.2*	6.4	3.9	2.1
Postponed or did not get needed medical care to avoid discrimination	10%	4%	3%	6%	2%	4%

Note:* Indicates a statistically significant difference from bi+ respondents of the same gender at the p <.05 level.
Source: See Methodology in Shabab Ahmed Mirza, "Disaggregating the Data for Bisexual People" (Washington: Center for American Progress, 2018), available at https://www.americanprogress.org/?=458350.

Fig. 5.1 Bi+ women report poorer health outcomes than their monosexual peers.

This material was published by the Center for American Progress.

Not disclosing your bisexuality to healthcare providers can also lead to negative sexual health outcomes. A 2014 study found that because biphobia contributes to bisexual men being less likely to come out and get tested for HIV, they are "disproportionately affected by HIV".[6] Closeted Bi+ people are also much less likely to find queer community and thus less likely to be aware of health and wellness resources that are discussed and distributed there.

Personally, my straight female doctor was one of the last people I came out to, and I soon found a gay male doctor who I felt more comfortable talking to about my sexuality and behavior. Based on his advice, I am on PrEP (pre-exposure prophylaxis), which involves a daily pill that is 99.9 percent effective at preventing HIV, as well as STD testing every three months. In my personal experience, almost all of my gay friends are on PrEP, while fewer of my Bi+ friends are.

Bisexual people are even more at risk of negative mental health outcomes, which many Bi+ scholars and researchers believe is related to minority stress and stigma surrounding bisexuality. ("Minority stress" refers to prejudice or discrimination of minority identities based on stigma held by the dominant group or culture.) All queer people face minority stress in our heteronormative society, but bisexual people face unique minority stress due to negative stereotypes and myths about what it means to be bisexual – that Bi+ people are confused, indecisive, promiscuous, unable to commit, going through a phase, or are vectors of disease. Bi+ invisibility and erasure also contribute to feeling unseen and unimportant, which adds to social isolation. In addition, Bi+ people face discrimination from "both sides", i.e. the heterosexual and homosexual communities, as you'll see repeatedly in the chapters ahead, which can lead to loneliness and defensiveness about our Bi+ identity, even within queer spaces.

All of this is borne out by current research on Bi+ mental health outcomes. A 2020 review of data by the American Psychiatric Association found that bisexual people report increased experience of depression and suicide than gay and lesbian people and are at slightly higher risk of alcohol abuse, drug use, and substance abuse disorders.[7] Bisexual women also reported higher lifetime rates of mood and anxiety disorders than lesbian women and straight women. While bisexual men and gay men reported similar rates of mood and anxiety disorders, both were significantly higher than for straight men, and the results could change with more data, as the review also found that bisexual people are underrepresented in research on mental health (despite being the largest group in the LGBT+ community).

A 2016 meta-analysis study in the UK found that bisexual people were more likely than monosexual people to be anxious or depressed – 39 percent of Bi+ people met the criteria, compared to 23 percent of straight people and 29 percent of gay and lesbian people.[8] A 2010 study in Canada found that rates of mood and anxiety disorder were higher among bisexual men compared to straight and gay men.[9] A 2010 study in the US found that 18.5 percent of bisexual people had seriously considered suicide in the past year, compared to 4.2 percent of gay and lesbian people and 3 percent of heterosexual people.[10] And a 2012 study found that only 5 percent of bisexual youth reported being "very happy", compared to 8 percent of gay and lesbian youth and 21 percent of straight youth.[11]

I could go on – there are many more studies (and new ones each year) confirming the current negative health outcomes for Bi+ people – but what about married Bi+ people? Are they doing any better? After all, studies of the general population have shown a "marital advantage" in terms of both physical and mental health. There are two main reasons for this: marriage protection, which means that having a spouse can provide valuable economic and psychological resources that make life easier and better, like pooling finances for stability or emotional support during difficult times; and marriage selection, which means that people in better health (physically and emotionally) and with healthier habits are more likely to be selected into marriage.

Given this, we might expect married Bi+ people to be better off than unmarried Bi+ people – however, research published by Duke University Press in 2019 found that this marital advantage does <u>not</u> exist for bisexual married couples, even though it <u>does</u> exist for gay and lesbian married couples.[12] The authors of the study attribute this to "pervasive prejudices and stereotypes against bisexuality" and "unique stressors that bisexuals face" in intimate partner relationships, like doubts about bisexual people's loyalty, commitment, or ability to be satisfied with monogamy. These conflicts within bisexual marriages can lead to relationship strain that counteracts the "marital advantage", and they are on full display in many of the chapters ahead.

In addition, the previously mentioned *Journal of Bisexuality* study found that the "illegitimacy of bisexuality was negatively associated with both partners' sexual and relationship satisfaction" (see note 2). In other words, bisexuality is often viewed as a phase before coming out as gay or lesbian, not as a valid identity, and even though this is flat-out wrong and not supported by evidence, it still leads to marital conflict when internalized by either partner. I've unfortunately experienced this personally, even years into my marriage, because biphobic stereotypes are difficult to avoid, and my wife and I sometimes get sucked in despite our best efforts not to. Even though I host a bisexual podcast, when I hook up with too many guys, my wife sometimes can't help but feel insecure and worry that I'm no longer interested in women – and even though I know I am, getting defensive about my attractions has at times led to marital discord and mental health struggles for both of us.

Despite all of these negative health outcomes, the Bi+ community receives far too little in terms of dedicated support and resources. According to the most recent Resource Tracking Report published by Funders for LGBT Issues, bisexual interests and groups received less than 1 percent of overall funding to LGBT+ communities and issues in both 2019 and 2020.[13] Gay men received 3–6 percent of those resources, and lesbian women received 2–5 percent, and in raw dollars, this translates to over 40 times the amount of money dedicated to Bi+ people in 2019 and over 200 times the amount in 2020. Though the majority of funding overall goes to general LGBT+ interests (59 percent in 2019 and 68 percent in 2020), which in theory should benefit the bisexual community as much as anyone else, the unique stigma and minority stress felt by bisexual people as well as our significantly worse health statistics show that we need more resources dedicated specifically to Bi+ people and communities.

Distribution of Domestic Grant Dollars by Sexual Orientation, Gender Identity, and Sex Characteristics, 2019-2020

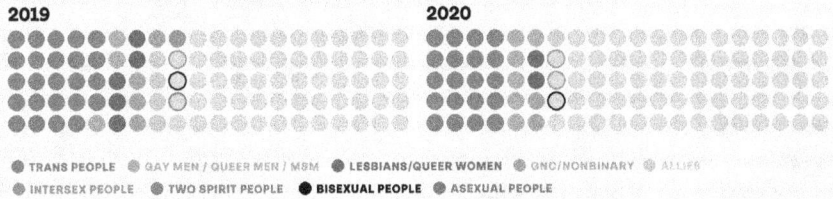

2019 2020

● TRANS PEOPLE ● GAY MEN / QUEER MEN / MSM ● LESBIANS/QUEER WOMEN ● GNC/NONBINARY ● ALLIES
● INTERSEX PEOPLE ● TWO SPIRIT PEOPLE ● BISEXUAL PEOPLE ● ASEXUAL PEOPLE

	2019		2020	
Trans People	$36,121,652	24%	$30,996,642	20%
Gay Men/Queer Men/MSM	$4,720,338	3%	$9,386,675	6%
Lesbians/Queer Women	$7,738,595	5%	$3,737,266	2%
GNC/Nonbinary People	$5,376,891	4%	$3,483,995	2%
Allies	$5,409,019	4%	$1,343,434	1%
Intersex People	$2,057,195	1%	$746,500	<1%
Two Spirit People	$63,913	<1%	$90,227	<1%
Bisexual People	$301,608	<1%	$58,333	<1%
Asexual People	$10,000	<1%	$0	0%

*This table excludes funds awarded for the purpose of regranting.

Fig. 5.2 Distribution of domestic grant dollars by sexual orientation, gender identity, and sex characteristics, 2019–2020.
Chart provided by Funders for LGBT Issues.

In addition, according to the minority stress model developed by Ilan H. Meyer in 1995, the degree to which someone integrates their minority identity and finds a community can impact their mental health, a theme you'll notice in the chapters ahead. Men who have found community and understanding have been better able to integrate their bisexuality into their lives and marriages, but many still struggle to find that. Making resources and community support more available to Bi+ people is vital.

FAMILIAL AND SOCIOCULTURAL FACTORS AFFECTING BISEXUALITY

Bisexuality affects many different spheres of our lives, as you'll see in many of the oral histories ahead. A helpful tool to visualize those spheres is Bronfenbrenner's Ecological Systems Theory Model, published by Russian-born American psychologist Urie Bronfenbrenner in 1977 in an attempt to broaden the factors that potentially affect child development beyond the individual and family, to include environmental and societal influences. This model names five ecological systems that influence our lives, all nested within each other.

Let's begin with the "macrosystem" and work inward (coming back to the "chronosystem" last), focusing specifically on Bi+ identity development. The macrosystem describes overall attitudes, rules, social conditions, and institutional structures of our culture. The most relevant component for Bi+ people is the pervasive homophobia we've discussed, which exists today for everyone on this planet (in my opinion), even those who live in more queer-friendly local environments. We cannot escape the stigma of homosexuality in our culture without completely closing ourselves off to the world. It is an unfortunate reality that provides a blueprint for the many regulations and social policies that constrain queer people, such as dictating who can get married based on gender (same-sex marriage was only legalized nationwide in the US in 2015 and may be overturned), among many other laws.

The macrosystem also includes another social institution that has intersected with sexuality for many men in this book: religion. While change is happening

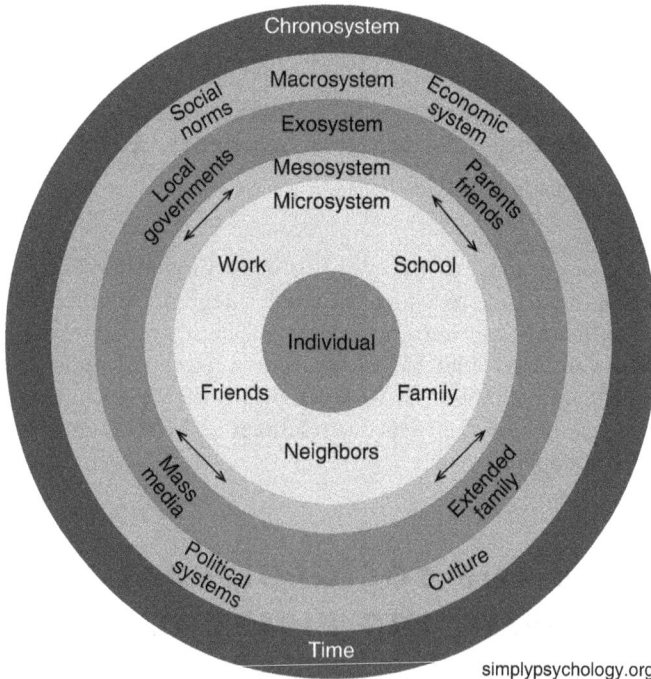

simplypsychology.org

Fig. 5.3 Bronfenbrenner's Ecological Systems Theory Model.

Chart provided by Simply Psychology.

among certain sects and denominations, many religious ideologies still conflict with acceptance of queerness and LGBT+ rights. Even for those able to find a queer-friendly church or other religious community, it is impossible to escape the anti-LGBT+ religious doctrines that have seeped into popular culture, media, and politics. Many of the laws currently being debated and passed in the US are justified by politicians' religious beliefs, despite our theoretical separation of church and state.

The next spheres are the ecosystem and mesosystem, which include structures like school, neighborhoods and community organizations, social services and healthcare, and local government organizations. Technically, the ecosystem refers to structures that we do not directly interact with on an individual level (like the school board or state government), while the mesosystem refers to things we do interact with directly (like the school we attend or local police), but they are of course interrelated, so I will discuss them together. Both are affected by location and economic status, which is part of why I've included that information for each interviewee at the beginning of every chapter.

School is perhaps most influential in Bi+ people's development – experiences and outcomes can change drastically due to victimization based on sexuality, overall safety from violence, anti-bullying practices, queer visibility among other students and teachers, the presence or absence of support groups like GSA ("Gay–Straight Alliance" or more recently "Gender and Sexuality Alliance"), whether queer health or queer history are taught in class, and whether the classroom climate allows for free expression. Jeremy's upcoming story, among others, provides a clear example of the challenges that Bi+ students face in certain school environments.

Neighborhoods and communities also have a huge effect. Some are very queer-friendly, with pro-LGBT+ lawn signage, publicly displayed Pride flags, events like Pride parades, the existence of queer bars and event venues, and queer visibility without repercussions. Others communities may lack those things, or worse: anti-LGBT+ assault and hate crimes are common throughout the US (and elsewhere), and they can have a chilling effect if they happen locally, especially for kids. Local laws and government organizations also have an effect, for example by adding legal barriers to same-sex adoption, by providing support programs queer people or for at-risk youth (or not), and by how local law enforcement views and treats the queer community.

Working inward, we then come to the microsystem, which includes our immediate environment and relationships. For queer development, our home lives play an incredibly important role, both growing up and in adult relationships. Our parents' attitudes and family norms are a primary influence on our gender and sexual socialization, comfort (or confusion) surrounding our identity, and sexual behavior. Almost every interviewee in this book was affected by their parents' perception of their sexuality (and their attitudes toward queerness in general) in one way or another. In my personal journey (and especially in psychotherapy), I always come back to my parents and my upbringing, finding memories that probably influenced why I was able to accept myself, come out, and thrive – but also why

I struggled for so long. Parental support, rejection, or something in between (the most common scenario!) can have a lifelong impact.

Our romantic relationships are another vital aspect of sexuality development. The men in this book are all married (or previously married), and their partners' attitudes, behaviors, and communication surrounding gender and sexuality are a huge influence, but prior relationships play an important role, too. A toxic, biphobic partner can be deeply traumatic and cause depression, repression, and worse – while an early experience of being accepted by a partner can be foundational in terms of self-esteem and a willingness to be vulnerable and explore.

Many other direct relationships and systems affect Bi+ development, such as friendships, relationships with coworkers and workplace environments, interactions with clergy or religious mentors, connections made at local support groups, relationships with doctors or therapists, and even interactions with strangers in our immediate orbit. Keep an eye out for all of these and more in the oral histories that follow.

Finally, at the center of Bronfenbrenner's ecological model, we have the self. Each individual interacts in various ways with the other spheres described above, and Bi+ people often see and hear messaging about fluidity that we internalize without realizing it, which can cause unique internal conflict. It's difficult to deal with the real-world challenges of a queer identity, so some people just don't – their brains don't let them. The internal struggle is as far as they get, and the fear of dealing with those real-world challenges prevents them from coming out or even acknowledging their own Bi+ identity. I know I battled with myself for <u>years</u> before I ever had to bring my queerness to the next sphere, and many men I interviewed did the same thing.

For Bi+ people especially, the "self" connects back in a unique way to the "chronosystem", which refers to changes that occur over our lifetimes. Generally, this sphere is used to discuss societal changes, which do affect queer development – attitudes about homosexuality and queerness have definitely changed over most of our lifetimes, as have laws and regulations, healthcare methods and opportunities, how queerness and sex are presented in school, and more. This is part of why the married Bi+ experience can vary drastically based on when you were born, which is noted in each chapter.

But because bisexuality is <u>about</u> fluidity and by definition incorporates potential change over time, Bi+ people experience the chronosystem on an individual level, as well. In order to fully understand ourselves, we must "check in" periodically and reassess, analyzing how all these other spheres (and how they're changing over time) affect our personal identity conception. This is something that I believe many straight people don't do, as heteronormativity often encourages "finding" oneself, implying a fixed destination rather than a lifelong journey. Bi+ people frequently have to accept that who they are and how they feel now may not be permanent, and this can have implications for their family, their community, their work, and more.

OVERCOMING THESE OBSTACLES AS A COMMUNITY

If we all have a universal capacity for queerness, then bisexuality is not only natural but could be quite common, perhaps even the norm if we could get rid of societal bi-negativity and stigma surrounding queerness. For me, it's a bonus, a positive addition to my life, but it takes a lot of work to get there, and even from where I sit today, it's not always easy. Entering into a straight-appearing marriage only reinforces the invisibility and repression that make a Bi+ identity uniquely challenging.

As a result, most Bi+ men don't know each other, and many don't even know that there are others like them to seek out. Though they face challenges that are unique to bisexuality in various spheres of their lives, they can't find support from like-minded people. This creates a self-perpetuating cycle of shame and isolation.

Many Bi+ men need to heal from the trauma of keeping part of themselves hidden during childhood – or the trauma of biphobic attitudes and attacks, if they came out early – and they need their life partners to be able to support that healing process. This can be challenging, especially if their spouse is unaware or reluctant to embrace queer issues or identities. But as you'll see, many men have found ways to live openly within a long-term partnership, even with a straight partner, and freeing themselves of that internal struggle is a necessary step for being more available to and supportive of their wives.

In the chapters ahead, look out for how each man's bisexuality affects his life in the various spheres of Bronfenbrenner's model. Their marriages and choice of partners have a huge influence on overall wellbeing, and I hope this book can provide models (and some cautionary tales) for how to successfully navigate bisexual-specific challenges together, at the family level. But these oral histories are about more than just marriage, and many of them point to the need for bigger societal changes. Based on almost every measure of health, security, and happiness right now, the Bi+ community is falling behind, and given that our queer identities can affect every ecological sphere of our lives, we're going to need change and improvement at every level in order to give Bi+ people the same opportunity to thrive as everyone else.

BE LIKE BONOBOS

I'll leave you with one example that illustrates the radical shift in thinking we need as a society, from *Queer Ducks*, which we heard about earlier. Eliot Schrefer writes about bonobos and chimpanzees, who both share nearly 99 percent of their DNA with humans but who are quite far apart from each other in terms of sexuality and its broader implications – unlike the polyamorous, bisexual bonobos, chimps have evolved a patriarchal and hyperviolent society.

While chimpanzees are brutally violent with each other, bonobos are known as the "make love, not war" ape … In a now-famous experiment, a primatologist tried introducing a source of honey to a group of chimps, and then to a group of bonobos … In the group of chimps, the strong young males took control of the honey and beat up any females or elderly males who tried to cut in and get food. This way the tough guys in control remained in control. Everyone else hid away, because the males were riled up by the exciting new treat, and riled-up chimps get aggressive.

When the same experiment was repeated with bonobos, it went very differently. First, they all circled the honey source. They got really tense, showing their teeth and shrieking. You could sense their anxiety: How were they going to distribute this delicious food without fighting over it?

… That's when, well, they started an orgy. Not just two or three or four of them, either. All the bonobos started having sex with one another. Male with female, female with female, male with male, young and old and everything in between… Soon they were all sharing the food … None of them got aggressive, because they were in too good a mood.

Both of these attitudes exist among humans today, but under capitalism, patriarchy, white supremacy, and heteronormativity, the chimp way is currently winning out. Too many people at the top (often rich, straight, white men) are hoarding wealth, resources, and privileges, creating unsustainable inequality that spills into every aspect of people's lives, from the microsystem to the macrosystem and everything in between.

Many of us feel powerless to determine our own destiny, but we do have the ability to resist dominant structures and conformity, even if it's difficult. We can choose how to live our individual lives, and when we share that choice with others, we can begin to effect societal change.

Sex, intimacy, and relationship structures have broader implications for humanity than many people realize, and I believe that sexuality and love can be foundations on which we build a more communal society. This will help determine our collective survival, and it will affect our experience of joy and fulfillment on the journey. In a world that often rewards chimp-like behavior, I hope that more of us will choose the bonobo way, which values collectivism, sharing resources, thinking before we act, pleasure, and empathy – even if we don't necessarily have an orgy before every meal.

NOTES

1.   Schrefer, E. (2022). *Queer Ducks (and Other Animals): The Natural World of Animal Sexuality*. Katherine Tegen Books.

2.   Mark, K. P., Vowels, L. M., Bunting, A. M. (2020). The Impact of Bisexual Identity on Sexual and Relationship Satisfaction of Mixed Sex Couples. *Journal of Bisexuality*. https://www.kristenmark.com/wp-content/uploads/2021/08/Mark_Vowels_Bunting_2020.pdf

3. Dyar, C., Taggart, T. C., Rodriguez-Seijas, C., Thompson, Jr. R. G. Elliott, J. C., Hasin, D. S., Eaton, N. R. (2018). Physical Health Disparities Across Dimensions of Sexual Orientation, Race/Ethnicity, and Sex: Evidence for Increased Risk Among Bisexual Adults. *Archives of Sexual Behavior.* https://link.springer.com/article/10.1007/s10508-018-1169-8

4. Mirza, S.A. (2018). Disaggregating the Data for Bisexual People. Center for American Progress. https://www.americanprogress.org/article/disaggregating-data-bisexual-people

5. Durso, L. E., Meyer, I. H. (2012). Patterns and Predictors of Disclosure of Sexual Orientation to Healthcare Providers among Lesbians, Gay Men, and Bisexuals. The Williams Institute. https://www.ncbi.nlm.nih.gov/pmc/articles/PMC3582401

6. Jeffries, W. L. (2014). Beyond the Bisexual Bridge: Sexual Health Among U.S. Men Who Have Sex With Men and Women. *American Journal of Preventative Medicine.* https://www.ajpmonline.org/article/S0749-3797(14)00186-X/fulltext

7. Noble, S. (2020). Mental Health Facts on Bisexual Populations. American Psychiatric Association. https://www.psychiatry.org/File%20Library/Psychiatrists/Cultural-Competency/Mental-Health-Disparities/Mental-Health-Facts-for-Bisexual-Populations.pdf

8. Semlyen, J., King, M., Varney, J., Hagger-Johnson, G. (2016). Sexual Orientation and Symptoms of Common Mental Disorder or Low Wellbeing: Combined Meta-Analysis of 12 UK Population Health Surveys. *BMC Psychiatry.* https://www.ncbi.nlm.nih.gov/pmc/articles/PMC4806482

9. Brennan, D. J., Ross, L. E., Dobinson, C., Veldhuizen, S., Steele, L. S. (2010). Men's Sexual Orientation and Health in Canada. *Canadian Journal Public Health.* https://www.ncbi.nlm.nih.gov/pmc/articles/PMC6974022

10. Conron, K. J., Mimiaga, M. J., Landers, S. J. (2010). A Population-Based Study of Sexual Orientation Identity and Gender Differences in Adult Health. *American Journal of Public Health.* https://www.ncbi.nlm.nih.gov/pmc/articles/PMC2936979

11. (2012). Health Disparities Among Bisexual People. Human Rights Campaign. https://assets2.hrc.org/files/assets/resources/HRC-BiHealthBrief.pdf?_ga=2.222807324.648274840.1677875464-1790989700.1677875464

12. Hsieh, N., Liu, H. (2019). Bisexuality, Union Status, and Gender Composition of the Couple: Reexamining Marital Advantage in Health. *Demography.* https://www.ncbi.nlm.nih.gov/pmc/articles/PMC7039402

13. Lawther, A., Wallace, A. (2022). *2019–2020 Resource Tracking Report.* Funders for LGBT Issues. https://lgbtfunders.org/wp-content/uploads/2022/06/2019-2020-Tracking-Report.pdf

6

Jeremy and How School Bullying Affects Identity Development

I was born in St. Paul, Minnesota, in 1978, right at the generational switch. I have two older sisters. [I'm] from a very working-class family, so one of the things that's impacted everything is having to move, first from Minnesota to Wisconsin and then eventually down to Georgia, for my dad's job.

Georgia was hugely problematic. Other than whiteness being its own little bit of cache, everything else, [I] was always an outsider. You speak with the northern accent, you're an outsider. You don't perform masculinity the way everybody wants you to, you're an outsider. Not politically conservative, definitely an outsider.

Jeremy is a white, bi, non-binary person (assigned male at birth) currently living in Maine. He primarily uses he/him pronouns, using they/them in more queer spaces, and in consultation with him, I've used he/him pronouns in this chapter. He was born in 1978 and was 44 years old at the time of our interview in 2023. He describes himself as non-theist and working-class.

Right away, Jeremy identified himself as an outsider on multiple spectrums, consistent with many other Bi+ married men I've spoken with, which likely affected his early awareness of his fluid sexuality – as well as his recent awareness of gender-non-conformity. Jeremy didn't identify as non-binary until the past few years, and I've included him in this book about married Bi+ men

DOI: 10.4324/9781003385585-6

because his experience overlaps primarily with masculinity. Jeremy presented masculine in many ways (beard, male clothing) but also feminine in others (like his long hair).

> I was six when we moved to Georgia. My father worked for 3M as a technical trainer. My mother was a bank teller early on, but was diagnosed with MS shortly after my birth. She stayed home most of the time. My oldest sister was the surrogate mom for much of my childhood. As soon as I hit 15, I had to do pretty much everything. Cooking, cleaning, you know.
>
> When I was two, I had meningitis, so I am profoundly deaf on my right side, and severely impaired on my left. I didn't speak very much, and I didn't necessarily want to, with the people that I was being confronted with.
> A lot of teachers in Georgia wanted to hold me back, repeat second grade, but I actually tested several years above grade level, so I was starting to get resentful.
>
> When I got to high school, I ended up taking 31 art electives. It was the one place where I could keep moving. My economics teacher gave me a nickname that persisted throughout high school: "that insufferable little shit". I wanna laugh about it now, but actually it's really horrible to be bullied by teachers. I ended up doing visual art, because that had been the refuge. I got a bachelor's in fine arts and a master's in art and teaching, then a PhD in curriculum and instruction. Now I'm an adjunct professor at three different Maine institutions, teaching art education.

Jeremy had to figure a lot out for himself. He had to step up around the house, navigate a challenging school environment despite being ahead of the curve academically, and deal with bullying from both students and teachers. All of this led to a lot of inward reflection, but in that environment, self-acceptance, let alone coming out, was much harder than self-awareness.

> Things started to feel different [in] third, fourth grade. Right when the playground games were picking up, where boys and girls were separating into their camps and making little flirtatious forays back and forth while everyone cheered. [For me], it just didn't feel right, didn't feel the same.
>
> There was certainly no language around it. And this was at the height of the AIDS epidemic. To have that sense that you're not following the same script as everybody else, then to see the real fear that was out there of any difference, particularly in the South … it was really virulent, the hatred around it.
>
> [Once,] an older student had been called a fag and was drinking from a fountain, and the teacher had the janitor shut off the water and spray down the fountain with disinfectant. This was probably 1987, and teachers were so worried about there being gay kids, equating being gay with having AIDS. It never made sense. For a few years after that, kids were still saying you could get AIDS by drinking from a fountain, like it was a really perverse joke. It

was awful in that respect, and it meant having to be pretty discreet. It was a very deep closet.

Though it seems that things are different these days, Jeremy's story also makes me worry about what else goes on in homophobic environments that never gets discussed or reported. Backwards, ill-informed attitudes like this still exist, and it only takes one teacher to traumatize queer students in lasting ways.

The first sets of crushes that I had, it was fast and furious, realizing that basically anyone who was quite pretty, I could have a crush on, and gender really had nothing to do with it. I always thought it was vaguely funny, the very first set of crushes I had were a young blonde girl, and then a redhead boy, and then a brunette. It just seemed there was infinite capacity there.

You have these electric charged moments, and then very much have to keep them to yourself, because the risk of even going to the other person with it was too great. For years, I would tell my own student teachers that I don't remember being bullied, and that's such bullshit. I was absolutely reeling from it. Basically third grade on, I never used the school restroom, because that was simply a place where I knew I was gonna get my ass kicked.

I asked Jeremy why he was bullied – was it because kids thought he was queer, or just "weird" in other ways?

The difference between just being weird and being queer could be pretty subtle at times. I was certainly called both. I was called a faggot. Kids could be absolute little shits.

It was also friendships that would fall apart. I had a set of male friends that in middle school completely dissolved, and only years later you find out the dynamics. Later, one of the friends, [Billy], would come out as gay, so he was obviously going through his own shit and didn't know how to handle it. When you don't want to be the target, the easiest thing you can do is find somebody else to turn on and throw them to the wolves. [Billy] set out to basically convince all of our mutual friends that I was a fag and therefore had to be exposed and outed and ridiculed.

In eighth grade, that culminated in this former friend group trying to convince me that some girl in science class had a thing for me, which they were totally making up to see if they could get me to show up for a fake date. I think they were trying to figure [my sexuality] out. I was very reserved and cagey at that point, self-defensively. When I said, "No, I'm not doing that", that was the sign to them that [I] must be gay, and then it just started coming fast and loose.

It's ironic for a bisexual person to be outed as "gay" in this way, and it hinged on the bullies' binary thinking, "testing" Jeremy's same-sex attraction by observing his attraction toward women, assuming that only one set of attractions could truly exist. Homophobia is often intertwined with biphobia and bi-erasure, though the latter can be nearly invisible.

> I'm an artist, and one of my friends would do drawings of me and spread them around, and in self-defense, I would do drawings of him. It certainly wasn't the best answer, but what do you do? Sometimes you bully back. There was one incident where I had done a rather unflattering drawing of him. Eventually he turned it around, made it about me, put a little word bubble that said, "I'm a fag", added pimples to it.
>
> It got confiscated by the teacher. She had him go home and kept me late. She didn't seem concerned that he had done that. She was more concerned that it might be true. I was deeply confused, like, "Does it matter if it's true? He's insulting me." Her reaction was, "We're gonna have to put this in your permanent file." There is no damn permanent file, but it's used as a threat for everything.

When I asked Jeremy about his relationships around that time, he mentioned a friendship that might have been something more – with a boy who was also a bit of an "outsider".

> [It] ended up not really going anywhere, because he moved away. It was the most emotionally fulfilling relationship that I had had as a younger person. His mother was a single mom and was very supportive of our friendship. I got the impression that she knew there was something more, that it was a deeper sort of friendship. But they had no choice but to move away. Not being able to experience that as an organic end, it set me up to feel really alone through the first couple years of high school.
>
> I really withdrew, very depressed. So nothing much romantically happened in high school. I still had crushes, but I didn't really act on them. The closest I got was being pushed into a relationship with a friend's sister. At that point, there was a real sense that if I can attach myself to this young woman, then it's done, I don't have to worry about any of this shit any more. And I so wanted to be done with it. Not a healthy foundation for a relationship.
>
> I did start to have my first friendships with other queer students. One in particular stood out, a young woman named [Hayley] who was out as a lesbian. [Hayley] was the first person who was like, "It doesn't matter, none of this matters. Love who you love, find attractive who you find attractive." I would find out years later that she ended up traveling with her family to Oklahoma, became a counselor, but eventually committed suicide because of the right-wing environment where she found herself.

I found it very difficult to come out as bisexual decades later, living in some of the most progressive, queer-friendly places in the country. If it was that hard for me, I can't fully imagine what Jeremy went through. To have the first person who normalizes queerness eventually commit suicide must have been extremely confusing and borderline unbearable. But there was more to come.

> There was one other guy who was at least rumored to be bi named [Simon]. I apologize if I break down while saying this. He was two years younger than me, and just watching him constantly bullied by football players, by young women, not just guys, by anybody and everybody . . . When I was a senior, [Simon] died on his bicycle because a group of seniors decided they wanted to play chicken and lost control of the car, slammed him into a tree. Police treated it as just a straight-up accident. I think two of the four or five people in the car died, and he did.
>
> There was no possibility that I was going to be out in high school. It just was not an option. I didn't want to die.

I feared coming out because of embarrassment, shame, and confusion, but I never thought it might get me killed. When we look at recent statistics and see more and more young people coming out as Bi+ or queer, it's important to remember how dangerous it was to come out in the past – and how dangerous it still is in certain areas today. I often wonder what these stats would look like if there were zero cost to coming out, and I hope we find out the answer someday.

Still, Jeremy wanted to be out. He told me another story about a Bi+ woman in high school who was in a terrible relationship, enduring biphobia from her obnoxious boyfriend (including many requests for threesomes), but Jeremy was still envious of her because she was <u>out</u>.

> There's something really dark about recognizing just how hostile and awful that relationship was, and envying it. For all that she was being fetishized and tokenized, she got to be out. You know?
>
> Things didn't shift until I went to college. Going to an art school is hugely liberating in so many ways. There was a vast permissiveness, people publicly identifying as pagan, having fun with that. One of the ways that I organized my friend groups was basically being as blunt and upfront as possible, and if they were assholes about it, then they're gone. I'm not gonna waste time on people that aren't accepting.

I found it fascinating how important your "world" can be in self-acceptance and setting boundaries. What was unthinkable in high school quickly became possible for Jeremy in college. He was able to develop more self-confidence and not put up with homophobia, biphobia, and bullying because of the liberated and open-minded attitudes of his classmates and teachers.

But that doesn't mean relationships got any easier.

> I had impossible standards. There was a guy that I had a crush on freshman year. We were really good together. Then I found out he smoked a ton of

pot. It was 1998, I was uptight, and I certainly wasn't open to it. So I said, no, we can't.

But I was so desperate to have somebody accept me for who I was, to hear somebody say, "I love you" and mean it, that the first person to come along, I just completely fell and convinced myself – and recognized as I was doing it that I was convincing myself. It was so intoxicating to be in what seemed to be a caring relationship. It wasn't until months in that I started to figure out why.

This was [Rachel]. She was more attracted to me initially than I was to her. She liked my butt, I remember that. It wasn't reciprocated at first, but again, just the chance to be accepted … that alone was so alluring. She seemed fine with me being bi. She was all for it. She wasn't demanding threesomes. She was just accepting. It was very cool.

That does sound very cool, especially after what Jeremy went through up to that point. And it's notable that Jeremy told her about his fluid attractions early on, perhaps because of the "permissive" college environment. But the relationship was not "very cool" for long.

Six months in, I had what I should have seen as the warning sign, which was she was asking about polyamory, and she seemed to be confused and think that bisexuality and polyamory were the same thing. And that just wasn't for me. In part because of my background, having to be so careful and so cautious, it just wasn't something I was looking for. But it was something that she was looking for.

We all tell little white lies and try to be who we think the other person wants us to be. I think that's sort of natural. But there's a level where it goes beyond white lies to really spinning fictions about yourself, and she had spun quite a few. I started to learn that she was from a very abusive environment, had grown up with a very broken home where her father had been given the nickname "Skip" because he skipped out on everybody. So on the one hand, she was looking for somebody who was very stable and steady, which I certainly fit the bill for, but then she also wanted permanent escape hatches.

That weird combination meant that what she really wanted was non-monogamy for her but stability for me. I tried to put the kibosh on it quite early and say, "That's interesting, but that's not what I want from this relationship."

Some weekend off, she cheated on me, and then it's a question of where you go from there. I didn't want to end the only stable relationship I had, and this was two years in, which seemed like forever. But at the same time, how can I trust you? Do you really want me for me?

If we had an argument, if there was something that went wrong, then she would immediately try and up the level of commitment. So she actually ended up proposing to me after all of this stuff happened. This is the only person who's actually said they loved me other than my family. Really difficult to understand. Is it real? If it's not real, what do I do?

It was obviously broken, but we continued to live together. She was not interested in consensual non-monogamy – there was very little consent going on there – she just wanted it open. And since I was sensing that things were on the outs anyways, I was looking around. I'm not gonna jump out of something unless there's some type of safety net.

But it seemed like anytime I got close to anybody, male or female, at a certain point, it would go wrong. They would be put off somehow. It didn't really make sense to me, but it happened three or four times. I thought, man, I must be deeply unlovable except for this one person. This is just not fair. How is it that the only person that that loves me is this not good person?

Statistics show that Bi+ people are more likely to be in abusive relationships, and while the rates are worse for women, we often forget that men can be victims, as well. According to a 2010 survey conducted by the CDC, 37 percent of bisexual men report experiences of rape, physical violence, or stalking by an intimate partner at some point in their life, compared to 26 percent of gay men and 29 percent of straight men.[1] Statistics on emotional abuse that include a breakdown of bisexuality are harder to find, but I have heard it anecdotally many times, and I've met many men who have been in emotionally abusive relationships with women. They frequently feel alone and powerless, because that dynamic is so often overlooked and not taken seriously.

I was in a relationship like that, just before I came out. I dated a straight woman (who I met on Tinder) for about one month, and when I tried to break up with her, she refused to let me go, eventually lying that she was pregnant. This prolonged our interaction for another month, during which she said, texted, and emailed me some of the most horrible things that anyone has ever said to me. Thankfully, I realized this was abusive and found a way out. (I was also scared to date women for a while after this traumatic experience, which may have contributed to my desire to explore with men.)

Though my bisexuality wasn't available as cannon fodder at the time, biphobia is often part of the abuse that bisexual people suffer from. Problems within a relationship get blamed on one partner's bisexuality, as if that were something they could "work on" or change. Rachel not only conflated polyamory with bisexuality, but she also straight-up weaponized Jeremy's same-sex attraction against him.

At that point, [Vanessa] stayed over for a weekend. She's a couple years younger. [Vanessa] stayed on the couch, and I think [Rachel] understood or could sense there was a mutual attraction, so when I was out, she pulled [Vanessa] aside and said, "Hey, you know that he's bi." [Vanessa] to her credit just looked at her and said, "So? It's not a big deal." And she said, "But he's attracted to both men and women – let me show you what's on his computer." She completely violated my privacy. And [Vanessa] is like, "Doesn't bother me. Why would that bother me?"

Rachel tried to use Jeremy's bisexuality against him – as if that made Jeremy so unlovable, only she could be with him. Thankfully, that biphobic smear didn't work on Vanessa, and the whole episode was instrumental in getting out of the abusive relationship with Rachel.

[Vanessa] had also seen her share of familial abuse, but sometimes it doesn't turn people awful, so [Vanessa] realized that [Rachel] was full of shit and told me about it. It was at that point that I realized what exactly had been going on. [Rachel] had always been asking me, "Is there anybody you're interested in?" The minute there would be, she would go out of her way to prevent anything from happening. When she sensed that I might be interested in [Vanessa], she pounced. It's just the one time it didn't work.

Then [Rachel] did her ultimate move, which was to get me fired. She outed me to my boss. Even though she had been basically relying on me for financial stability. I was working at a toy store in Savannah. Georgia's a right-to-work state, so you don't have to be fired for [a] cause, you can just be let go. What [was] relayed to me was, "He just makes everyone uncomfortable." I think I can fill in the blanks.

We had a couple other friends, one wanted to get me away from [Rachel], and they conspired to get [Vanessa] and [me] together. On a road trip to Atlanta, [they] made sure that we were stuck in an apartment together, completely alone, while the rest of them found other couches or whatever, just to see if we would hook up. And we did. Their manipulation worked.

As soon as I officially ended it with [Rachel], she did some of the classic stuff. Even though it was my name on the lease, she went down to the leasing agency and demanded to change the keys. I had provided all the furniture, not that it was worth much, but she tried to steal as much of it as possible. I was a bit of an ass; I think I said, "I'll leave you the bed, because I don't wanna sleep on anything that you've slept in, but I'm taking all of my stuff, my computers, my clothes," and I piled it all into a U-Haul [truck] and got the hell out of there.

[Vanessa] and I ended up staying in a long-haul hotel for the semester to take the last couple credits I needed to graduate. What a remarkable difference. I mean, everything that had been wrong and off with [Rachel] suddenly seemed to be right. And the most important part was that [Vanessa] didn't care.

It was clear that Jeremy meant she "didn't care *about my sexuality*", but I thought his phrasing was interesting, and I've heard it before. It's almost as if bisexuality doesn't need to be named because it's so obviously the thing that a potential part-ner would "care" about, simultaneously making it a vital aspect of identity and also an invisible one by omitting the actual label.

In some respects, it is both: it's vitally important even when it fades into the background. As Jeremy learned, having a partner who is open and accepting – and maybe even recognizes their own fluid potential – is liberating.

I remember being very free to talk about, like, the typical Hollywood crush, right? It was Angelina Jolie and Johnny Depp, you know. [Vanessa]'s sexuality, the way that she tends to say it is 80/20. She recognizes the potential in herself to be attracted to and appreciate more than one gender, even though she's never been in a same-sex relationship. One hot kiss at a convention, that was fun. But never a relationship. But just being able to recognize that potential and to see in each other that little bit of fellow feeling ...

Jeremy trailed off, but it was clear that this meant the world to him. Though we didn't get into many details about why else they were attracted to each other, they clearly had a solid foundation and were off to the races. I asked how old Jeremy was when the relationship began:

I was 22. I married [Vanessa] at 26. We've been together 20 years, married 17. And it is a monogamous relationship.

After I graduated, I ended up moving with her to North Carolina where I started as a long-term substitute and then a public school teacher. Over time got my master's degree, then my PhD, and she has been hugely supportive all the way through.

This was one of the few interviews where non-monogamy didn't come up. Jeremy and Vanessa both wanted to be monogamous and have stuck with it throughout their marriage. We also didn't get into many other details of their partnership, but Jeremy described it as happy, healthy, and committed.

Still, he deals with biophbia — and more recently, transphobia — from people outside his relationship, to varying degrees depending on where he's lived.

When I was in Minnesota, one of my colleagues — I didn't know the terminology [then], but I can use it now — she's very much a gender-critical TERF [trans-exclusionary radical feminist]. She was opining that no person expressing masculinity should ever be a teacher. It's a little out there. If you said, "[Don't] young men need good male role models? Can we present a vision of masculinity that is non-toxic?" Her answer would be no, because men are centered enough in society, and they would do far better to just have women teachers. There is a little bit of evidence that a lot of queer folk teach elementary, a lot of gay and bi men [are] in more caring professions. She was deeply uncomfortable with that, so if you were a male teacher, you needed to keep your door open, 'cause you can't be trusted to have your door closed with your students. Stuff like that.

When I was teaching in North Carolina, it was like straight back into the closet. In North Carolina, another right-to-work state, they were willing to accept a lesbian, [but] much less willing to accept gay men, because of a perceived ... I mean, the whole groomer term may be new, but the discourse is old. If I had been out, I would've been fired that afternoon.

While I was there, students ask, people figure it out. If you're sort of cagey, they figure out what it is you're not saying. So I ran an art club that ended up basically being a better GSA than the GSA, because the GSA was really transphobic and biphobic. But otherwise I had to be very strictly closeted, for professional consideration. That limits an awful lot.

As a teacher, Jeremy began to encounter more gender fluidity and trans identities among his students, which helped him reconsider his own gender identity.

It's always been the sense that I didn't fit in with the other guys. Something there, or something not quite there. Part of it, very honestly, was just how toxic the expressions of masculinity were. And so to always have that tension between expression and identity, to me, "non-binary" fits best.

I asked how long he's identified as non-binary and why he chose to come out publicly.

Just in the past decade. In part because I think we need to be more out and public, particularly for students. That's what all of this recent legislation is about, making everyone invisible to try and make it not possible. If something's not possible because it's not seen, I think it's really important to do the opposite. It's always been part of me, but it's not been public until I was in a position where that could happen. Once I started in higher education, it became possible.

I asked how his wife reacted to him coming out as non-binary.

She's the one who first proposed it. It's nice to be with someone who's figured you out.

Throughout Jeremy's relationship, being fully understood and accepted by his wife has helped keep him going – and sane. This type of support is urgently needed for other Bi+ and queer men, both on an individual level and as a community, if we're going to survive and thrive as Jeremy has.

The idea that somehow being married means that I've stopped being myself . . . Like, huh? I understand why people want that to be the case, but we're something like 20 times more likely to end up in a heterosexual-seeming relationship than not, simply because of the odds. Damn it, we exist. Visibility is important. We can't be over 50 percent of the queer community with 1 percent of the funding and none of the visibility.

Having somebody that you can be completely open and completely honest with, that's what's made it work. It's not always easy. I don't think you ever fully recover from trauma. We both had parents [who] were severely ill. We both have been part of abusive environments. We have encountered difficulties, and it's the same difficulties that any long-term couple encounters, mostly around money – losing a job is never fun, being temporarily unhoused really sucks – but having someone to go through it with matters. It's [about] recognizing yourself in somebody, not just sexuality, not just gender, but all of it. I think that's why it's worked, because I don't have to hide anything. We can just go through it together.

NOTE

1.   Black, M. C., Basile, K. C., Breiding, M. J., Smith, S. G., Walters, M. L., Merrick, M. T., Chen, J., & Stevens, M. R. (2011). The National Intimate Partner and Sexual Violence Survey (NISVS): 2010 Summary Report. *National Center for Injury Prevention and Control, Centers for Disease Control and Prevention.* https://www.thetaskforce.org/bisexual-women-have-increased-risk-of-intimate-partner-violence-new-cdc-data-shows/

7

Kaiko on Surviving Abuse and Embracing Change

I was born in '92 in Lancaster, California, in the desert. My dad was in the military, so he worked on Edwards, and my mom worked on the base in LA, so they split the difference.

I'm an only child. I can't compare it to anything, 'cause it's all I know. It's a little strange in the sense that you don't have someone to relate your experience to. Having to process your parents' stuff, I wish that I could do that with a sibling sometimes.

I'm 30. We're embracing the 30s, but 30 was hard for me, I don't know why. It was a weird one. It felt like I couldn't just dick around any more, you know what I mean? I had to be like an adult and take my life seriously.

Kaiko is a bisexual, cisgender man who described his race as "super-mixed". He was born in Lancaster, California in 1992, currently lives in London, and was 30 years old at the time of our interview in 2022. He described his religion currently as "ex-vangelical and slightly pagan". He grew up and remains middle-class. He is not a military veteran, but he comes from a military family.

Already, I identified with Kaiko's story, because the turning point in my Bi+ journey was right around the same age. I remember wanting to explore with men before I hit 30 – it felt like a "now or never" moment. I did that privately for a

DOI: 10.4324/9781003385585-7

year or two, and I started coming out by age 32. As it did for Kaiko, 30 equaled adulthood in my mind, and I finally had to take this stuff seriously.

But bisexuality wasn't the only thing that Kaiko decided to confront in his 30s.

Last Christmas, I was at a very British thing, the "pantomime", which is like a play [for children] and the audience cheers for the good guys and boos the bad guys. They had these sweet little children, they were these little woodland creatures, and I was hit with this thought, "Those people are so small and so vulnerable and tiny." And then I had the thought, "How [could] my dad treat me so badly when I was that age?"

He was so scary at the time. But now I look at it and I feel like he's more a coward who can't really deal with his own emotions and anger properly. I use the term abusive, but it wasn't ever a constant thing. It was more like, whatever pissed him off that day, if I said something or looked at something wrong or sat on the couch wrong, it could have been anything, then an explosion would happen. So I feel like I grew up walking on eggshells because you never really knew what was going to happen. Am I going to get yelled at or smacked around or whatever form it took that day?

My mom, I feel like I've always really loved her and felt like her sidekick. I still have all that love for her, but I also think, "How could you let that happen to me? How could you observe that and not really do anything?" But at the same time, I think she also felt powerless, and she sometimes justifies his behavior, because they both had worse situations growing up. So the cycle continues.

Kaiko grew up in an abusive home, and though he half-joked that the cycle continues, his awareness of this dynamic puts him in a good position to stop it. He qualified the abuse as "not constant", but of course that doesn't mean he wasn't abused or traumatized, and this may have affected his attachment style.

One of the most impactful books I've read since coming out is *Polysecure* by Jessica Fern – even though it does focus on polyamory, it is mostly about how our attachment style (developed in childhood) intersects with and affects our romantic relationships, including monogamous ones. (I highly recommend this book for everyone, regardless of your relationship structure or orientation.) Fern writes:

We learn how to self-regulate through our connections with our attach-ment figures. So, if our parents were unable to regulate their own emotions (whether from their current stress levels or their previous unresolved trauma), and therefor couldn't support us in regulating our own emotions, we lost a foundational developmental experience ... We have to figure out how to identify and then articulate our emotional states and then find ways to self-soothe as a healthy response instead of pulling away, shutting down or lashing out in emotional reactivity. We also need to learn how to healthily rely on others and to figure out when it's appropriate to seek support from them to help regulate our emotions.[1]

This concept is relevant to every story in this book, but it's particularly useful in understanding Kaiko's trajectory. Thankfully, it seems like he's made a ton of progress in terms of emotional regulation – thanks in part to his wife (whom you'll meet soon) and therapy they've done both alone and together – but there are also moments in his story where he describes "pulling away" or not fully engaging emotionally in relationships, which could be a response to the trauma of abuse and a form of self-protection.

My dad is Creole, which is a mix of French, Native American, and African. My mom is Hawaiian, Filipino, and her dad's parents were from Germany and Sicily. My mom grew up Catholic but doesn't practice now. My dad dabbled in Buddhism for a minute. They would occasionally come to church with me if I went, so they're not opposed to [religion], but they're not actively gonna pursue that.

My dad's old. He was born in '46. He had me when he was 45, my mom was 26, they're 19 years apart. My mom was an Air Force recruiter, she retired as a master's sergeant. My dad was in Vietnam, which I think is where a lot of the instability comes from, because it was like you just went to war and then you came back and you can't talk about your problems – only weak people go to therapy.

Though Kaiko eventually did go to therapy, his father's old-school attitude no doubt influenced how Kaiko dealt with challenges growing up. Especially paired with his dad repressing the trauma of war and not talking about any post-traumatic stress, it's understandable that Kaiko might initially repress his sexuality and try to "tough it out". (Reading this just before publication, Kaiko remarked: "This is probably true. I've never thought about it that way. I had no space to just be. I could hardly go beyond existing and be myself when my dad would scold me or yell at me for the most banal things." This makes sense to me – when we're dealing with abuse, we have no space to "just be" and focus on ourselves, and things that don't fit with the environment get repressed. Kaiko's father likely also lacked the space to "just be" and address his own trauma, but because he was unaware of that, perhaps willfully, he perpetuated it.)

My parents got stationed in Hawaii when I was seven, and we moved back to Lancaster when I was ten. I was really behind, so they put me into a private Christian school. I learned how to be a certain way, like we had a dress code, and we had chapel every week on Thursday. [One day] they were talking about sex, it was like, "Let me glue these two pieces of paper together, because that's what you're doing if you're having sex with someone that you're not married to", and then [they] ripped them apart and [said,] "Look at that, isn't that so terrible?" So my ideas on sex and sexuality were just so fucked up for the longest time.

My favorite was the Oreo. It was like, if you're not married and you're having sex, it's like someone taking a bite out of you, so eventually you just disappear. Which logically is so funny … [laughs]. But when you're in seventh grade, it's not funny.

On top of physical abuse at home and religious trauma at school – not easy for any teenager – he was also dealing with confusion about his sexual orientation.

I feel like I was always bullied for my sexuality because I've always sounded like this. I didn't pick that up. I came out of the womb like this.

Kaiko was referring to his voice being slightly higher-than-average for men, with a bit of sibilation – a very mild version of the so-called "gay voice".

People would assume that I was gay or make fun of me for being gay. But I couldn't be that, because you would get kicked out of the school for that. It was also a term that felt like it never really fit, because I [was] realizing I just thought everybody was hot, but I didn't know how to put that into words.

I think it was second grade, I remember thinking, "Oh, this boy's so great, I wanna be his friend." But I think I wanted to be more than his friend. In fifth grade, I remember finding a few of the girls in my class attractive as well. I was just in denial for the longest time, and I didn't know what to do with it. Then the church was like, you have to be straight and that's the only option. I didn't even know the word bisexual was an option, so I was like, okay, my options are straight and gay, and I feel both things, but I'm just gonna go with the one that makes sense with my community right now. So it was "straight" – you know, in quotes.

I asked Kaiko whether he'd had any romantic relationships growing up, with women or men.

I was a good Christian boy, and I was also really driven and academic-focused, so I didn't really have time or didn't wanna make time. I've only had one serious relationship other than my wife, and that was in high school, which I even hesitate to call that serious. We were friends for a really long time, since fifth grade. I think it was our senior year, the attraction just grew, so we started dating.

There was a little bit [of a physical relationship], but never sex, because that was never an option. We were never naked together. I don't really remember why we broke up. Isn't that terrible? I just remember at some point it didn't work out or it got weird. We're also Christian school kids, so we're not used to talking about our feelings, because you're not supposed to have your own personal feelings. You have to relate everything back to God, so it's hard to process your own emotions. It's always like, "What is God telling me?" I didn't even know what to do with myself.

I also identified with Kaiko being unable to process his own feelings. As a "people pleaser", I spend so much time attuned to others, I sometimes repress my own emotions without even realizing it. But for Kaiko, it was more extreme:

The repression feels like it went beyond people pleasing. Church deprived me of outside influence and ideas. I could only believe the things they believed.

Our environment has a huge effect on our worldview and sense of self, and when we're in a constrictive one, it can suck up all our mental energy and leave us with little in the tank to focus on ourselves. Thankfully, high school doesn't last forever.

Other than my high school relationship, I've only dated my wife. We started dating when we were 20, and then we got married at 23. We were young, which has its challenges, because you don't work out your own shit, you know? The church tells you, if you're both focused on God, it's gonna be great. And that's not really true. I think compatibility is a myth – it's always going to shift and change. I don't think using God as a scapegoat is going to keep your marriage together. Now I prefer to be more open and honest about what's going on and how I actually feel, how we're actually relating to each other.

Kaiko hit the nail on the head: marrying young means you haven't necessarily "worked out your own shit", and you'll have to work it out together. This offers some benefits – you have someone to help support you, guide you, and grow with you – but it can also be challenging, because the stakes of self-discovery can be higher, especially if those discoveries affect your partner. This may have contributed to Kaiko's hesitancy to enter a relationship at this time.

We were in the same dorm [in college] and going to the same church. She was interested initially, and I was focused on [getting] a degree. Being a musician's not easy, and you have to say no to a lot of things in order to make it work. I started a degree in piano performance, and it's cutthroat.

At some point I had to say, "I think you're interested in me, but this isn't going to go anywhere." She didn't want to be my friend, because she said it felt like a breakup in a way. Then I realized that maybe I'm the asshole, maybe I'm the idiot. Eventually I was like, I have a good time with this person, I like this person, I'm attracted to this person, so what's holding me back? I got to the point where I was like, even if this doesn't work out, I don't wanna let the opportunity go.

I thought we would go on a couple of dates, and she was like, Facebook profile official, we are dating. And I was like, I've probably messed this up too many times to backpedal any more, so I just let it be. And then it ended up working out. We got married in 2015, after dating for two-and-a-half years.

We had two years in Colorado. They were great. Then we moved to Italy for my master's degree, and that was hard, as gorgeous as it is. That's when some of those conflicts that we never dealt with in Colorado came to the surface. That was a lot to work through.

She took a trip to London in 2018 and was like, "Look, if you're ever going to apply to any PhDs, you need to apply here, because it was great. I wanna move there." And I was like, okay. So I applied to one school, and I got in. We moved in December 2020, in the middle of the pandemic. [Now] I teach piano in London, and I'm doing a PhD in historical musicology.

We eventually got to a point where I was like, if we don't do therapy tomorrow . . . I'm not saying I'm gonna leave you, but it's not working. The positive thing is, we did it, and we're doing it, and we work our shit out. We have worked on developing a growth mindset around things so that it's not like there's this narrative that was always fed to us, like, "I want to be financially stable before I date", or "I want my own place before I date" – that's not realistic at all, because life doesn't give a fuck. [Life] is gonna throw whatever [it] wants at you, and you have to find ways to cope with that.

Many of us feel that our relationships and lives are supposed to follow certain scripts, and milestones like marriage or achieving financial stability are evidence that you're "healthy" and "successful". But in reality, those milestones and structures can sometimes mask deeper problems and communication issues. As Jessica Fern writes in *Polysecure*:

The narratives people have about love, marriage, primary partnership and how to achieve relationship security are powerful, so much so that just the idea of being in love, married or in a primary partnership can lead us to think we are experiencing attachment security when in reality we might not be … Structural demonstrations of security can be signs of genuine commitment … but they do not ensure high-quality attunement, presence and responsiveness that foster secure attachment at the interpersonal level … Allow your direct experience with a partner to be the vehicle to secure attachment instead of having certain relationship concepts, narratives or structures be the vehicle.

This is exactly what Kaiko and his wife were able to do once they let go of meeting societal expectations. Writing your own script with a partner takes brutal honesty and negotiation, which they were able to achieve with the help of a therapist. This is not an easy process, but the hard work eventually paid off and brought them closer together, because they learned to communicate through conflict and be their authentic selves with each other, without fear of rejection or abandonment.

Feeling a newfound sense of authenticity and safety within his relationship likely gave Kaiko more space to notice his queerness and soon verbalize it.

> I remember having to do the census in January [2021]. There was the drop-down of sexuality, and I was like, "Hmm, what happens if I click on bisexual?" So I clicked it, and I was like, "I feel okay." And my computer didn't explode, so I guess it's all right.

This moment has happened to so many Bi+ people I've met (although the census is certainly a unique catalyst). We dip our toes in the water, expecting it to be terrible (or for our computer to explode), but it's actually … fine, which gives us confidence to go deeper.

> Then I started listening to your podcast, and I cannot tell you enough, it was so helpful for me, because it's just this nebulous thing that you're feeling. It's not even anything that you can grab out of society because it's not there. You have to shave off or deconstruct or smash it apart and then take the pieces and build something up for yourself that actually makes sense. So that's what that year was.
>
> I didn't come out until I was 29. I didn't want to go into 30 not being myself. I'm realizing it was for me, which I think is okay, like it's mine to have and it's mine to give and it's mine to own.

Not only is this "okay", it's a perfect way to think about sexuality – it is yours, you don't owe anyone anything, and you get to choose who you "invite in" to know your true self.

> I told my wife first, in October [2021], which also happened to be national coming-out day, which was just a coincidence but worked out perfectly. She was like, "Oh my God, babe, that's so great." She was really supportive. Which was kind of shocking, because in the past she said things like "bisexuality just means that you can't pick a side." So I was nervous to tell her, but I also knew that she'd grown since then. She doesn't even identify as a Christian any more, so I felt like it was safe to tell her.

Despite Kaiko's fears, coming out to his wife was an overwhelmingly positive experience. For many others, it's a lot more complicated, but thankfully, his wife had unlearned some societal biphobia by that point and was supportive. This is part of why we need more Bi+ visibility and representation, not just for Bi+ people, but for their partners, lovers, friends, and family. In my opinion, sharing our authentic stories and knowledge is the best way to combat pervasive biphobic misinformation and stereotypes.

Then I told my friends here [in London], because that's easier to do. I just met them, so you can present, "This is me", as opposed to having to add something in later. Telling [old] friends and family was scarier for me.

I told my mom in April [2022], and interestingly enough, she was like, "I think your dad is, too." And I was like, "What the fuck?" She was like, "I don't think he'd ever say that, but I think he is." I was like, that's interesting. I don't know what to do with that.

I never had a conversation with my dad, because I don't really wanna have conversations with him. I told my mom, "You can tell dad if you want to." Which is sad. So he knows, but he never mentioned it to me, never wanted to talk about it. So there it lies. It's just a word that he can attach to me.

I was almost as shocked as Kaiko to find out that his father might be bisexual. I'm not sure how much to read into that, but keeping difficult emotions "private" does seem to be a theme in his family, perhaps even a tactic for survival. There also may be some relationship between the mental health toll taken by this type of repression and the abuse Kaiko's father perpetuated.

Though Kaiko had good initial experiences sharing his sexuality, it wasn't all sunshine and rainbows when he came out to his wife's family.

It was my turn to pick the book for family book club with my wife's family. I picked a book by Celeste Ng, it was *Everything I Never Told You*. Everything we read is written by white people – I'm like, "Can we not? They're not the only people who have things to say." I was also saying there's a Bi+ character, and I'm really excited to read things with more bi representation, because I'm also bi. And then just left it at that.

Her younger sister was actually very supportive, and her dad, surprisingly also cool. Mom – horror story. [Her] mom always thought that I was gay, and I swear to God, she still thinks that I am. She was like, "I'm always gonna protect my daughter", like I'm a threat now. I wanted to invite them in to this information, you know what I'm saying? But instead it didn't go well.

The next day, she was saying things [to my wife] like, "I wouldn't be surprised if he is sleeping with [his] best friend", and" Are you sure he wants kids?" Because queer people don't want kids? I do want kids, because I feel like I have a lot of love to give. They basically said, "We will help you get a divorce if you want", which was a massive overstep and just incredibly inappropriate. So [my wife] didn't want to talk to her parents for a long time, about six weeks.

They eventually did apologize to me, but it was mostly her dad trying to save face. Her dad [said], "We won't bring it up again", and I was like, "No, that's not the point." The point is to bring it up, because it's not just something like, oh, I'm attracted to that person. It's more of a worldview. You look at things differently. The grass is greener, the sun is brighter, and the sky is bluer, you know what I mean? There's so much freedom that comes with actually being able to say it out loud and to feel good and have some conviction behind it finally.

Maybe Kaiko's thoughts remind me of my own because he listened to so much of my podcast, but I couldn't agree more. So many people think that sexuality is just about sex – even some of the older Bi+ men in this book, who shy away from discussing sexuality with their kids or parents because they think it would be a conversation about sex – but to me, it's a complete shift in worldview that affects much more than sex. Once I realized that having sex with men was not just okay but pleasurable – and I didn't explode! – it reshaped how I view the boxes that society puts us in, why we follow so many unwritten rules, and how much power there is in subverting authority. I gained a new understanding of all marginalized identities and experiences, and my politics shifted toward radical inclusivity.

Once you realize all that (and more), it's hard to keep it to yourself. But talking about it often makes people uncomfortable, because they think you're just talking about queer sex acts. Don't get me wrong, I love talking about those, too, but my bisexuality is about so much more. It's like I found a buried treasure and want to share it, so it's emotionally challenging and confusing when others aren't interested.

As it often does, non-monogamy eventually became a topic of discussion.

She did have a moment where she was freaking out that I would want to be non-monogamous. If you know the podcast *Sex with Emily*, we did her "yes, no, maybe" list, it's like every sexual act you could possibly imagine, and it's like, anal, yes or no, and then blowjob, yes or no. When it came to group sex or a threesome, I was like, "maybe?" I think she's still processing that.

She feels like monogamy is the only option for her, and I've told her, I've committed to you, we've been through too much shit to mess this up, and I really like being around you, so I would never do anything unless you approved of that. But I wouldn't mind exploring that. I don't even really know where that would start or what that would mean. I think we're still working through that.

Because Kaiko came out so recently, they're still at the early stages of that discussion. I don't doubt that he's committed to monogamy if she is, which would be a valid decision even if Kaiko has at least some curiosity about exploring sex with other people. I asked him if he had ever explored sex with men in his life, and he shook his head.

Nope.

There was a pause. I asked how he feels about that.

Part of me feels … I feel great about being married, and we work really well together, and we always have a good time together. I think I'm not sad about not being able to do that now. I'm more sad about not being able to do that before we met. To just figure that out a little bit more, because everything was so rigid and black-and-white for me. So that's more of the bummer.

I asked if Kaiko has met other Bi+ people since coming out and moving to London, a particularly bisexual city where many of my podcast guests live.

I would love to build more bi community, because I know they're out there, especially here. The thing is time. When there's a bisexual meetup, I'm often teaching, or I have to go to a concert, or work on my PhD, or whatever. But it's something that I would really like to do.

My best friend, he first came out to me as gay, and then I came out to him as bi, and then he thought, "Oh, maybe that fits me better". I don't quite know where he's landed, but it's been kind of cool to go through that stuff together.

I'm out everywhere else. Work, school, which so far has been positive. My old friends know – I was originally like, I don't know if I can tell you this, because some of our friends are still in church. I told our friends who have a baby, and they were like, "Okay, great, we're leaving our church because we want to be supportive for you." I was like, that took a turn, I wasn't expecting that. I think I was the final straw for them. It's like a dance when you put that out there, to see what kind of reactions happen and what kind of ripples it has.

I know what Kaiko means. Before I came out, I had so much anxiety about how different people would react, but overall, I was surprised by how supportive most people were. I was also surprised by how many people came out to me in response, either telling me they're Bi+ also or by sharing some other, unrelated secret. It reminded me of how hard it is to be vulnerable about things we've repressed or are ashamed of – and how wild it is to feel so alone when other people close to us are going through something similar.

I asked Kaiko if they're planning to have kids.

We've always wanted them, and that hasn't really changed for me. I teach kids, I've taught them for a very long time. I feel like I've learned so much about how to navigate kids that I could have my own. I don't like the idea of getting older and being like, "What do you wanna do tonight? I guess we could go out?" I don't want that to be our only thing. I feel like I have love to give in that way.

I asked if he was happy with his journey so far and if there was anything he wished he had known earlier. His answer was classically bisexual in its acceptance of conflicting emotions.

I'm okay with the journey. Am I? I don't know. I think I am and I'm not, because not to be dramatic, but I feel like I have to hold a lot of pain in my heart and love at the same time, because of my dad and how I was treated, because of how [my wife's] mom feels toward me, because of church. But I have to find some way to move forward.

I guess I would tell myself that it's okay to hold both at the same time. I would also say that your identity and sexuality are yours to have and to keep and to own and to love. You get to choose who you want to share yourself with, and it's okay to not share yourself with everybody.

One thing that I love about the Earth is that it's constantly changing, and I think if we were more honest with ourselves, we would realize that everything is constantly changing all the time. Accepting that and going with it is better and more natural, because that's what the planet we live on does constantly. I garden, and even to look at my garden today versus tomorrow, it's gonna be different. There's gonna be different things in different places. Something is going to change, and I love that idea now. That used to be so uncomfortable for me.

An important aspect of Bi+ discourse is understanding that sexuality can be fluid, and this extends to more than just gender preference, including things like overall sex drive, how we prefer to experience romance and emotional intimacy, our orientation on the monogamy spectrum, and more. When we understand and embrace this fluidity within ourselves, I believe it makes us kinder and more empathetic toward others, in all area of life. This is one of our Bi+ superpowers, and it allows us to appreciate the full spectrum of the evolving human experience. Kaiko summed it up nicely:

I feel like the more I know myself, the more I am able to relate to people and value their experiences and not try to fit it into my lens. It's all valid, which is super cool. I feel like that's what bisexuality has given me, is not having to look at things so painfully black-and-white, but everything is a lot more fluid and a lot more flexible. All the options can be valid.

NOTE

1.   Fern, J. (2020). *Polysecure: Attachment, Trauma and Consensual Nonmonogamy.* Thorntree Press.

8

Scott on Lost Opportunities and Navigating Infidelity

I was born on the East Coast. I grew up in a fairly liberal college town in [the Midwest]. There were a lot of cultural events going on, so it didn't feel like [a] small town, even though it was. My parents were very liberal, it wasn't some conservative environment in which I felt repressed. My family is a family of academics, so I'm kind of the odd one out. But it was a very pleasant childhood.

S cott is a white, Bi+, cisgender man who also identifies as queer and pan. He was in his mid-40s at the time of our first interview in 2020 and late 40s during a follow-up interview in 2023. He was raised Protestant but currently describes himself as agnostic. He grew up middle-class and now considers himself upper-/professional class.

Scott is also a lawyer, which is why he described himself as the "odd one out" in a family of academics, and as we've seen already in other interviews, self-identifying as "different" for any reason often leads to introspection about queerness.

The first time I was aware of anything sex-related, I knew that there were at least two sides to me. From the very beginning it was clear that there was something … initially I described it as, and this is only to myself, something is wrong, something's off, there's some issue or problem.

DOI: 10.4324/9781003385585-8

I was 13 or 14 and I was feeling attraction. The non-scary part of it was that I was feeling attraction to girls. The scary part of it was that I was feeling attraction to boys, and that was the part that felt wrong. And I kept on waiting to grow out of it, which I have been unsuccessful at.

Scott's story began with a common refrain. For most bisexual men, it feels like part of our sexuality is confusing or even "wrong" – the same-sex attraction part. The other part – opposite-sex attraction – feels more "normal", not scary, and is generally accepted by those around us, so we often lean into that.

I know I did. Especially the year or two before I was out, it felt great to be with women. The relationships and sex felt natural, pleasurable, and validating – and as a bonus, they were a good distraction from my more confusing feelings about men. Because I was still locked in a binary, being with women felt like "evidence" for me that I was straight, which unfortunately allowed me to ignore and minimize my same-sex attractions.

Scott also leaned into the "non-scary" side of himself for a while, but his experience was still fairly limited, and because he didn't see bisexuality as a valid option, he had trouble integrating his feelings.

In terms of my sexual experience, I slept with one woman when I was a freshman in college, I lost my virginity, and then the only other person I've slept with, at least until more recently, and we'll get to that … is my wife. I was certainly repressing in a number of different ways because I was scared and I didn't know how to deal with it.

Although I knew there was something going on, I had difficulty putting a label on it. I'd also seen, to the extent people did come out that were within my age group, they frequently identified as bi, but then it was pretty clear they were gay. That's not an uncommon story, and so I resisted that label as well, because my experience is that it was just another lie.

I would say, other than that, I had a pretty decent childhood.

It was interesting that Scott occasionally went back to discussing his childhood as "pleasant" and "decent". I am sure it was overall, but it also reminded me of myself and of something I've been working on in therapy: I frequently think of my circumstances as "fine", I downplay discomfort, and I think of myself as "strong" and able to handle anything.

I see these as common coping mechanisms for queer people in a heteronormative world, and especially for Bi+ people in an ultra-binary world. We experience very basic human needs – attraction, connection, pleasure, sex – in a unique way that is often stigmatized and erased, so most of us have <u>had</u> to downplay our own feelings at times to survive. We've had to repress ongoing trauma and microaggressions related to our sexuality because biphobia is so pervasive and accepted. We give others the benefit of the doubt because sometimes it's easier to accept that we're "different" or "confused" instead of most of the world being misinformed.

But eventually, there comes a day when we can no longer ignore this incongruence.

> Ignoring was my default. Although I did admit to myself, I think around freshman year of college, that this was a permanent side of me. My hope that it was going to disappear was not going to happen. That said, that doesn't mean I dealt with it or addressed it or that it was a healthy thing. I just acknowledged it and then said, okay, I will force myself to ignore it. Yeah, I know. Not a psychologically sound strategy.

Okay, maybe we <u>can</u> keep ignoring it even after that initial light-bulb moment … but in Scott's case, consciously ignoring is different from subconsciously ignoring, and it's difficult to sustain. Awareness plus repression adds up to cognitive dissonance (or internal tension caused by our thoughts not matching our behavior), and this is one of the biggest reasons why Bi+ men suffer from mental health issues.

While lifelong repression is possible – and probably common, unfortunately – I do not recommend it. Sex, connection, and attraction are important to your identity, perhaps fundamental, and it's worth some initial discomfort in order to navigate them authentically.

> [My wife and I] met on a night in which everyone was drunk except me, 'cause I had to study. Instantly, there was attraction. It was not even a question. We were very casual for a number of years. She certainly had lots of boyfriends. My experience was kind of … I was fairly limited, in terms of basic sex [laughs].
>
> It was a really good relationship, in many respects. There were bumps in the road at the beginning, but I felt very satisfied. With one caveat, which is that I would … this was back in the day when you actually had to physically go somewhere and buy porn, I did accumulate a fairly large and very pointed collection, which, um, [my wife] found, and that's how I came out to her.
>
> [My wife] did think very seriously about leaving me, and sometimes I wonder if she would have been better off to have done so. We ignored it for a little bit, and then we had a sit-down conversation and she was like, "Okay, I can deal with this." That's when I made promises to her and to myself that I shouldn't have made and that I ended up not being able to keep.

When we repress such fundamental aspects of ourselves, they're bound to spill through the cracks somehow. In Scott's mind at the time, his accumulation of porn, including gay porn, was not a big deal – it was one small caveat in a life he was otherwise very satisfied with – but when his wife found out by accident, it almost ended the relationship right then and there. Scott admitted what he couldn't deny, but he also still minimized his desires, which were bound to pop up again.

I didn't have a "playing the field" experience at any point in my life. And so I cheated. I first started cheating with women when I was in my early 30s. It was an overseas business trip when I first had the opportunity to cheat, with a woman. I think that was tied in part to the fact that sex [with my wife] had dried up. We'd had a kid at that point. It's just a different experience. And I was still relatively immature emotionally, despite the fact that, by all outward appearances, everything was going well.

And then around age 36 was the first time that I had sex with a man. It's something that I'm not proud of. But at the same time, looking at the trajectory of my life, the choices I made early on set myself up for failure. I was not going to remain someone so limited. The regrets continue to this day. I'm definitely not saying it's an excuse, but I was not making it my whole life without having sex with other people.

As we've seen, many Bi+ married men today did not have a chance to explore their sexuality before marriage, and I can understand the power of that lost opportunity, unrequited longing, and unrealized curiosity. Once I accepted my bisexuality and decided to explore, it was like floodgates opening, and I finally got to experience things I had fantasized about for years. It's hard for me to imagine opening those gates in theory but still trying to stay dry.

When Scott read this interview almost three years later, before publication, he had some reflections on his own words above. As he wrote:

I fully understand and appreciate that I was a douchebag. The "sex had dried up" because we had a kid, so I cheated … that is a horrific thing to say. Re-reading this now, I cringe. I had gotten to an inflection point at the time of this interview, but I didn't fully appreciate the implications of what I was saying, namely, that sometimes I was the villain of my own story. It's been very important to my growth as a bi man to recognize and accept that, and not try to excuse it, minimize it, or explain it away (I did all three here).

I also wasn't proud of cheating with women, and it's curious why I made [that] comment only with regard to my first experience with a man. I honestly can't tell you if I was still expressing some form of internalized homophobia, but I do find it curious.

Scott was clearly processing a lot during our initial interview, but his awareness while re-reading shows the progress that is possible when we accept ourselves – he knows that he has made mistakes but also that his identity and attractions are not a mistake, which is a vital distinction that now allows him to live more authentically.

In our initial interview, I asked for more details on the first time Scott had sex with a man, and in addition to shame, he also had positive, joyous feelings about the experience. He was clearly fighting internally with that incongruence, highlighted by his repeated euphemisms surrounding sex instead of explicit descriptions.

I was in San Francisco on a business trip when I just said, fuck it, I'm gonna try this. And I really, really enjoyed it. It was different and exciting because it was new, and, I mean … it's fun to play with the tech, honestly. I enjoy playing with mine. It turns out I enjoy playing with others. So that was fun and new.

At least for me, it's frequently more animalistic and more aggressive, in terms of the sexual aspects of it. I assume the same role with men as I do with women. I mean, I'll just say it: I'm an exclusive top, pretty much. That's always been my only interest. So sexually it's actually similar, it turned out. Remarkably similar. It was a lot more similar than I thought. That was kind of shocking. The very first time, I was afraid I'd be nervous, but once we got going, no, I'm not nervous. This is very simple.

So that continued, off and on, for a number of years. It was, um … it was great [laughs]. It was great. It's always while I was traveling. Some were one-night stands. If I find somebody I click with, we do come back to each other. So probably more frequently it was like a friends-with-benefits situation.

Then I met a guy. Saw him enough to start to develop feelings, and it turned into a full-blown affair. We clicked, got along, it just was easy. It lasted a couple of years and ended prior to the pandemic. We do exchange texts from time to time. He's always been an extremely positive influence. That kind of opened my eyes, because that was the first time I was not only sexually attracted to a guy, but also romantically attracted. Before it had been purely physical. Falling in love with a guy and having that affair I think is what finally made me decide that I'm actually gonna do something.

I started looking back at the layers and the defense mechanisms I had built up, and all the lies that I told myself, and all the things I was ignoring, and decided I've got to start making changes. I'm not going to go through the rest of my life … I'll literally put a bullet in my head if I don't get some of this stuff fixed.

Studies show that queer people are more at risk of suicidal ideation than straight people, that Bi+ people are more at risk than gay and lesbian people, and that those who are not out are more at risk than those who are. It's understandable that many people living through what Scott is describing – or something similar – might go down a rabbit hole and not see a way out. This is part of why Bi+ community is so important, so that you can talk to someone who understands what you're going through, doesn't think you're crazy, and can help you find a way out. If you're in the US and haven't found that community or support yet and need immediate help with suicidal thoughts, you can call or text the National Suicide Prevention Hotline by dialing 988, the LGBT National Hotline at 888–843–4564, or the Trevor Project (for LGBT+ youth) online or at 866–488–7386.

I obviously identified with Scott's story – I also imagined sex with men and women as categorically different, but that view quickly fizzled for me once

I experienced both, and eventually, the same became true for romantic relation-ships. Gender actually didn't make much of a difference for me at all. Once I real-ized this, it wasn't long before I was screaming it from the rooftops, but unlike Scott, I wasn't married when I began exploring, so I didn't have to worry about how my coming out would affect a partner, much less our children. Interestingly, though, becoming a father (to two kids) is what nudged Scott to begin exploring, because it helped him feel more valid in his identity.

> Originally, we weren't going to have kids, but they turned out to be really nice. Sometimes mistakes happen and they're good.
>
> Here's the irony: [kids] have actually been enormously freeing, because once I had kids, I felt I could better claim that [bi] identity. For a long time, I was scared that "Am I really secretly gay?" It's kinda like proof that, no, this is a real thing, I'm not misleading myself, I can calm my ass down. Until I felt that yes, I was attracted to both [and] wasn't secretly gay, I didn't feel comfortable telling people that [bi] was my label. [Having kids was] proof positive I've had sex at least twice [laughs]. Without them, I don't think I would have gone onto the next stages.

As I was coming out, I often felt like I needed some sort of "anchor" to my "straight side" in order to acknowledge the other side. For example, I often was more comfortable watching gay porn if I had recently slept with a woman. I remember imagining that marrying a woman would allow me to accept my bisexuality fully, because it would be "proof" that I wasn't gay. Many Bi+ men feel validated by milestones like marriage and kids, which can sometimes give them the necessary space to notice and accept other attractions.

But for those who are not out to their wives, that secret usually begins to take a toll, affecting more than just sex and intimacy. As Scott learned the hard way, it's further exacerbated when infidelity is involved.

> One of the other big problems of [being in] the closet and behaving unethically in how you approach your sex life is that it inevitably bleeds into other aspects of your life. All of a sudden I would not tell my wife that I was going to the gym, or lie to her about going to the grocery store. Why did I do that? She'd prefer me to go to the gym. I think once you get into a habit, you start applying it. It was corrosive. I spent most of my time not liking myself and dealing with that by self-medicating, which also is not helpful. I was very compartmentalized, but eventually it was coming through the walls, so I said, I gotta stop.
>
> We ultimately broke it off [the affair], because he didn't want to be somebody's side piece, and I respect and understand that. I really, really hurt [him]. I was in love with him, and he was just as in love with me. He's the one who broke it off because, on some level, I was using him. It's painful to be the "other person" to a marriage.

I felt like I couldn't continue living this double life. It just wasn't fair to anybody, including myself. So I think we ended it for the right reasons. Still, I miss him.

The first time we spoke, Scott said he was out as bi to his wife on a "surface level", but had not come clean about cheating. Nevertheless, he wanted to share his story with me anonymously for this project, and I'm grateful that he did, because I'm sure there are many men in a similar position who think they're completely alone. Here is how Scott described the status quo at that time:

> [My wife] knows [that my bisexuality] exists. We joke about it from time to time. But besides that, no other deep, emotional conversations, nothing that's more than surface level. We don't sit around and talk about hot guys [laughs]. She may have suspicions, but I don't know.
>
> It's ridiculously difficult to talk with her about it because the stakes are so enormously high. It could inevitably lead to questions that I wouldn't want to provide a lie to. "Have you done this before?" I don't want to be untruthful. If I say yes, though, that could be a marriage-ending answer.
>
> I have regrets, 100 percent. I should have been more open. I should have dated more women. I should have allowed myself to date guys. It's not been all bad – I mean, I've had a great life. But you never get those years back and you never get those experiences back.

Even then, Scott knew that a change was coming. Perhaps he was preparing himself to be fully honest with his wife, even if he didn't know when or how that would happen. He was clear about one thing, at least:

> The one certainty I will tell you is that I've established, I think definitively, [I need] some version of ethical non-monogamy. Because I've been unethically non-monogamous, and I don't see, over the course of my remaining life, that never happening again. So I have to negotiate something that aligns with what inevitably is going to happen again, with my promises to the people in my life who are important.
>
> I'm nervous beyond anything, because again, the stakes are so high. And with kids involved. There's nothing wrong with her saying, "No, that's not the kind of relationship I want", but if she said that, then it could trigger a bunch of stuff that I don't want, like the end of the marriage, when I prefer to be in it. So it's a terrifying conversation.

So many Bi+ men have gone through exactly what Scott is describing. The stakes of coming out to your wife feel enormous, and it can end the marriage, especially if you add infidelity to the mix – but repression takes its own toll, and Scott was nearing a breaking point. In addition to his sexual fluidity, he was beginning to understand that he might be non-monogamous by nature, and he wanted to be honest with his wife. He also expressed a desire to be more open with other important people in his life.

I'm out to maybe a dozen people. It's still pretty selective. I just simply say, "Oh, by the way, man, I'm bi" or "I'm bisexual", and the reactions have been uniformly positive. So that's nice. I like to think it's that I'm not friends with assholes [laughs]. But I've also been selective. I've gone for the low-hanging fruit, the people who I know are going to react fine.

I'm a member of [my firm's LGBTQ+ pride organization], and some of them do know. Others probably look at me and say, "He's a straight ally." So it's inconsistent there. We've actually had discussions about how we can help people who are in my situation feel that this is a welcoming space and that they have resources to assist them.

I'm not out to my parents, and quite frankly, I really don't want to talk to my parents about sex, period. Unless something changes in terms of my marital status, I doubt I'll ever mention it to them. They're wonderful, lovely people, but I don't have the emotional energy to have that conversation. I have not told [my kids], but at some point I will. What I have told them is that, however they feel, I support them.

I tell myself, just come out. It can't be as bad as living a life like this. That's easier advice to give now in 2020. In the '90s, that was much more difficult to do. So I'm trying to forgive myself a little bit because the times were very different. I've also recently started therapy for the first time. I should have started about age 14, but I'm trying not to beat myself up too much for ignoring stuff for so long.

I saw this project and immediately thought I should participate, [because] I'm just a big fucking cautionary tale, right? Don't do this. This is not the way to proceed. I've got harder work to do now than I would have had to do if I did this in my 20s. I'm not done with this. This is going to get resolved, and I'm probably going to be unhappy for different reasons [laughs].

I kept in touch with Scott after we talked, and given how much was unresolved in his story, I wanted to get an update, so I interviewed him again almost three years later. I gave Scott the transcript of our initial interview to read before the follow-up, and when we began, I asked how he felt about it.

It was like reading someone who was familiar to me but didn't feel like me, if that makes any sense. I knew that guy. I read it several times actually, 'cause I found it interesting. I was definitely processing a lot of stuff. I would frame things a little differently [now]. My inclination is to leave in as much as possible, because I do think that the flaws and the processing are important and could be useful.

I agree! And I'm so grateful that Scott was vulnerable at such an inflection point and willing to share his story for this project.

At that point, I was still mentally thinking of myself as half-straight and half-gay. What I have concluded is that that is probably one of the most unhealthy ways to look at yourself, 'cause if you're always half of something else, you're never a complete human being, and you never land anywhere.

The second thing, and this parallels what I've heard on your podcast as well, is that shortly after that interview, I started thinking of it more in terms of gender and starting to really interrogate gender. I don't have gender dysphoria at all, I don't feel trans or non-binary or anything, but I do experience gender in a way that's different from other people.

Particularly since I've been doing a lot of work with the transgender community, I don't really care what your genitals are, you know? If I'm attracted to you, I'm attracted to you. Everything is okay. What matters is the person inside. That to me is not dependent upon whether they express themselves stereotypically masculine or stereotypically feminine, or not stereotypically anything. That's not what attracts me to people, and I don't think it ever has. Looking back, that was always what I was experiencing: I just didn't care that much.

I will say, I think we've got to fight for the trans community foremost. In part just because we experience gender differently, and many people who identify as Bi+ can understand it better than somebody who's only attracted to a certain gender or expression. I think that they quite literally are our closest kin in this very diverse coalition of queer people.

Scott had clearly processed a lot more about his relationship with gender, but at the same time, he acknowledged that he had some way to go.

It's worth noting that I'm still not completely "there". It takes years to undo a lifetime of mistakes.

Updates. At the time, I was out privately to friends. Now I'm out publicly and professionally. You can Google my [real] name and find me as a bi person. I found that to be extremely liberating and the right choice. It was not a choice that was available as recent as maybe ten years ago, to be that out [as bi] professionally.

[It] has been very gratifying to have people come up to me to be like, "I didn't think there was anyone else out there, and I didn't think that you could even talk about this stuff." To the extent that I can make someone feel less alone or let someone forgive themselves for making similar mistakes or better yet keep them from making those mistakes, I think I owe that to the world. I'm an evil lawyer [laughs], if I can do a small mitzvah every once in a while, I'll do it.

I'm out to my kids. I suspect my parents know. I told our kids very nonchalantly. This generation is so chill with gender and sexuality that it had zero impact on anything. It was a nice experience.

Weirdly to me, the most negative reactions I got were from gay men. Not all of them, but it's a little bit like you're cheating, not in the sense of betraying anybody, but you can disappear anytime. If it gets too rough, you could just hide so easily. I think there's some suspicion. "You haven't gone through what we've gone through." I can fully understand it. Although some of the reactions were shitty-feeling, the fact that I feel shitty doesn't mean it's not a valid reaction.

I can understand those reactions, too, but I'm not sure they're "valid", since they're based on a pretty big misconception – Bi+ men can't hide their queerness "easily", and "disappearing" into a straight-passing marriage can do serious mental health damage. Scott's story exemplifies this, so it's no wonder these reactions made him feel shitty.

I then asked Scott about his relationship with his wife.

I made a very conscious decision that I wanted to be in the marriage. And she made the conscious decision that she wanted to be in the marriage. So we had a discussion. It didn't touch on every subject that it probably should have or could have. There's still a chance that I could blow up everything by being a little too honest.

Being bi was part of it, as well as my intent to be out. I think that was a relief to her, because what I didn't realize is that it wasn't just my secret, it was also her secret. It was her burden as well as my burden, because she then had questions of her own that she had to face. Seeing the impact on others was just another reminder of how corrosive the closet is.

I asked if Scott and his wife have specifically talked about non-monogamy.

We have started. But that has been left more as kind of "don't ask, don't tell". That might be me being overly hopeful. When you have a self-interest in something, you have to be careful that you're reading the other person the correct way. So I can't say that we're necessarily there yet. It feels to me like we're there, but because we haven't put it into words, I think I'm an unreliable narrator – until it actually comes out of her mouth …

She has said things that suggest that she strongly suspects that I've been not monogamous in the past. Ironically – or maybe not ironically, because I feel so much freer – our sex life has improved. It's not quite where I'd like it to be, but it's gotten better for sure. Which is nice. I've gotten better, but I sense that I'm still conflicted. I'm still not quite where I need to be.

Clearly their relationship dynamic isn't fully settled or resolved, but Scott's story again exemplifies that addressing a Bi+ identity – and various intersecting aspects of sexuality – is not like getting over one giant hurdle and then you're in the clear. It's a long process, perhaps lifelong, and there are many steps to coming out and fully integrating your queerness into your life.

Scott is still clear that he wants some form of non-monogamy, but he doesn't want to cheat any more, so I asked if that means there must be an explicit discussion with his wife at some point.

Yeah, there has to be. There has to be. And if for whatever reason that ends the marriage, then I have to be brave enough to accept that. I have to be brave enough to say that being truthful is important, and I need to be truthful about all things. I'm getting there. But I'm not there.

Whatever I needed to get out on my system in terms of playing the field, which I felt like I had missed out on, that's gone. No desire. So I don't think that I'm talking about wild craziness. But if the opportunity arises, it feels right, it's the right circumstance, it's safe for all involved, then I don't see a reason not to do it, I guess is what I'm saying. For whatever it's worth, I'm a lesser slut, on the sluttiness spectrum. I also think that a lot of bi people are more open to that possibility, you know, not treating sex so seriously. I guess I just don't [either]. It's a fun thing to do.

I say this only because I'm now facing down the end of my 40s in a very direct way ... losing a little testosterone is not the worst thing in the world. Part of the reason why I say sex is not such a big deal is that you just have less sex as you get older. The drive is not as much, the need is not as much. You can think about other things from time to time – not frequently, but sometimes. So that's been a pleasant consequence of getting older.

It also makes you value other things more, such as being a good partner, being kind to others, how you raise the kids and how much you invest in them. When I look at my wife now, I appreciate other qualities so much more, which is one of the reasons why I decided to recommit to the marriage, and she also decided she was gonna recommit.

I don't know what will happen with Scott and his wife, and I definitely don't know what "should" happen, but if they both continue checking in with themselves, are honest with each other about their needs, and are not afraid to risk the relationship in order to live authentically, then they'll be on the right path. Scott's decision to confront his bisexuality has allowed him to understand himself better and ultimately accept himself for who he is, which is a benefit to his wife, as well, no matter the outcome. As RuPaul says at the end of every episode of *Drag Race*, "If you can't love yourself, how in the hell you gonna love somebody else?"

9

Bisexuality and Intersectionality

As you've likely noticed in the stories so far, Bi+ people often have similar experiences, desires, or belief systems surrounding sex and relationships, but at the same time, there are many (if not infinite) unique expressions of bisexuality. People realize it in different ways, come out in different ways, receive different reactions, and develop different thought patterns, and this is all potentially influenced by various intersecting identities.

On *Two Bi Guys*, I begin every interview the same way: I ask how my guest identifies, on any and all spectrums they feel are important. Guests usually discuss some combination of their racial, religious, and gender identities, with some including additional intersections like disability, age/generation, economic class, or political ideology. While these facets of identity are not the be-all-and-end-all of who someone is and do not dictate experiences, they do frame and give context to each story, and each intersecting identity has the potential to affect the Bi+ experience.

I identify as a bisexual, white, upper-middle-class, millennial, bicoastal, progressive, Jewish, cisgender man (in no particular order). Though I found commonalities between my Bi+ journey and every other in this book, my overall experience differs greatly based on these identities. In this chapter, I will outline some of these intersections (not to explain how people of other identities experience bisexuality, but simply to highlight possibilities) and explain how my unique combination of identities has influenced my personal experience and worldview.

DOI: 10.4324/9781003385585-9

BISEXUALITY AND RACE

One of the biggest factors affecting an individual Bi+ experience is race. Fluidity may be natural and enduring, but "bisexuality" as an identity is a cultural construct of this moment in history, so the modern Bi+ experience will vary greatly depending on the culture we're brought up in as well as how we're perceived by those around us.

Bisexual people are a minority, and we are often "othered" by straight people and by gay and lesbian people, so growing up as a racial minority can double-down on the experience of being othered. Interestingly, this can affect people in opposite ways: some men of color in this book felt marginalized due to their race, and because of that, they resisted further marginalization by repressing or downplaying their sexuality and not coming out until they were in a safer environment, like Drew in Chapter 15, but others were already comfortable being an "outsider" and embraced their bisexuality earlier, like Gregory in Chapter 2. Some men tied their race or ethnic background to the way they structured their relationships, like Nelson in the following chapter, whose family and culture valued monogamy and having children, which led to conflict when he opened up his marriage.

It's worth noting that sometimes, similar things happened to men in this book across racial identities, so more data is needed to uncover overall trends, as there is limited research investigating the influence of ethnicity on sexual identity development. In the few studies I've been able to find, the sample sizes were too small to disaggregate the data by orientation and still end up with significant results for Bi+ people.

That said, there is anecdotal evidence of a negative interaction effect for Bi+ men of color. Certain interviews on *Two Bi Guys* highlight the unique challenges of being marginalized within a minority community – for example, I interviewed J. Christopher Neal, a Black Bi+ artist and activist and the first Bi+ Grand Marshal of Pride:

> Intersectionality is a bitch. There was a period of time when I was "Chris, the bi guy", but first and foremost, [I'm] a Black man. The specter of racism impacts every aspect of existence for people of color. When I was looking at the disparities within that LGBTQ tent, there are still a lot of disparities around race.
>
> I was listening to the radio one morning, and there was a young white woman talking about this newfound acceptance for bisexual people, people are embracing bisexuality, and all this very glorious conversation. I was thinking, not in the Black community. Because in the Black community, bisexual men are held as responsible for the rising HIV rates among straight women, because of the "down low" and stuff like that.

Another guest, J. R. Yussuf, a Nigerian-American writer, actor, and Bi+ activist (and author of the upcoming book *Dear Bi Men*[1]), connected his Black identity to how his masculinity is perceived, which is intertwined with his bisexuality.

When I'm in the Black community, generally speaking, I'm seen as on the feminine side, so because of that, my sexuality as a bi man is not believed. It's like, "Come on, we know you're gay, stop playing. Who are you fooling? Look at how you act." Whereas in spaces or with people who are not Black, because I am Black, that's automatically a masculine boost. Because they perceive me as more masculine, they are more willing or more likely to believe that I am in fact bisexual. It's easy to be erased as a bi man when you're viewed as being feminine, and it's racist to associate being Black and having dark skin with masculinity. It's really weird.

In each individual story in this book, racial identity plays a role, but the interaction with bisexuality is often more complex than overall trends could capture. This is also true, perhaps especially so, for white people – whiteness has a huge impact on the Bi+ experience, but because it is often considered another "default" identity, this usually remains unexplored.

My whiteness intersected with my sexuality in ways that were mostly invisible to me for many years – which in my experience seems common for white people. Because we have white privilege and are not generally marginalized due to race, our whiteness can fade into the background and go unexamined. But that privilege actually affected my sexuality development in huge ways, and coming out helped me unpack and understand my white identity better, alongside my bisexuality.

Growing up, I noticed that many white spaces I spent time in were very homophobic – but also quite homoerotic. These included sleepovers at friends' houses, high school sports team, Jewish youth groups, fraternity parties in college, and especially summer camp. No one was even out as gay at my summer camp in the 1990s, let alone bisexual, but there was a ton of homoeroticism, from horseplay in the shower house to naked forfeits for losing bets and even discussions of late-night circle jerks (which I never actually witnessed … but the topic came up often). It almost felt like gay activity was a joke or a test – if you could talk about it without getting nervous, be naked around other guys but not self-conscious, then it was "no big deal" and it solidified your straightness.

All those things made me nervous, and I avoided them. I didn't realize that I had same-sex attractions at the time, but my anxiety likely stemmed from that. I was extremely confused, because it seemed like the straightest, most athletic guys – and interestingly, the ones hooking up with girls more than anyone else – were also the most involved in homoerotic activity and discourse. They were also the most homophobic, denying that they were gay.

I struggled with this confusion for years, but it finally all made sense when I read what I've referred to as my "Bi Bible" – *Not Gay: Sex Between Straight White Men* by Dr. Jane Ward. Though it is not specifically a book about Bi+ identities, it is about sexual fluidity and why it's so invisible: Dr. Ward's thesis is that straight white men in particular are able to use their status and privilege to engage in gay sex in specific, culturally recognized ways that actually maintain or <u>strengthen</u> their straightness.

Homosexuality is an often invisible, but nonetheless vital ingredient... of heterosexual masculinity ... I am going to argue that when straight white men approach homosexual sex in the "right" way – when they make a show of enduring it, imposing it, and repudiating it – doing so functions to bolster not only their heterosexuality, but also their masculinity and whiteness.

... This book is based on the premise that homosexual contact is a ubiquitous feature of the culture of straight white men ... white straight-identified men manufacture opportunities for sexual contact with other men in a remarkably wide range of settings, and ... these activities appear to thrive in hyper-heterosexual environments, such as universities, where access to sex with women is anything but constrained.[2]

This behavior is not necessarily a deliberate attempt to boost their hetero-sexuality, but rather a way to actualize their desire for same-sex intimacy, which Dr. Ward argues is incredibly common if not universal (remember her "universal capacity for queerness" theory), without it affecting their public sexual identity and thus without it affecting their relationships or sex with women. It's how queerness pokes through the cracks of a heteronormative society – in secret, when drunk, as a joke, because they "have to" (to get into a frat or club), but never because they actually <u>want</u> to or have queer desires. Dr. Ward argues that these var-ious "explanations" are especially available to white people, while people of color do not have as many culturally accepted scripts that can re-categorize gay sex as "not gay". This is part of why many men of color talk about the "DL" or "down-low", as J. Christopher mentioned, which describes men who have sex with men but are "discreet" about it, because that's sometimes the only way to be sexually fluid but not be seen as gay.

Learning about all this helped me accept my same-sex attractions and decide to act on them, but once I had, I didn't want to be like the guys Dr. Ward described in her book, so afraid of losing their privilege that they led hidden lives and rel-egated their fantasies to jokes and occasional random interactions. I enjoyed my same-sex experiences, I wanted more of them, and I didn't want to hide or down-play them, but I also didn't want to negate my attractions to women or lose my ability to be with them – so I came out as bisexual.

I understand why so many white Bi+ men don't come out – we're at the top of multiple social hierarchies, and it's scary to be marginalized and lose certain privileges – but I believe we have a responsibility to do so precisely <u>because</u> of those privileges. We should not hoard our unearned status but rather use it to effect change and lift up the rest of our community. I would never urge an indi-vidual to come out if they do not feel safe doing so, but collectively, if we want to dismantle white supremacy and patriarchy, we have to be honest about our place on the sexuality spectrum. This could help normalize fluidity and reshape the sexual hierarchy into a more level playing field so that each point on the spectrum is equally respected.

Of the 13 men interviewed in this book, seven identified as white or Cau-casian, five identified as Black or mixed-race (two of whom also shared AAPI identities), and one identified as Latino (Mexican-American). This roughly reflected the demographics of the approximately 150 men who volunteered to be interviewed – the majority identified as white, a significant portion identified as Black, very few identified as Hispanic or Latinx, and none identified primarily as Asian, Pacific Islander, or something else. I did my best to collect a diverse sample of stories (some men I wanted to include did not respond to emails or were unavailable), but more stories are needed from Bi+ people of different backgrounds to understand the full landscape of our community, and I hope this book is the first edition of many.

BISEXUALITY AND RELIGION

Religion is another huge factor shaping the stories in this book, and it often intersects with queerness – but not always how you'd expect.

In my lifetime, I've witnessed most major religions directly or subtly promoting heterosexual, monogamous marriage and the nuclear family. Over 60 percent of people in the United States identify as Christian, and homophobic (and transphobic) movements and activism often have ties to various sects of Christianity – but Judaism, Islam, and other major religions, especially the more traditional or orthodox sects, preach homophobia, as well. In some ways, upholding heteronormativity in this way this makes sense: religion is often an attempt to bring order to a community through norms and rules, which is antithetical to queerness, a rebellion against dominant culture. Unfortunately, many men in this book who grew up in extreme or traditional religious environments ended up suppressing their same-sex desire for years, like William (Chapter 11) and Kaiko (Chapter 7).

But this intersection is more complicated than religion simply keeping people closeted, and in my opinion it's important to differentiate religion from "spirituality", which can manifest in totally different ways. In my view spirituality is a personal belief system and an experience of something greater than our individual selves, and while spirituality thrives in community, it is not necessarily the same for each person, even during a collective spiritual experience. Religion, at least in my mind, is the organized structure that comes out of spirituality, including written histories and laws, physical structures like churches and temples where people congregate, and actual communities of people who interact and worship together. This distinction is especially important for Bi+ people, because in my opinion, spirituality overlaps nicely with the definition of bisexuality (in that it is personal, fluid, and unlimited by rules and norms), while religious doctrines can be hit-or-miss in terms of queer acceptance (and right now, they usually miss).

Indeed, a 2014 study found that higher self-esteem scores for non-straight people and openness about sexual orientation correlated with higher levels of spirituality.[3] At the same time, having attractions to people of the same sex was correlated with identifying as bisexual at a younger age <u>and</u> being less likely to view religion as socially important. In other words, Bi+ people tend to gravitate away from organized religion but towards spirituality – or put another way, spiritual people who don't view religion as important are more likely to identify as Bi+. (The study showed a correlation but did not determine causation.)

This is true for many men in this book, especially in an upcoming chapter featuring William, who left the Church of God in Christ once he realized he was bisexual and began following "mystical" religious traditions, which emphasized spirituality and openness. You may also notice a large number of men who identify as "agnostic" or something similar at the beginning of each chapter, despite sharing stories about traditional religious upbringings, indicating that after coming out as queer, many of them no longer identify fully with the religion they were brought up with. Still, many of them identify as spiritual and even religious, like Rich, Quentin, Kaiko, and William, but now on their own terms, often picking and choosing aspects of multiple religious traditions that work for them.

I have felt this within my own Jewish identity, which has certainly evolved over time. Growing up, I was immersed in the "religion" aspect: going to temple, attending religious school, celebrating holidays, and becoming a Bar-Mitzvah. My temple was "reform" by denomination and relatively progressive, with a female assistant Rabbi, guitar music during services, joint worship with a local Black church, and a focus on social action and charity work. Still, my Judaism overall felt like it was about a shared history, traditions, and community – religion over spirituality.

But in high school, my interests shifted toward the spiritual. My Rabbi encouraged us to ask questions and challenge authority rather than follow Jewish laws and traditions blindly. I learned how to celebrate the aspects of the religion that resonated with me while setting aside those that didn't. While I had internalized the common idea that God is a physical being who controls the world in mysterious ways (which never made logical sense to me), certain biblical scholars led me to re-imagine God as an <u>idea</u>, a collective belief that we can choose in order to create community, connection, and meaning beyond ourselves.

I see all of this as intertwined with my Bi+ identity. In fact, re-imagining my religion was a test-run of sorts for re-imagining my sexuality and integrating my queer desires. I used the lessons my Rabbi had taught me: I questioned the status quo, I challenged authority and dominant culture, and I researched a broad range of beliefs to find what fit with my experience and worldview. The idea that I could <u>choose</u> what God meant to me helped me realize that I could choose what bisexuality meant to me, too. I now see my sexuality as a spiritual identity, connecting my spirit to the Bi+ community at large and to all our queer ancestors.

At the same time, my religious upbringing was devoid of explicit queerness. I didn't know a single person at my temple through high school who was gay or lesbian, let alone bisexual. I didn't know that queer Rabbis or queer Jewish scholars existed. I wasn't taught any explicitly queer Jewish theory or interpretations of the Torah. All of that existed, and I've found it since, but it was invisible to me at the time.

So my religious identity is another example of duality – it gave me the personal tools to eventually recognize my own queerness, while at the same time keeping actual queerness hidden from view. As many men in this book have experienced, there are progressive, spiritual sects of most religions that can similarly give people the space to explore their queerness, even when more traditional denominations are preaching homophobia and gender conformity. Religion is a spectrum, and its complex intersection with the sexuality spectrum is present throughout this book.

BISEXUALITY AND MASCULINITY

In my experience, bisexuality seems to conflict with traditional conceptions of masculinity, at least on the surface, but doing the work that bisexuality requires by digging deeper into our authentic identity often opens up new ways to express masculinity.

I view masculinity as a set of traits that fit into a conventional "box" of what men are expected to be – strong, stoic, providers – and how we're expected to present – athletic, muscular, with facial and body hair, conforming clothing (i.e. the business suit). Much of this felt natural to me growing up, and a lot of it still does, so it was easy to ignore any fleeting desire to behave or present differently.

But masculinity has also been very tied to power dynamics for me. Though I wasn't always consciously aware of it, for a long time I viewed masculinity as a "dominant" role, probably because we live in a patriarchal society – men <u>do</u> have more power and privilege currently, and in most cultures, the majority of men are actively holding onto that power and keeping women (and others) in submissive, subservient roles.

In hindsight, I never liked this. Especially in relationships, I played a dominant role by default, because I thought that was the only way that heterosexual relationships worked, but I hated it. I didn't want to be in charge – most of the time I wanted an equal partner, and when it came to sex, I even had submissive fantasies. Only after coming out as Bi+ was I able to start expressing some of these feelings and re-imagine power dynamics in relationships.

With other men, I was forced to write new scripts and have open conversations about what power dynamics I preferred, and from there, I was able to use those communications skills with women and non-binary folks as well, finally breaking free of default patriarchal relationship structures. Formally exploring these new roles with women helped me understand why I had been drawn to so many "strong", independent, and sometimes more masculine women in my past.

Social hierarchies are bad for everyone, even those at the top who receive tangible benefits. Patriarchy hurts women and trans/non-binary people the most – and the most directly – but it also hurts men by boxing us into specific ways of interacting and creating relationships. It gives us power by default, and even though many us wouldn't choose that power, we don't know how to refuse it, so I believe patriarchy sometimes creates oppressors. Men need more examples of proverbial off-ramps in order to dismantle patriarchy, and this starts with greater visibility of men who are re-imagining their masculinity (like Bi+ men!).

Shiri Eisner, a Mizrahi genderqueer Bi+ activist living in Israel/Occupied Palestine and author of *Bi: Notes for a Bisexual Revolution* (another book I highly recommend), summed this up nicely in an interview on *Two Bi Guys*:

> I think bisexuality gives men a really great opportunity to step aside
> from masculinity as a dominant structure. It gives a way to reevaluate the
> construction of what masculinity is and the requirements of society from
> men, and that opens up a lot of options. I feel men are often trapped in very
> rigid structures. Society locks them in, and of course all these rigid structures
> are meant to qualify men to their role as oppressors, but that also very much
> harms men. It requires them to mutilate a lot of emotional and behavioral
> parts of themselves to fit the role.
>
> It's not just that bisexuality is outside dominant masculinity, it's also the
> fact that bi people in general can often experience what it's like to be at the
> bottom of the hierarchy, for example in LGBT communities, or what it's
> like to be erased from culture. I think that opens up a lot of opportunity for
> solidarity with other groups and for a broader political understanding.

The "mutilation" of our authentic inner lives in order to fit the masculine mold is extremely damaging and similar to repression of sexual fluidity, so it's no wonder why the two experiences are often linked. When you learn to conform in terms of gender expectations, it feels natural to conform in terms of sexuality, too – and vice versa. Only when we step outside these structures – by identifying as something other than straight, or by overtly exploring non-conforming versions of masculinity – can we understand "what it's like to be at the bottom of the hierarchy", as Shiri put it.

For me, stepping outside was incredibly scary, so like many Bi+ men, I didn't do it until my 30s. Once I did come out, it was liberating (I no longer had to work so hard to keep secrets and fit the straight or masculine boxes), but it also gave me a first-hand understand of being marginalized and erased, it taught me to believe other people's experiences without judgment, and it changed my political worldview to be more radical and inclusive. While I understand the fear, I'd argue that continuing to conform and "perform" could be even worse for your mental health, whereas stepping aside from dominant masculinity or straightness will help you connect with other people's struggles and create more opportunities for political solidarity, which is needed now more than ever.

My bisexuality helped me re-imagine my own masculinity and play with my gender expression. Before I came out publicly, I began wearing bright red sneakers to work – my subtle way of dipping my toes into non-conforming attire. I got tons of comments from coworkers (my shoes were so "loud" they couldn't hear me speak, for example), and I loved it. I had always dressed to fit in, but suddenly, I was flattered by the attention – and I enjoyed looking at the bright color on my feet all day!

I began dressing more colorfully, and soon after coming out, I began experimenting with nail polish and makeup. I purchased more feminine and flashy outfits to wear in queer spaces. I switched from a black suit and gray tie to a blue suit and pink tie in formal, straight spaces. My current favorite pair of pants are my women's purple bell-bottoms. These days, I am rarely seen without nail polish, and mascara is my secret weapon for nights out.

Honestly, I'm still pretty conservative in expression compared to others, but I've gained the <u>potential</u> for anything, without shame. I've overcome the stigma of "standing out", and this has helped me re-imagine other aspects of my masculinity, as well. I am less afraid of showing emotion and crying – in fact, I think it's necessary, and I try to embrace my authentic emotions rather than push them down to appear stoic. While I consider myself athletic and strong, I no longer shy away from activities I used to consider "feminine" (like dancing or yoga). I have embraced my love of Broadway musicals and showtunes. In general, I am more able to follow my instincts rather than censor myself out of fear I'll be perceived as feminine or gay.

Many men in this book have stepped outside of traditional masculinity, as well, including Rich, Quentin, Jeremy, Kaiko, and in upcoming chapters, Bennett and Carter. All of them have found joy and authenticity by exploring their authentic expression, even if they're occasionally met with resistance. While it is not always safe to come out or express yourself in non-conforming ways, especially in certain areas or communities, I do believe that on both an individual and societal level, it is often worth the risk. These hierarchies are so ingrained and internalized that the fear is often disproportionate, which is how these structures are maintained. But if more Bi+ and gender-non-conforming men could take that leap, it would more often than not benefit them in the long run, and it would make a huge difference toward dismantling patriarchy and other social hierarchies.

A NOTE ON BI+ MEN V. BI+ WOMEN

I've found that internally, bisexuality manifests in similar ways for men, women, and people of other genders, or at least it has the potential to. At the same time, outsiders' perceptions often vary based on gender, and this can affect the Bi+ experience in important ways. I could write an entire book on this subject alone (and we've done numerous *Two Bi Guys* episodes focused on this), but let's take a brief moment to explore it and how it affects Bi+ married couples.

As discussed, male bisexuality is often viewed as fictional – a stepping stone to a "gay" identity. It is perceived as more feminine, regardless of a person's actual gender expression. Bi+ men are often seen as confused, insecure, or hypersexual. Many women see Bi+ men as vectors of disease, which has roots in how bisexuality was portrayed during the HIV/AIDS epidemic, and that fear is reflected in multiple interviews in this book when couples have talked about opening up their marriages.

By contrast, female bisexuality is typically viewed more positively. It is seen as more sexy, and it reinforces femininity rather than conflicting with it. Many straight men see Bi+ women as <u>more</u> desirable than straight women (a phenomenon that is much less common in reverse), often intrigued by the promise of MFF three-somes – which of course may or may not be on the table, because bisexuality does not equal non-monogamy. Many Bi+ women are perceived to be "really straight", a harmful misunderstanding but an interesting one, because it centers attractions toward men and minimizes attractions toward women – exactly the same assumption people make about Bi+ men. In a patriarchal world, fluid people's attractions toward men must be "real" and their attractions toward women must be "fake", right? (All of the above attitudes are reflected in a 2012 study, *Gender and Binegativity*, among others.[4])

Even though some of these attitudes about Bi+ women may seem more positive, they are not necessarily accurate and they often prevent Bi+ women from expressing themselves authentically. While some mental health statistics show that Bi+ women fare slightly better than Bi+ men, this is a generalization that doesn't apply to everyone, and it often obscures <u>worse</u> outcomes for women in specific areas. For example, according to the Human Rights Campaign, Bi+ women in particular face higher rates of cancer, heart disease, and obesity (possibly related to disparities in preventative care); higher rates of emotional stress; increased drug and alcohol use and a greater likelihood of pairing that with sexual activity; and increased rates of sexual assault and intimate partner violence.[5]

A book about Bi+ married women would thus be very different from this one, especially as it relates to bi-negativity and biphobia, but these attitudes are still relevant to these oral histories, especially because they involve different-sex marriages and because some of the women involved are Bi+ themselves. A 2014 study found that bisexual respondents had lower levels of bi-negative attitudes than straight people and gay/lesbian people.[6] In the chapters ahead, you'll meet a few men who are married to Bi+ women, and you'll notice how this changes the experience, often allowing these women to be more sensitive and attuned to their husbands' bisexuality (and vice versa).

Women are also more likely than men to have positive attitudes about bisexuality overall, according to a 2016 study.[7] In addition, overall attitudes in that study were more positive toward bisexual women than toward bisexual men. These two data points can come into conflict within a straight-passing marriage – wives might be more likely to accept sexual fluidity overall due to their gender, but less likely to accept it in their husband because of his gender. Perceptions of fluidity based on gender play out in complex and sometimes unexpected ways in the stories in this book, but these overall trends are important to keep in mind.

BISEXUALITY AND TRANS/NON-BINARY IDENTITIES

Though sexuality and gender identity are separate spectrums, they intersect heavily, with one often affecting the other on an individual level, and because of that,

I tend to see a natural and necessary alliance between the Bi+ and trans/non-binary communities. Both identities are built on the same foundation: a conception of gender as a spectrum, with the potential for fluidity or change. This is part of why we see such a huge overlap in terms of identity. In a 2015 survey of transgender, non-binary, and other non-cisgender people, 14 percent of the sample identified as bisexual, 18 percent identified as pansexual, and 21 percent identified as queer (that's 53 percent total who potentially fall under the Bi+ umbrella), while only 15 percent described themselves as heterosexual, 16 percent as gay or lesbian, and 16 percent as asexual or something else.[8]

It makes perfect sense to me that Bi+ people are overrepresented in the trans community, and vice versa. Since sexuality labels are often based on your own gender, if you transition, that may necessitate a re-examination of your label or

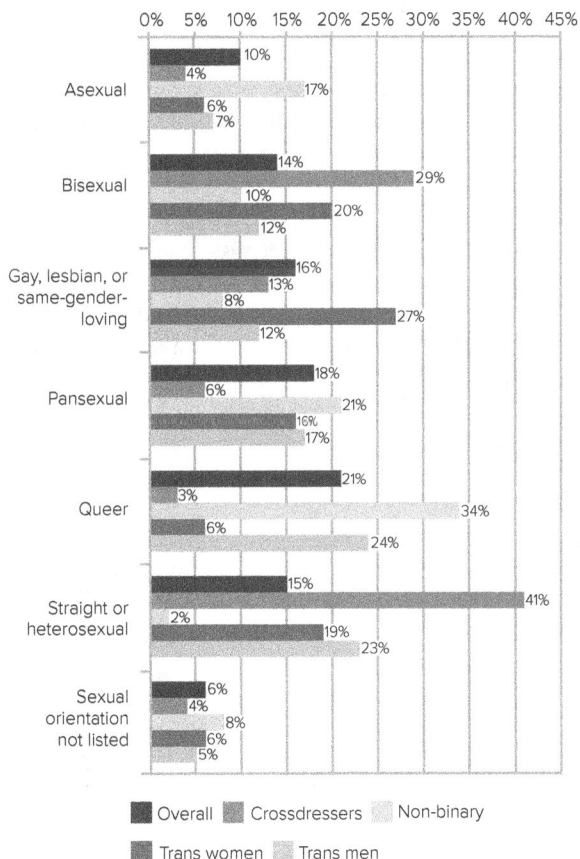

Fig. 9.1 Sexual orientation (among a sample of people who identify on the transgender identity spectrum).

© 2016 The National Center for Transgender Equality.

even your attractions – which happened to Carter (Chapter 13). On the flip side, many Bi+ people I've met have transitioned after a deep examination of their sexuality spilled over into examining their place on the gender spectrum, and others have adopted a non-binary identity (like Jeremy in Chapter 6), particularly since this has become more visible and understood.

Personally, my Bi+ identity caused me to reflect heavily on my gender identity, and while I am still re-evaluating every day, right now I feel comfortable in my cis male identity. Though I do like to play with my masculinity and express myself in gender non-conforming ways, I also feel like a guy at heart, and I haven't experienced gender dysphoria. I feel strongly that my place as a Bi+ activist and creator is to push the boundaries of what it means to be a man rather than to adopt a non-binary identity myself, which doesn't feel authentic for me (but someday could!).

In addition to the individual intersection, I've also seen a lot of crossover in relationships – many Bi+ people have trans or non-binary partners. This also makes sense to me: because Bi+ people are open to more than one gender (and most often to any gender), a partner who transitions or who has a non-binary gender identity is not a threat or a disqualifier. In addition, both partners will likely share an understanding of gender as a spectrum and potentially fluid.

My own marriage is a good example of this. I met my partner before she transitioned, and as she moved through a non-binary identity and to a trans-femme identity, my love and attraction toward her was unaffected by her gender. I also think my bisexuality gave her more space to explore her gender without fear of abandonment. I remember that when we met, she had only ever dated gay men, and her interest was aroused by my bisexuality (we met at Pride in New York City, where I was marching for the first time ever with the Bi+ contingent). Dating gay men may have contributed to repressing the doubts she had about her gender, but knowing that transitioning wouldn't affect my feelings – something which we discussed explicitly in the first few months of dating – gave her more space to fully explore her authentic self.

The Bi+ and trans/non-binary relationship is also necessary on a broader level in today's political environment, where both communities are particularly marginalized. If you thought the negative health outcomes for the Bi+ community were bad, the landscape is even more dire for the trans/non-binary community, especially when it comes to depression and anxiety, self-harm and suicide, and it doesn't take a law degree to see that trans people are one of the most targeted minority groups in today's culture wars. According to the Trans Legislation Tracker, over 485 anti-trans bills were introduced in 46 states of the US in the <u>first three months</u> of 2023 alone, compared to 170 anti-trans bills in 2022, which set the previous record.[9]

Because we share a fundamental understanding of the gender spectrum and fluidity, Bi+ people must stand in solidarity with the trans/non-binary community as they face being erased by legislation and hate. Though our actual experiences are different and should not be conflated, we are oppressed by heteronormative structures for many of the same reasons, and fighting back against either transphobia or biphobia benefits both communities. Though cisgender Bi+ people often have a greater ability to "pass" and remove themselves from queer culture and backlash, doing so leaves behind the most vulnerable members of our community, and it ultimately harms us, as well. As many stories in this book prove, living openly and authentically as a Bi+ person is vital for our physical and mental health and well-being, and we'll only get there if we stand in solidarity with all LGBT+ people who are being marginalized and attacked, because our fundamental struggle is interrelated.

A NOTE ON THE BI V. PAN "DEBATE"

There's a frequent "debate" about the meanings of "bisexual" and "pansexual", but I put "debate" in quotes because, spoiler alert, I think they're very similar words with huge overlap, and focusing on this "debate" takes away energy and resources from working together toward collective queer liberation. Still, let's take a moment to clear things up.

People with multi-gender attractions have always existed, though the word "bisexual" did not always describe this experience. On *Two Bi Guys*, I spoke with Mark Wilkinson, a queer linguistic researcher, about the evolving uses of the word – before the 1960s, it was primarily used in medical texts pertaining to animals that displayed both male and female sex characteristics, i.e. intersex. In the 1960s and 1970s, it began to refer to people who were attracted to men and women. Though it was initially referencing "both" or "two" genders ("bi" literally means "two"), that is primarily because trans and non-binary people were not as visible or accepted until more recently, and the word evolved over time in usage to mean "attraction to more than one gender", similar to the Robyn Ochs definition I prefer today.

The word "pansexual" became popular in the 1990s – "pan" meaning "all", "pansexual" meaning attraction to all genders – in response to concerns about the "bi" in "bisexual" upholding the gender binary, but both of these things were hap-pening at the same time, and proponents of the "bi" label were inclusive of trans and non-binary people as their understanding of the gender spectrum increased. Long before the word "pansexual" was coined, there were many trans and non-binary members of the bisexual community – in fact, some were leaders of bisexual and queer liberation movements, like Marsha P. Johnson and Sylvia Rivera.

Mark Wilkinson also weighed in on the rise of the word "pansexual", which was first used in the 1990s but which rose to prominence after 2007, in a research article he published in 2019[10]:

In a new linguistic landscape that has opened up and deconstructed the gen-der binary, the term bisexual again finds itself in a tenuous position. Namely, if bisexuality is perceived as upholding the gender binary, it is possible that its colloquial use may become less popular among those who no longer subscribe to the binary gender paradigm. On the other hand, bisexual people may increasingly redefine their sexuality, emphasizing that their sexual identity falls within a group of 'plurisexual' identities whose objects of attraction are extended beyond the bi- in binary to any number of gender identities.

So even though "pansexual" might be more linguistically appropriate, I believe we should also remember and honor the history of the word "bisexual" and allow it to evolve with the community. The existence of the word pansexual does not mean that bisexual people are only attracted to two genders, male and female. In fact, even in the 1990s, prominent bisexual thinkers were urging the community not to be divided by linguistics; as the 1990 manifesto for the Bi+ magazine *Anything That Moves* stated:

> Bisexuality is a whole, fluid identity. Do not assume that bisexuality is binary or duogamous in nature: that we have "two" sides or that we must be involved simultaneously with both genders to be fulfilled human beings. In fact, don't assume that there are only two genders.[11]

That said, we must acknowledge that there are some bisexual people who are not attracted to trans or non-binary people, and some of them do not believe that gender fluidity is real — in other words, they are TERFs, or trans-exclusionary radical feminists. It's quite common today on social media to see TERF organizations co-opt the word "bisexual" and insist it refers to only two genders, cis men and cis women, ignoring the history and evolution of the word. With people like this targeting and misrepresenting our community, I can understand the impulse to re-identify and promote the "pansexual" identity, which explicitly includes and validates all genders.

But I also believe that these TERFs are attempting to drive a wedge between the Bi+ and trans/non-binary communities, and we should not give in to that pressure. Abandoning the word bisexual would leave it to the TERFs alone and do incredible damage to our collective understanding of the gender spectrum. So while it's appropriate to embrace the word pansexual, because it is accurate and has a history of inclusivity, we should also continue to honor the history of the word bisexual, use its inclusion in the LGBT+ acronym to our political advantage, and explain its evolution and what it means to us today to counter anti-trans rhetoric.

I'd also like to briefly note that there could be some people who identify as bi but not pan because they've only experienced attraction to cis men and cis women, but they are not TERFs. This is logically possible, and I've met a small handful of people who have identified this way, but in literally every case of those I've known personally, their identity has evolved as they've learned more and actually <u>met</u> more trans and non-binary people. They usually realize that gender fluidity is not a barrier to attraction, even if they haven't experienced it yet. I thus see this as an issue of visibility, not necessarily transphobia.

Overall, I view this debate as distracting, and it obscures more important issues like visibility, awareness, addressing the health and wellbeing needs of queer people, and converting our collective strength into political capital. Bisexual and pansexual people have so many more similarities than differences, and those differences are often manufactured and amplified by TERFs and biphobes who hope to divide the Bi+ community. In terms of organizing around shared experience and values, and in order to gain the acceptance, rights and freedoms that we deserve, we must work together and not segregate ourselves over semantics. "Bisexual" is not inherently transphobic, and "pansexual" is not inherently biphobic – they are just slightly different words describing similar but not always identical experiences. The umbrella term "Bi+" is an attempt at unification for visibility and political purposes, and I find this much more useful than getting into the weeds over the definitions of every term under the umbrella. While the differences are important on an individual level, they pale in comparison to the collective strength we'll need to counter right-wing homophobic and transphobic attacks on our ability to live freely and prosper. At this moment, when trans and gender-non-conforming people are being targeted by hate groups and with legislation designed to eradicate their identities, the Bi+ community must come together and stand up for them, as I hope others will do for us. Our collective understanding of gender as a spectrum is a powerful idea that could up-end patriarchy and other unfair social hierarchies, and we should be united in defense of all queer people, no matter what label we choose.

The big intersections I've outlined here – race, religion, and gender – have an impact on Bi+ identity development in nearly every oral history I conducted. There are other important spectrums that intersect with bisexuality for some men I interviewed, including age/generation, disability, geographic location, economic class, and political ideology. But ultimately, with only 13 subjects, this book is more about the depth of each experience rather than representing every possible intersection. However you identify, my hope is that you will find connections with other people in this book; that even if no one is exactly like you, you will recognize certain moments, experiences, or thought patterns similar to your own based on unique intersecting identities; and that perhaps you'll feel more connected to this beautiful, historic, multi-faced community. And when the stories in this book are far from your own, I hope they'll help you understand the experiences of others and work toward a world in which we all have the ability to live safely and thrive as our authentic selves.

NOTES

1. Yussuf, J. R. (2024). *Dear Bi Men: A Black Man's Perspective on Power, Consent, Breaking Down Binaries, and Combating Erasure.* North Atlantic Books.

2. Ward, J. (2015). *Not Gay: Sex Between Straight White Men.* New York University Press.

3. Rodrigues, E. M., Lytle, M. C., Vaughan, M. D. (2014). Exploring the Intersectionality of Bisexual, Religious/Spiritual, and Political Identities from a Feminist Perspective. *Journal of Bisexuality.* https://www.ncbi.nlm.nih.gov/pmc/articles/PMC4251592

4. Yost, M. R., Thomas, G. D. (2012). Gender and Binegativity: Men's and Women's Attitudes toward Male and Female Bisexuals. *Archives of Sexual Behavior.* https://pubmed.ncbi.nlm.nih.gov/21597943

5. (2012). Health Disparities among Bisexual People. Human Rights Campaign. https://assets2.hrc.org/files/assets/resources/HRC-BiHealthBrief.pdf?_ga=2.191342952.354486474.1647302316-46451389.1647302316

6. Friedman, M. R., Dodge, B., Schick, V., Herbenick, D., et al. (2014). From Bias to Bisexual Health Disparities: Attitudes toward Bisexual Men and Women in the United States. *LGBT Health.* https://www.ncbi.nlm.nih.gov/pmc/articles/PMC4283842

7. Dodge, B., Herbenick, D., Friedman, M. R., Schick, V., Fu, T-C., Bostwick, W., et al. (2016). Attitudes toward Bisexual Men and Women among a Nationally Representative Probability Sample of Adults in the United States. *PLoS ONE.* https://journals.plos.org/plosone/article?id=10.1371/journal.pone.0164430

8. James, S. E., Herman, J. L., Rankin, S., Keisling, M., Mottet, L., Anafi, M. (2016). *The Report of the 2015 U.S. Transgender Survey.* National Center for Transgender Equality. https://transequality.org/sites/default/files/docs/usts/USTS-Full-Report-Dec17.pdf

9. (2023). Trans Legislation Tracker. https://translegislation.com

10. Wilkinson, M. (2019). 'Bisexual oysters': A Diachronic Corpus-Based Critical Discourse Analysis of Bisexual Representation in *The Times* between 1957 and 2017. *Discourse & Communication.* https://journals.sagepub.com/doi/abs/10.1177/1750481318817624

11. (1990). About our Name ... *Anything That Moves.* https://atm.silmemar.org/manifesto.html

10

Nelson and How Pornography Can Trigger a Bisexual Awakening

I was born and raised in Chicago, Southwest side, known as back of the yards. I'm a first-generation Mexican[-American] – my parents are both from Mexico. I have a brother, five years younger than me. My parents were strict with me 'cause I was the oldest. I think I pretty much had a normal childhood. I was a mama's boy. My dad worked at a factory. My dad was always working, working, working. My dad was involved with us very little – physically, emotionally. My mom worked for McDonald's for a long time, then for Old Navy. I was very attached to my mom. I'm more comfortable with women than with men, especially in an environment where I don't know people. I was my mom's favorite, and my brother was my dad's favorite.

School was fine. I was kind of a nerdy kid. I was in the band, I played trumpet. I played jump rope. I wasn't into sports. I didn't really have a lot of girlfriends, but I hung a lot with girls. When I went to Mexico to visit my family, a majority of my cousins were girls, so I played with Barbies. I had one male cousin, and we would play Ninja Turtles or He-Man or whatever he had.

I went to classes, I got decent grades, I didn't talk back, I didn't sneak out. I was your good boy. I was seen as the guy to marry. That's what everyone was telling me. I'm the guy to get married to.

DOI: 10.4324/9781003385585-10

Nelson is a Latino/Mexican-American/Chicano, cisgender man born and raised in Chicago, where he still resides. He was born in 1979 and was 41 at the time of our interview in 2020 – at that time, he identified as bisexual, but now he is "not sure". He grew up in a lower-middle-class Christian household, and he still describes himself as lower-middle-class but not religious.

Like me and other men in this book, Nelson had memories of not conforming to traditional gender roles growing up. Whereas I learned to please others and conform subconsciously, tamping down feelings before I could even deal with them, Nelson had an early awareness of non-conforming desires, at least privately.

I was curious at a young age. I knew there was something about men that sparked that curiosity at four, maybe five years old. We call it a bath house, where you change at the beach, and I remember looking over while guys were changing but not being obvious. Or looking at guys without shirts on TV. On a lot of Mexican soap operas, [guys] are usually without shirts, women were in pretty much nothing, and I remember coming up to the TV and trying to see if I could see anything lower. But of course it's a TV – you can't see anything lower.

My parents were religious to a certain degree. They never said, "Hey, if you're gay, we don't want you", but my dad would make comments and make me feel that I shouldn't come out. I remember I dyed my hair blond, red, blue, and he said, "You look like a faggot."

I actually experimented with a childhood friend in high school. You know, "Hey, my dad has porn. Can I come over and watch porn with you?" And one thing led to the next, you show me yours, I show you mine, and we both masturbated. We would meet regularly. It was mainly oral or mutual stimulation. But looking back, I thought that's all just curiosity. You're telling your friend, "Hey, now I have hair here, I have hair there. Do you?" I thought that's all it was.

Honestly, after that, I didn't really do anything with any guy at all. Of course, there were guys that I was interested [in], but I was still trying to pretend to be that straight guy through high school.

I didn't think my curiosity affected me wanting to be with a woman. I did have crushes on women. I did have some on guys, I just didn't act upon it or express myself to a guy. I did it more to girls. I maybe had four girlfriends in high school.

It's around this age that many gay and lesbian people become aware that they are gay or lesbian. Having same-sex attractions and nothing else fits into a relatively well-known script – but that isn't the case for most Bi+ people. Nelson still had feelings for and relationships with women. These "dueling" attractions can be confusing, especially because it's hard to find other bisexual people, bisexual resources, or bisexual narratives in media – even more so in decades past. Growing up in the 1980s and 1990s, Nelson had to figure it out mostly on his own.

My first girlfriend lasted maybe a month. We didn't even hold hands, we didn't even kiss. My [first] kiss wasn't until my sophomore year. My personality was more flirtatious versus trying to date. There were a lot of girls I was interested in, but when it came to relationships, I was a bit shy.

Back then you didn't have the internet. I remember one time in high school, I found a pornography magazine on the floor. It was a bisexual magazine. I opened it and … you know the rest [laughs]. That was my first visual contact with bisexual sex. I had always fantasized about being with a man. I had a lot of sexual dreams. Now, the magazine had visuals, pictures, to see what they were actually doing. I'm like, this happens for real now.

Even though I knew I was attracted to men, I had restrictions. I didn't want to kiss a guy. I didn't believe that gays should adopt kids. I was very anti feminine guys. With the trans world, I didn't know anything about that.

It's frustrating, 'cause I did want that physical intimacy with another man. I would have a lot of sexual dreams being in the bath house, being in orgies, being in public somewhere with multiple men. So it was satisfying watching porn, but still, it was that physical contact that I missed. I wanted to experiment with that or feel embraced.

I was single my freshman year in college. I didn't date anybody. I did have interest in a girl back then, and she did ask me once if I was interested in guys. I told her, "No, I'm not. I'm straight." 'Cause I wanted to date her. But we never took that step.

Nelson's queerness initially included some internalized homophobia and biphobia, which I think is common for Bi+ men. We both desire intimacy with men and we're a bit repulsed by it. Anxiety about our sexuality can easily transform into arousal. Nelson looked down on male femininity and queer adoption while fantasizing about gay orgies. These internal contradictions usually lead to one of two things: going deeper into the closet, validating your internalized homophobia, and hating queer people (including yourself – I don't recommend this option); or it can lead to exploration, self-examination, and ultimately an acceptance of this duality.

As discussed in the previous chapter, Dr. Jane Ward believes that nascent queer desires are often paired with disgust and repulsion, allowing someone to experience gay sex while maintaining a straight identity – but it is primarily straight white men who have the privilege to follow these scripts. Nelson was likely aware of these scripts, because he was fantasizing about gay sex while resisting it at the same time in order to maintain his straightness, but perhaps because of his race, he struggled to find a setting where he could actually engage in those acts and not be seen as gay or on the "down low", and his sexual fluidity remained mostly unrealized.

Like others in this book, Nelson met his wife early, and his story again illustrates the complicated nature of coming out as bisexual with potential life partners.

My wife, she was in the [high school] band as well. She played the flute. She was a year younger than I was. We started hanging out with each other more my senior year, when she joined the marching band.

[We went to the same] college, and at the end of my freshman year, that was when we started hanging [out] a lot. It was pretty much her and I, her and I, her and I. We both majored in biology. We had classes together. We did everything together. She was my first long relationship. She's the one who I lost my virginity to. And to this date, she's been the only female I've had sex with.

When my wife and I started dating, I pretty much told her that she had saved me from being gay. I had told her that I was curious about men, and she forgot about that, and we moved forward. Even though we were dating, I was still looking at pornography, straight and gay.

Coming out is an important step in every Bi+ married man's journey, but we often fall into the trap of viewing this is another binary: you either come out to your wife before marriage, or you don't. While some men can't tell their wives because they haven't even figured themselves out yet, they often drop hints, perhaps unintentionally, and while others try to lay themselves as bare as possible before marriage, there are always hidden aspects of sexuality than can only be revealed with time and intimacy.

In other words, it's not so black-and-white. (Are you noticing a theme?) No one I interviewed has done this part "perfectly" and revealed every aspect of their sexuality, and no one has hidden from it entirely, either. Being "out" is a spectrum, a continuous series of tiny decisions, especially for bisexual people – not a single, binary moment.

How these conversations go – if they happen at all – <u>does</u> often affect the marriage in a big way (although nothing is irreversible), but for Bi+ men, there is no standard model and no traditional narrative to cling to. Nelson and his wife dated through college, but his internal struggle continued, manifesting in a new technology of the time: the internet.

[After] high school, that's when the internet was all over the place, so of course we had a computer lab in college. We didn't have to log in. They wouldn't keep track of who was doing what. So that's when I found AOL, I found Yahoo chats, and of course there's the gay rooms, there's the straight rooms, the Chicago rooms, the LA rooms, and I would just check a random room. I actually started having phone sex with men, exchanging phone numbers in the chat rooms.

Before we got engaged, one of our best friends was living with us, and he was gay. My computer was in the bedroom where he was staying. I had downloaded porn [from Sean Cody], and [my wife found it], and I'm like, "No, no, that's not mine, [it's his]." That night, we went out to Boystown, which is the West Hollywood of Chicago. They were playing porn, and one of the titles on there was that website, Sean Cody. And she looked over at me and just gave me that face.

Some of our best friends were gay, so we would always go to clubs. We would alternate, straight clubs or gay clubs. I'd be walking around, checking out guys but trying not to be obvious, 'cause I didn't want to hurt her feelings. One time, I had sunglasses so I could disguise my eyes. I remember walking around, nervous 'cause I'm with her, checking out guys.

Nelson was exploring his desires online, but he still had "restrictions": he kept it virtual and didn't plan to act on it in person. Still, he was leaving behind clues, and while I doubt he did so purposely, he could've had a subconscious desire to be found out. Lots of queer men I've met need to "get caught" even if they don't want to, and their actions sometimes do the work that their voice isn't ready for.

> She was getting hints. One night, I left a Yahoo chat open. I was chatting with a guy, exchanging pictures. We were just going to meet to talk, no sexual activities, no kissing, nothing like that. She came home and saw [the chat] and called me right away and said, "Hey, this is what I found." We talked about it and I told her, "Look, I can't hide it any more. I could prevent myself from acting out, but yes, I'm bisexual. I'm attracted to men. But I'm still attracted to you. I love you."
>
> Of course, she got very mad, very sad. We broke up for a day. We got back together. This was before we got engaged. [I said] I was going to try and not pursue that at all, that I wanted to focus on her and get married and have kids and have a future with her. She was hurt, and I don't blame her, the way that she found out.

I don't blame her either, because Nelson wasn't just coming out about his sexuality – he was also planning to meet up with someone. Even if they weren't going to have sex, he was planning to discuss intimate things with him – things he was too afraid to share with his own partner.

In addition, Nelson only moved the needle a bit in this conversation – he didn't fully come out, because the truth was that he did want to act on his desires and be with other men. Perhaps he couldn't yet access that knowledge because he still felt so much pressure to conform and have kids. It seems his wife viewed this as a confession of some sort, but not as him coming out and adopting a queer identity.

> She says she did remember that conversation years later, but she thought that I had put that in the past.

So they moved on and looked to the future.

> We got married in 2006. I wanted my own biological kids. I was trying to portray that straight side to people. I wanted to be the good parent, the good son, the good husband, the good family man.
>
> I was always a person that never expressed my feelings. I didn't tell her how I really felt. I did tell her, "I want a social life." She said "No, no, no, I don't want you out there cheating on me." If I did go out, once or twice a year, I would get texts and texts and texts, voicemails and voicemails. So it got frustrating. After a while it was like, okay, this is my life. It's the family. And that's it.

Nelson and his wife were out of sync both in and out of the bedroom, and being limited in his social life likely led to some resentment that decreased his sex drive. That's no excuse for dishonesty and infidelity, but that's where they were headed.

> Getting more and more into the marriage, my desire for sex declined. After a while, sex [with my wife] became a routine, became boring. I would actually make an excuse not to have sex with her. I would tell her my stomach hurt. And I got tired of fantasizing and watching porn.
>
> [It] was never my intention to cheat. It was just a meetup with a guy, have a friend, and one thing led to the next. We started meeting a little bit more regularly for lunch, just flirting. I told him one day, "Why don't you let me over?" [He] was the first man to touch me in a sexual way. And then of course, curiosity, I wanted more … we ended up kissing, and a secret relationship started there.
>
> My wife told me she was pregnant [a month later], with the youngest one. And, um, I cried. I cried 'cause I knew I didn't want the marriage any more. I was done. So I told her I was done. I didn't want this any more. My main thing was: I want a social life. It's not the fact that I'm bisexual that's affecting me, it's that I want a social life, and that's something she didn't understand.

Nelson seemed very clear about his marriage at this point in his story (even though he wasn't being clear with his wife at the time). He cried because he knew he wanted out of the relationship – which deeply conflicted with his wife getting pregnant.

Many other men still want to remain in their marriages, and they fight to do so. Even more are confused about it – they can see both sides, and they aren't sure what to do (probably the most common reaction for Bi+ men – go figure). But Nelson had a visceral reaction that he remembers clearly, which resonated with me. It's often hard for queer people, myself included, to understand our own complex, non-binary emotions, but occasionally, our bodies clearly tell us things that we aren't ready to acknowledge intellectually.

For better or worse, Nelson didn't submit fully to that reaction at the time. He was still locked into his idea of a traditional family, and he did some work to keep it intact.

> She found out that I had actually met the guy. I would always delete the messages before I got home, and one time I left my phone in the garage and a text message comes in. He said, "I love you, man." She ran [in] with the phone, and she's like, "Who is this asshole?" I lied. "It's just a friend, somebody I've been talking to for a while." "Well, why don't I know about him?" And I go, "If I told you he was bisexual, you're going to get upset and assume something." She said, "I want to talk to him. I want to make sure you guys are not doing anything." Of course, we denied it.

When she met him a month later, he comes over to the house, I drop him off at home. She leaves her cell phone in the car, recording our conversation. So, yeah, um … we talked about that being our last night of doing anything sexually, any romantic relationship. The next day, she calls me. "I recorded your conversation last night. Do you have something to tell me?" Of course, I can't deny it. I can't deny it.

I came home. She's about two months away from giving birth. I didn't get kicked out of the house. I kind of moved away for two weeks and she said, "Either you stay away and don't come back, or you come back home and we'll work on it." From pretty much mid-July through Thanksgiving, we slept in the same bed, opposite each other. The baby was born in September.

She hated herself. She felt bad, ugly. She was scared that I was gonna leave her. First of all, I cheated on her. Her dad cheated on her mom a lot. Her dad had multiple kids with various women. So that all was part of her growing up.

Because Nelson was hiding the truth, his wife resorted to checking his phone and secretly recording him for answers, but doing that probably hardened Nelson's defenses even more and caused him to only admit as much as he had to. Neither was providing a safe space for the other to be vulnerable and open up of their own accord, so it was an uphill battle to figure out what type of relationship they both actually needed.

But by outward appearances, things were on track, so they kept it up and hoped for a change.

The baby was born. We co-parent, [but] there was very limited sex. There were issues with the sexual chemistry. We were still portraying the happily married family. People called it a "Disney family"'cause we were always at a Disney park or doing family things together. But it started taking a toll my life. I detached from Catholicism. I would pray every single night. When I cheated on her, that was the last time I prayed.

She told my parents that I was "done", and my mama asked me, "Are you seeing somebody? Who was this woman?" I told her there was no woman. "It's a guy." My mom said she kind of always thought [so]. [My wife's] mother actually told me do it, go out there, experiment. "If that's what you want, that's what you want. If you don't like it, you don't like it."

We had three kids, and it was work, kids, work, kids. I love my kids, I enjoyed the parenting, but it was just a routine. I didn't really have a social life. Whenever I wanted to go out with the guys, it was a "no". I told her, it's not meeting somebody and having sex with them, it's just hanging out, going to a baseball game, going to the bar. I wanted that. I didn't get to experience much with my dad – I feel I missed out on that. So that took a toll on me as well.

While bisexuality was initially blocking Nelson, the whole ordeal helped him get clear about what he was really missing in his marriage, and it wasn't just sex, it was companionship and community, especially with other men. Nelson's wife prevented that because she was afraid he would cheat with a man (but not a woman – a unique and challenging form of biphobia).

I talk a lot about how much therapy has helped me, and I typically recommend it to sort through issues like the ones Nelson was going through. Unfortunately for him, their couples' therapist only complicated things.

> We had actually started seeing a therapist prior to her finding out that I was cheating. Both of us, together. I didn't like the guy from the first meeting. I told him I was bisexual. I told him I wanted a social life. I needed an outlet. His thing was: bisexuality does not exist, and once you're married, there's no such thing as a social life. I didn't like that answer.
>
> We officially stopped [seeing a therapist] when she told him I had cheated on her. He's like, "I can't do anything any more. Once you guys cheat, that's it. You pretty much need a divorce. You guys aren't happy together." Our friends were telling us the same thing, and I'm like, "No, why? I love her. I want to be with her."

Though the therapist was ultimately right about one thing (a broken clock is right twice a day), he was very wrong about bisexuality, and he may have overstepped his bounds in telling them what they "needed". Because no one could help Nelson sort through his conflicting (but real and valid) desires, he continued to struggle and lead a double life.

> Everybody was saying, "Do whatever makes you happy." My thing was, I wanted the family still. But at the same time, I continued to see the guy. I would deny it to her, [but] I didn't stop at all. Not only was I still seeing the guy, I was actually going out there and finding [other] men to experiment or play around with. So that was my outlet.
>
> It was just mainly oral. It was very few guys that I actually had sexual intercourse with. If I did have, um, anal, I … even though I was kind of turned on or aroused, it wasn't satisfying. There was no connection.

Thankfully, they tried again with a new therapist.

> We started seeing a family therapist. I thought it helped us. We seemed to reconnect. He told us, "You guys need date nights. Find a babysitter, get out there, spark this flame up again." We started to go a little bit out, we felt better, but sex still wasn't there. I had started taking testosterone, and I told her, "It's not you, it's me. I can't maintain an erection." That created an issue with her. She was very insecure.
>
> 2017, Pride comes around, and she's like, "I'm proud of you being bisexual. Put it out there." So I started coming out on social media, little

by little. Our immediate family knew already. I posted, but people didn't question it. I didn't really say, "I'm bisexual", I just said, "Happy pride month", you know?

Once they were feeling more connected and able to be more honest with each other, non-monogamy came up.

In 2017, I expressed to her how I wanted to have a threesome with another guy. So she found somebody, through one of the apps. He was very attractive, very hot. We started fantasizing, and we were having sex every single day for a while. It was like we reconnected. We were going out every weekend together. We went out to the bars drinking and we would sit there and check out guys. It was fun.

Even without going through with it, just the idea of a threesome – and the freedom to talk about it openly with each other – reignited their attraction. I've found the same thing in my marriage: just talking about sex with other people increases my arousal for my wife. For me, sex drive is not a finite resource that gets depleted, as I used to believe, but rather a muscle that expands the more it's used. I'm sure that's not the same for everyone – while Nelson may be closer to my side of that spectrum, unfortunately his wife was not.

We brought a guy home, a straight guy, and it was all right. I was very nervous because it was our first threesome. I pretty much watched her have sex with the guy, and it was hot. But it was hard to find true bisexual guys. Every guy had his limit. They don't do this, they don't do that, or it's just you doing it to me. It's supposed to be a mutual thing.

She went on and she found a guy, and it was just her by herself. Towards the end of the summer, I started going on Grindr again, Growlr, any of the apps to find a guy just for me. But our rules were always to come back home to each other. That's where it started going downhill again. She didn't want to have sex with me 'cause she was with somebody else, or she was holding herself off to meet somebody else. [So] she said, "Let's just stop." I didn't want to stop, 'cause I was finally enjoying myself, having my guy time that I've always wanted.

She did warn me and said, "I may get attached to somebody." Mentally I'm thinking, "No, we love each other. We're happy. We're talking about renewing our vows." But that's where our marriage started declining.

She would deny me sex. I was getting upset, jealous. She met a guy, started seeing him more and more. She started asking me to wear a condom, and I'm like, "Why are you asking your husband to wear a condom?" She wasn't with the other guy. And literally four years after I had told her I was done, she told me she was done. She didn't want a marriage. She didn't want to be with me any more. I went through some dark moments. We separated January 2019, officially divorced as of Halloween.

After realizing it and then denying it to himself for four more years, Nelson finally had to accept that his marriage was over, because his wife wanted out, too. I can understand the "dark moments" he's describing, and I can imagine he was kicking himself for not arriving at this realization sooner. But hindsight is 20/20, it's easier said than done, and your journey is your journey – it's what makes you the person you are. Because Nelson had experienced and processed so much, he was in a better place to be more authentic with his next partner.

Around Memorial Day, I met my current boyfriend. We've been together for almost a year. We met through Christian Mingle [laughs]. I always say that, but yeah, through Grindr. I was upfront, I told him, "Look, I want a friend. This is what I'm going through. I am recently separated. I have kids." We just started talking, hanging out more, and feelings came about.

It hasn't really been hard dating, coming from a woman to dating a man. It's the same thing. The anatomy is a little bit different, there's things that I've had to understand, but other than that, to me, it's just dating somebody new. The one thing that is a little bit different is being out in public and being affectionate. We tend to watch ourselves a little bit more, especially now with what's going on with discrimination and racism. I'm Mexican, [my boyfriend's] African American. Chicago was heading towards racial war, especially with the riots that were going on [in summer 2020], so we don't really hold hands. There's not much PDA [public display of affection] when we're out, and I am used to the PDA, the holding hands, kissing, so it's been a struggle. We're very careful.

I went to a ball last year, 'cause my partner's in a house. Just being surrounded by people that are part of the community, it's like, wow. It opened my eyes, my mind. And yet at the same time, I'm seeing the discrimination in the community as well – you're bisexual, or you're overweight, or other discrimination.

We actually found a church, it's primarily African American, but it is LGBTQ-friendly. It felt amazing. I felt welcomed, very different from a basic Catholic church.

Nelson was in the early stages of his new relationship when we spoke, and it remains to be seen if he'll want to get married again. Either way, he seems more clear about his needs and more able to communicate his situation and identity to potential partners. He also realized that dating men and dating women are "the same thing", as he put it – an epiphany I also had – and this knowledge, which he felt in his body, helped him solidify his Bi+ identity and come to terms with the totality of his journey, setting himself up for more authentic relationships in the future.

I can't go back and relive my life. You gotta be happy. You can't make others happy. That's what I did for a long time, making others happy versus myself.

It's hard. Especially being bisexual, especially for a man. Especially when it comes in a marriage and having kids, it's hard.

I'm upset, 'cause I'm the one that caused the marriage to [end]. Eventually we would have divorced, yes. Both of us wanted change. A second mother is pretty much what she was, and I don't need that. I'm an adult. I miss having another parent, especially with three kids, but the more we're separated, I don't miss her as much. It took me a while, but I can honestly say now, that's the past.

Sexuality, I think, did play a role. But when I tell people I'm happy now, the thing is, happy to me is not being bisexual. Happy to me is not being with a man. It's just, I'm myself. You know? I'm happy just being myself.

People are always going to want to label you as something. My friends ask me, "Are you sure you're not gay?" My thing is, even when I'm with my partner, I don't see him as a man, I just see him as somebody I love. I don't see myself as a bisexual man, I'm just myself, I'm [Nelson]. Why put a label on it? You have one life, and life goes extremely fast. Always be true to yourself.

11

William and Sexual Fluidity in the Military

I was born in 1971, in Washington, DC, Southeast. Southeast is the rough part, the ghetto. I grew up with a single mom. My elder sister, who was 19 years my senior: I lost her when I was seven. My mom took jobs that she could get. She was a waitress, a short order cook, Toys "R" Us, a lot of cashier work. Before I was born, she was a singer in a nightclub. Our relationship was really good. We were friends. I wasn't afraid to go to her with an issue, even if I was the one that was wrong.

I had a decent relationship with my father, as well. I knew who he was. When I was smaller, he would come pick me up on his bicycle, ride me around to the store, get a little bag of potato chips, you know, spend that father–son time. Periodically he would scoop me up, spend a weekend at his house, drop me back off.

We moved from DC to Rockville, Maryland in the 1980s. We moved from there to Germantown, Maryland. We just kept moving higher and higher, upper and upper scale. Then my mom's boyfriend, who she did all this growth with, he decided to split, and we just kind of tumbled back down the economic ladder again. Started staying with family in Alexandria, Virginia, and from there I joined the military. Had my first little experience there … more on that in a minute.

DOI: 10.4324/9781003385585-11

Willam is an African-American, bisexual, cisgender man living in Alaska. He was born in Washington, DC in 1971, and he was 51 at the time of our interview in 2022. He was raised Christian (Church of God in Christ) but now describes himself as Mami Vodou (an African traditional religion/ spirituality). He grew up working poor and now describes himself as middle-class. He is a military veteran and spent most of his career in the Army. He has ADHD.

William was eager to talk to me. He said he had never been interviewed before, but he was working on transparency and authenticity, and he hoped his story might resonate with others. He was also the only person I interviewed with a military background – an environment rumored to be both homophobic and homoerotic – so I was eager to get to his "little experience".

> I was 19 when I joined the Army. Military intelligence. That was rocky. First off, I was walking around with ADHD and didn't know it. In the military, if you can't pay attention to detail, you will have a hard way to go. Luckily the Army was great, because they really do cater to the lowest common denominator, and with me, it was kind of hard to tell whether I was smart as a whip or dumb as a box of rocks. They couldn't tell – I couldn't tell.
>
> It wasn't until 2019 I found out I had ADHD, so the entire time I'm like, I know all the right answers, I can get everything done, but somebody has to walk behind me, because there's always a shoelace untied or something that got passed over. That was my military experience. It sucked, and it really did cap my ability to grow there.
>
> I'm recently learning … it was Shiri Eisner, she said there's a link between neurodivergence and bisexuality, and as soon as that was made known to me, it was like, click, click, click, click, click. "That explains everything!" I was such a social chameleon, and I didn't understand that that's one of the ways people with neurodivergence cope with social situations – they learn to mask. Now that makes sense.

Similar to almost everyone I interviewed, William had the experience of being othered and of not quite fitting in. Moving a lot during his childhood contributed to this – he was the "new kid" over and over. When he joined the Army, his ADHD made him "different", but it was his 2019 diagnosis and awareness of this difference that finally helped him connect to other unique aspects of his identity and eventually come out as bisexual.

For most of his life, though, William had sexual and romantic experiences that he struggled to categorize and understand.

> I probably found love anywhere I could, because relating to people emotionally and sexually was a difficult thing to do, because I didn't fit molds.
>
> My first sexual experience was when I was five, if that. It was with an older child. Looking back now, I realize that that young lady was a victim of sexual assault. She asked me to pee in her, and that didn't make any sense to a

five-year-old child. My male cousins and I "explored", and I had a best friend that I was exploring with. All of this happened before first grade. It was creepy now that I look at it, but it's what the kids were doing back then.

After fifth grade, I did come across my stepfather's porn stash. That's when I saw my first porno, which was an Army movie. That's funny, how that all played out for me. That was the first time I saw ejaculation, so I was like, "That's what happens?" Because all of this happened before I could do that. I did realize that the prostate could be, uh, manipulated directly. I learned that on my own in that timeframe.

William was definitely a curious child – I didn't explore prostate stimulation until my 30s! He's not the only Gen X-er I interviewed who explored sexual contact before puberty – perhaps he's right that "it's what the kids were doing back then", but there was likely less awareness and openness about it, as well as less acceptance of homosexuality, so he couldn't fully contextualize what was happening until adulthood.

William soon had an experience at summer camp that could've been formative for his identity.

I don't know how my stepfather managed to work this, but he got me sent to a summer camp. I couldn't have been more than 12, 13. It was something like eight or nine boys in this cabin, in bunk beds, and we're all just sitting there talking about sexual identity. A lot of guys were like, "I'm straight, I'm straight, I'm straight." There was this one dude who said, "No, no, I'm bisexual", and we were like, "Ooh, what's that?" "That's a guy who likes girls and he likes boys." And I said, I think that's me, too. I like that. And it was as simple as that. Nothing crazy came out of that. I didn't hook up with anybody. It was just a bunch of kids talking about who we are and what we found interesting and what we thought life was about. That was awesome.

Though William remembers this clearly now as "awesome", unfortunately it didn't help him solidify his identity at the time. I sometimes think that sexuality is actually much simpler than it seems (of course you can like more than one thing – why not?), but because our society constantly sends us heteronormative and binary messages that are not in line with overwhelming research on the existence of sexual fluidity, we have to do a ton of work to unlearn all that. Kids haven't learned or internalized as much misleading information, so their thoughts about sexuality are often clearer.

Soon, we got to those military experiences I was curious about. Though William didn't see himself as "bisexual" yet, he certainly had some awareness of his attraction to other men.

I was terrified when I got to basic training, specifically because I knew I was gonna be with other guys my age, in a huge shower bay, naked. What if I get aroused in there, you know? 'Cause by then, I knew who I was, I knew what I liked. I didn't have the vocabulary for it necessarily, but I knew.

Basic training was one of the first places I learned fraternal relationships with men, like brotherhood. 'Cause I was an only child. I had a sibling, but she died when I was seven. In the military, I found out what a brother was, which was awesome. Kind of sucked because now I'm attracted to my brother … that's just really weird.

Nothing happened in basic. AIT (Advanced Individual Training), lots of opportunities with girls. I had fun with them. That was awesome. Then I reclassed to Military Intelligence. It was all male. When I got to my first duty station, I got introduced to boys as an adult. It was one thing to look at guys from a distance. It was something totally different to have some guy take interest in you. At my first duty station in Germany, that's exactly what happened.

I know what he means about attractions suddenly "becoming real", and I think many Bi+ guys do, too. Most of us start with porn – completely non-reciprocal – then move on to watching, staring, brooding, fantasizing … but it still doesn't feel "real". Eventually, someone is going to stare back, maybe even talk to us (or more), and suddenly we have to respond in a very real way. I was terrified by that at first (I remember quickly denying any attraction by declaring "I'm straight" with multiple prospects), but William was a bit braver.

It started like this. August, 1992, my birthday. I called my mom who didn't pick up the phone. I called one of my girlfriends who was busy. I called my other girlfriend, she was busy. I was upset and depressed. I walked out of the building and down the hill, and they were having a cookout, so I invited myself, and folks figured out that it was my birthday. One guy said, "It's your birthday, let's go for drinks. Have you been downtown yet?" So he takes me off post, just me and him, and we go to this club.

I'm enjoying myself, I'm dancing. It's a quiet club, I'm in my own zone. But I do notice that he's sitting there at the table drinking, looking at me. So I get off the floor, he wipes down my chest with a towel or a shirt or something. I'm like, hmm, okay, cool. We go back, and I'm thinking, this dude's hot, but I'm also thinking I don't have a shot, because I haven't been having shots with guys all this time.

We get back to his room. I'm drunk. He said, "Hey, you're drunk. Lay down here, sleep it off. Go back to your barracks in the morning." I'm like, cool. No problem. Go to sleep. Wake up in the morning. Somehow, some way, we're in the same sleeping bag. Things just did what they did from there. I don't think we did much more than make out and grabbed on each other and tugged a little bit. I think that's about it.

That might not seem like much, but if you've been through it, it can feel like a complete transformation. Being intimate with another man felt to me like stepping through a portal into an alternate universe. I had suddenly done something that I had told myself for my entire life was forbidden. The world didn't crumble – in fact, it felt very similar to fooling around with a woman – but suddenly I was confused for a new reason: why had I been so afraid of doing that in the first place?

It sounded like a similar portal opened up for William.

I went back up to my barracks confused. But after that, he took me around to all the gay spots, introduced me to gay lifestyle. I didn't know anything about that. And given how hard I fell for that dude, I thought I was gay.

But I couldn't stop thinking about the girls. As a matter of fact, one of the things that soured things between me and him is that I had this bad habit of sleeping with his girlfriends. He identified as gay, but he was having sex with men and women. He was messing with a senior enlisted guy in his unit, which is a big no-no, and [that guy] identified as gay and had kids. It turned out that there was a lot of gay, bisexual guys in that building. I made up for lost time, I'm not gonna lie [laughs].

That was all before "don't ask, don't tell", so it was a prosecutable offense to do it, which at the time added to the hotness of it. It's forbidden, you can't do this, you're gonna go to jail. It was nuts.

Many men in William's story were having sex and relationships across the gender spectrum while identifying privately as gay and publicly as straight. Bisexuality was likely not as popular a label then, and many were not even aware of it as an option, but I also think the fact that gay sex was officially forbidden contributed to a binary view of sexuality among servicemembers. You're either following the rules against same-sex fraternization … or you're not. Being with women didn't change the fact that you were breaking the rules with men, so for all professional intents and purposes, fluidity was irrelevant.

So for years, William viewed himself as gay, even though he was fully aware of – and indulged in – his attractions to women. He downplayed his fluidity, and he was careful to hide his same-sex behavior from his superiors. Being so aware of your own feelings but unable to express them to others often causes intense cognitive dissonance, so it's no wonder William ended up admiring guys who were more "out" than he was.

There was this one guy who was openly gay, he worked in human resources. This dude could walk around with a tiara on and nobody would say boo about it. He was amazing. The level of respect and admiration I had for that guy, he stuck in my head all these years later. We never had a thing going on. But he could be himself. He was an example of what I wanted to be one day.

I wasn't scared, but I wasn't stupid either. I was very into my boyfriend, so it's one thing to play with my life and my career, totally different conversation to play with his. So I made sure that I kept my nose clean.

The soldiers on the ground levels, they already thought I was out there sucking dick. I got upset one time 'cause they were right, they hit the nail on the head. But they never ran it up the flagpole. As long as I did what I had to do, I pulled my weight, they didn't care. Plus, it's hard to make that allegation knowing the luck I was having with the females, as well, 'cause I didn't stop messing with the girls.

It's interesting that William's bisexuality saved him from more intense homophobia, although I'm not sure if that's a lucky break or a precursor to long-term struggle (probably both!). Either way, it's an example of how a binary view of sexuality leads to the minimization of same-sex exploration, especially in environments like the military. Other soldiers didn't view William's same-sex "transgressions" as material or worth reporting at least partially because he was still "messing with the girls" – it's not a gay <u>act</u> that's viewed as sinful, but a gay <u>identity</u>. This view also helps soldiers rationalize the gay sex and homoeroticism that is common in the military: it's "normal" and accepted as long as those engaged in it (ironically) maintain a straight identity.

Of course, men like this with multi-spectrum attraction or behavior can always claim a Bi+ identity – but William wasn't there yet, still stuck in a binary way of thinking.

I initially labeled myself as gay, because in the African-American community, you are either straight or you're gay. But gay just didn't fit me. The gay culture did not fit me.

My boyfriend took me to a festival in Germany. It ended up being this big gay orgy, it was awesome. This guy showed up in drag and glitter and fabulous, and I'm like, "What in the hell?" 'Cause that's just not me. When we went over to where the orgy was at, he was like, "I don't like your name. We gonna change your name to Stella for the rest of the night." And I'm like, "I don't wanna pretend I'm a girl. I don't want to be effeminate." All this on top of the fact that I still like girls – gay's not what I am.

After I left Germany, I broke up with [my boyfriend], then went through a whole phase. Tried to pray the gay way. I'll give you three guesses of whether or not that shit worked. It was torturous. I had so much self-loathing at that time. I remember just bawling my eyes out, crying like I had been beaten, asking God to make me not like men no more. I wouldn't wish that on nobody. The existential dread that came with that . . . Oh man, I hated everything. I hated me.

William was equating being gay with being feminine, which I can understand given his experience, although they are completely separate spectrums. It's also interesting that even after William's experience at camp understanding the word "bisexual", and even after years of sex and relationships with both men and women, he couldn't come to terms with his same-sex attractions. This speaks to how difficult it is to deal with an intensely homophobic society – especially in decades past – and to how confusing the Bi+ experience can be. There are often many layers of acceptance and shame rolled together, and the path to coming out is usually not a straight line.

Thankfully for William, that rock-bottom period of self-loathing and existential dread helped him finally turn a corner.

By the time I left Germany, I had given up on trying not to like guys any more. But I had also wrapped my head around the fact that I'm not gay. I tried gay, gay don't work. I'm bi.

I hooked up with my best friend's girlfriend, and that's when I found out that I wasn't possessive. She slept with other people, and I was like, "You still like me? You still want to still wanna be with me?" She's like, "Yeah." "A'ight then, I don't see the issue. Next time, bring 'em over." We could both sample a flavor, see what happens. She knew that I was mess messing around with guys – she was the one I was crying to about it, you know? Eating ice cream and shit.

William finally found a relationship in which he could be himself without fear of rejection, and it was transformational. Though it wasn't a perfect match in the end, she did help him get to the next phase of his journey.

Me and her didn't end up well, 'cause she got religion. Then I went into this phase where I really wanted to understand how I did not magically get made straight. I was Church of God in Christ. [Then] I investigated Judaism, 'cause it was the closest one actually. And from there, Kabbalah, Daoism, Confucianism, Hinduism, hell, all the -isms you could think of, trying to find a spiritual footing. When I went to Fort Drum, I became a Muslim.

I always found myself attracted to the esoteric pieces of the traditions. So Christian mysticism; Kabbalah, Jewish mysticism; Sufi, Islamic mysticism. I saw these common threads. Apparently, all these mystics saw what was common, too, 'cause they never beefed with other mystical traditions. You would get the presumption of validity and tolerance.

I realized that I'm going to be who I am, how I am, what I am, the way I am, because I was made this way. I was supposed to have this perspective. I was supposed to be this kind of fluid. It's not an aberration. It's not wrong. How I conduct myself may be right or wrong, but the way I feel or what I want, that's not a right or wrong thing. That was a difficult lesson to learn, but it was so very rewarding.

William had many relationships up to this point, but once he accepted his sexual fluidity, he was quickly ready to be in a more open, authentic relationship. I've seen this among other Bi+ men, and it happened to me, too – my relationships before coming out usually lasted three months maximum, because I was subconsciously afraid to open up further, but after coming out and getting more comfortable with myself, I met my wife within six months, and we've been together for five years now.

William also met his future wife soon after his big realization, while stationed in Italy.

I am a Dungeons and Dragons geek. There was this female Sergeant that I was having illegal [in the Army] sex with. She had a Dungeons and Dragons group, and one of the guys in that group met this Italian girl, and they got engaged. So I did what any red-blooded American man would do: "Hey, your girl got a friend or a sister you could hook me up with?" She's like, yeah. And that happened to be my wife.

He introduced me to her, and we played some cards, got some pizza, went back to her spot. She was like, this was good for a "F", you know? He'll never call me back. I called her back. I think I waited a day.

She had a daughter from a previous relationship. The little girl loved me, her parents loved me, and I loved all of them. I decided I'm gonna marry this lady. I moved all my stuff off post and into her house. I dated my wife for three months before I proposed to her. I knew what I wanted. That was 23 years ago.

Before we got married, she asked me, "You ever been with a man before?" I think she was being funny. I was like, this is gonna be a long term thing . . . I don't know how you felt when you first jumped off a high diving board, but it felt like that, taking that first step off of there. It's like, here we go. And I said, "Yeah, I've had sex with a guy before." I didn't go into details or anything like that.

She was surprised. I think she didn't know what to ask after that. I told her, "Yes, I did, but right now, I'm just with you. It's just us." If I'm being honest, I don't know if I made it a 100 percent clear ... I know I didn't lie about it, but I don't think I was clear that this was an ongoing condition with me.

Like Quentin, Scott, and others, William was afraid of losing the love of his life if he revealed too much, too soon, so he didn't make it clear that fluidity was an ongoing part of his identity. Whether it's due to lack of self-awareness or fear of abandonment, coming out is frequently not a "one and done" event for Bi+ men, but rather an ongoing conversation that gets deeper over time. Of course, that initial fear and censorship can lead to conflict further down the road.

We got married, and it was good for a while. My wife has a work ethic that you would not believe. She was a security guard. She sold wine on post, did real good there. My wife was amazing in the military.

Then we hit a couple of bumps. She found me entertaining myself to gay porn. That was rocky, 'cause she didn't think it was something I was still interested in, and she wasn't prepared for me still to want that.

Those bumps lasted for quite a bit of time. It turned our marriage adversarial. I was 28, she was 25, so I had the advantage of being older. I don't know if I was wise with that position. Instead of taking a lead and getting us to a space where we could understand each other, I just kind of browbeat her. You know, "Woman, don't be asking me what the fuck I'm doing." Not the best version of me at all. I still made sure I could take care of her, but when it came to us sexually, I caused the real rift there, and that lasted for five, six years maybe.

At a certain point, I crept out, started doing my own thing, you know? Not at all proud about that shit. There wasn't a lot of incidents, but one was too many. And it was more than one. We sought counseling, we got therapy. It didn't work, 'cause I wasn't honest. And that went on until we got to Georgia.

[In] Georgia, my wife was like, "Get it together, or we're done." I had a come to Jesus moment. I had to ask myself, did I want this marriage? And the truth of the matter was that nothing in the world was more important to me than her and our babies, 'cause by then we had two. I was like, I gotta make this work.

So we went to therapy together. Came clean, transparent with the therapist, so the therapist knew what the hell she was working with. Every infidelity, every dirty magazine, everything. The therapist told us, "You know, William, you fucked up. The ball is in her court right now. Your job is to prove to her that you want her back." So I did.

It took years for William to fully open up to his wife, and doing that took mutual trust, which had to be established slowly, step by step. Over time, William learned that being vulnerable created space for his wife to be vulnerable, as well, which led to more intimacy and connection.

When I told her that I was bi, she was like, "Hmmm, okay." A little while after that, she was like, "I'm bi, too". Because she didn't have the word for it either. She's born and raised [in Italy]. When we first met, she didn't speak English, and I didn't speak Italian. I think this contributed to us being successful as a couple, because communication was such an intentional thing. We had to work really, really hard to communicate to each other.

I came up on orders to go to Korea. You could bring your family to Korea with you. I asked my wife, "Baby, what you want to do?" I knew and she knew if she stayed, we were done. It didn't matter if I kept my nose clean while I was there, she wouldn't have no reason to believe it. So she said, "I'm coming with." She had just had a baby, she was pregnant going through therapy. We packed up all three of the kids, we all went to Korea.

By this time, we were no longer tip-tapping and lolly-gagging around what's going on: I am a bisexual man. What I didn't understand was that monogamy is a different animal. My wife is bisexual, but she's monogamous and I was not, and I didn't understand that.

It's common for outsiders to conflate bisexuality and non-monogamy, but in this case, it was William himself who made an incorrect assumption about his wife and was disappointed to learn that she preferred monogamy. In my experience though, it's possible for our orientation on the monogamy spectrum to be fluid and change over time, especially when we feel emotionally safe with our partner.

While we were in Korea, I left no doubt in my wife's mind that I'd cut my whole dick off if I thought that's what it took to keep her in my life. And she was like, "No, no, no, no, no, no! You gonna keep that, 'cause I need that." Through those ups and downs, my wife was like, "You wanna be ethically non-monogamous?" I'm like, "Yes." She's like, "Okay, we'll see. It might not be for me, but we'll see."

We had been talking about it off and on for a decade-and-a-half, but last year, we put the feelers out there. We got two bites. I went off with one guy on my own once, and me and her went off together with this other guy. We're keeping it to these two, which I'm cool with. We lead really busy lives, we got three kids.

It seemed like something changed in William's marriage at some point during his time in Korea, so I asked what made the difference.

Radical honesty. You'd be surprised, when you got somebody that loves you, and they tell you, "I'm gonna be there with you no matter what, just tell me the truth" … I didn't believe it when I was younger, because it hadn't been my experience, but my wife is the real deal. Me being open, honest, and transparent made her feel safe and let her be herself, so then she could say, "You know, I've always wanted to do this and experience this." She had to know that she wasn't going to lose me, and she could only feel that if she could believe the words coming outta my mouth. I had spent a long time convincing her that she couldn't. We're there now.

One day she was like, "I always wondered what you looked like with a dick in your mouth." I'm looking for the cameras, I'm waiting for the other shoe to drop, you know? It's easy to talk about your spouse not trusting you, but a lot of times that comes from you not trusting your spouse. I had to deal with that.

Establishing enough trust to talk to your wife about sucking dick is no easy feat. Until a few years ago, I never thought that would be possible for me – it seemed like a crazy idea! But in my opinion, bisexuality is so fundamental to who we are, many of us will go crazy if we <u>don't</u> talk about it eventually, so we find a way. This not only relieves tension surrounding sexuality and gender, but it can open a door to communication about other things that we fear talking about.

Even after coming out and discussing non-monogamy, William had a lot more to unpack – and doing so helped him feel a sense of freedom in his marriage and life.

There's a lot of things that I'm just finding out. A lot of traumas I was carrying around, a lot of internalized biphobia, homophobia, racial crap, social economic crap. When you realize that you can't be you, you see how that impacts you in the bedroom.

It may have been one of your podcast interviews, I remember somebody talking about how common it was for bisexual men to have performance issues in bed. I was like, "Yo, why is this motherfucker telling my story, and I don't even know him like that?" It's true. You get imposter syndrome. When you feel like you are not being who you're supposed to be, your performance in the bedroom suffers. You're naked and you're exposed, you can't hide it, and your partner doesn't know what that is. Your partner's thinking, "You're just not into me." Now you're worried about what she's thinking. It's a spiral. It's horrible.

Right now, I'm experiencing a sense of personal freedom that I never felt before. I don't even wanna rip and run out in the streets no more. I'm too old for that shit. But I'm happy and satisfied with me and my wife just being me and her. I realize that there's another dimension that can't be ignored, 'cause it's been ignored too long, but now we found that there's a healthy way to express this, and that means the world to us.

I asked William if he talks to his kids about his bisexuality.

I don't go into detail with my children about my sexual habits, naturally. But I do normalize it. I don't hide it. My eldest, she knows I'm bisexual. My son, he should know. My youngest recently said, "Dad, I think I'm a lesbian." I'm like, "You like girls? I do too." And my wife was like, "I like them, too." My daughter was like, "That's a thing?" "Yeah, I'm bi, your mom's bi, it makes sense. What else?" I didn't want balloons and a party coming out. I just didn't wanna get beat up, you know?

William's attitude with his children, both normalizing bisexuality while downplaying its importance, could be tied to the compartmentalization that was necessary for his survival. Despite this, he and his wife have recently recognized the importance of finding their own queer community – and how difficult that can be where they now reside: Wasilla, Alaska.

This was a conversation I had with my wife not too long ago, that we need to meet more LGBTQ+ people, specifically bisexual people. Not for hooking up, but because we need to be around people who make being bisexual normal. We don't feel normal. We've been talking about going down to this local LGBTQ bar. It's 45 minutes away in Anchorage, but Anchorage is the next closest city. I don't personally have anybody that I would call a friend that's bisexual. So that piece is lacking in our lives. We don't have a community, but we're open to building one.

William has come a long way on his Bi+ journey and in his marriage, but I expect there's more to come. Sometimes the way he phrased things reminded me of myself early in the coming out process – I still saw bisexuality as "sexual" more than a holistic identity, I hadn't quite disentangled fluidity from non-monogamy, and I hadn't fully experienced the diversity within the Bi+ community. For me, learning more about sexuality and gender has been like climbing to the top of a hill only for the next peak to be revealed. I find it beautiful that there's always more to discover, and I have no doubt that William will continue on his journey.

12

Bennett and the Journey from the "Other Side" of the Spectrum

I was born in 1980 in Oakland, California, to a liberal lesbian mother. I was raised in a rather idealistic gender-neutral format that my mom was really committed to. She was a midwife. I was raised by her and her various partners. She didn't have a primary partner, but over the years had different partners. [I had] two older sisters, so a lot of feminine influence there.

I was also a donor baby, so there was this real heightened desire to be accepted by men along with that over-saturation of feminine energy. That really pushed me toward men from an early age.

I brought a Barbie doll to school to my first show-and-tell, which my mom was totally okay with, and it just went horribly wrong. They all laughed, and I was no longer accepted. I became an outcast basically. It was a pivotal moment in my life where I'm like, "Oh God, this is not okay. Who I am is not okay." My mom did not prepare me for that. "You betrayed me" was the basic thought in my little five-year-old brain. And I knew it was connected to not having a father.

For me, sexuality was never really an issue. I didn't really have to come out – I was raised in an alternative family, basically. Still, I struggled a lot with society and in high school in the mid-1990s. I did feel like I had to come out to my school, because I was rather feminine. I was the only out queer person in my entire high school of like 3,000 people. I just thought of myself

DOI: 10.4324/9781003385585-12

as queer, basically. I don't think I used the word "gay" – I didn't want to pigeonhole myself like that.

Bennett is a white, bisexual, cisgender man from Oakland, California and currently living in New York City. He was born in 1980 and was 40 years old at the time of our interview in 2020. He was raised non-religious and middle-class and still describes himself that way.

Though the majority of bisexual people identify closer to "straight" on the Kinsey scale than they do to "gay", of course this is not always the case. Because the options for sexuality feel binary to most young people, many who are aware of their same-sex attractions end up identifying as gay, even if other attractions are also present.

This is exactly what happened to my former co-host on *Two Bi Guys*, Alex. He knew that he was attracted to men, so when his parents found gay porn on his computer and asked whether he was gay, he said "yes" even though he also knew he had crushes on girls. As a teenager, he wasn't aware of the bisexual option, so he fell into a gay identity that didn't tell the whole story.

Most of the messages we've received at *Two Bi Guys* come from previously straight-identified men, but as we've continued, more and more messages have come in from gay men. They tell us that their label boxed them in, too, and that as they've grown older, they've understood that their attractions have a degree of fluidity. Some, like Alex, didn't make a conscious "choice" to identify as gay but rather got pushed into it by default or circumstance. Many keep the "gay" label – for various reasons – even while exploring with people of a different sex or gender. While it can be healthy to come out early in life, coming out as gay if you're actually fluid can lead to repressing an important part of your personality – just like for closeted Bi+ men who pass for straight.

Bennett's trajectory reminds me of others who come from this side of the spectrum – but his story is still unique, since he never actually identified or thought of himself as exclusively "gay". Perhaps because he grew up in a progressive, LGBTQ+ household, he became aware of his same-sex attractions (and accepted them) early, but he adopted a "queer" label, understanding that the word "gay" might pigeonhole him.

Still, many people assumed he was gay, and Bennett did feel like he was part of the gay community. Though this made him an "outcast" in school, his interest in the arts kept him in relatively safe and tolerant environments as he grew up and got to know himself better.

I'm an artist, I'm a musician, a fashion designer, performer, circus, stilt-walker, painter – all the arts. Fashion has been the most lucrative of my artistic expressions, music has been my biggest passion, and I've kind of gone back and forth between the two. I've had multiple clothing companies. Before the pandemic, I was primarily in nightlife here in New York, performing, go-go dancing, living statue, stilt-walking, all sorts of stuff.

In Bennett's case, his journey toward understand his complete sexuality was complicated by a traumatic sexual experience.

I had some rather deep stuff going on around men, especially being raised by women and then going into school and being ostracized. My earliest sexual experiences, besides pre-teen experimentation [with friends] … I was 14, with a much older man. It was illegal. There was coercion and force involved. And it was super-traumatizing. I didn't see it like that for years, but as I started to unpack it and detangle it, I realized that it was molestation, if not assault.

That coupled with this yearning for male affection, male acceptance, no father … it was just this perfect storm. After this traumatic experience, I normalized it and continued to seek out experiences like that with people [who] didn't care. Some of my earlier sexual experiences with men were just retraumatizing this wound.

That made it really confusing around my bisexuality, because there was this trauma with men that didn't occur women. So for a long time, I was like, well, am I even gay? Do I even like men? Because when I have sex with men, this doesn't feel right, because I was reacting to this trauma, and then with women, it feels great because there was no trauma. But because of our society and bisexuality, it became really murky. I was like, is this just internalized homophobia? Or am I really just not gay at all and just traumatized from these experiences?

I had sex with women occasionally. I had some short-term affairs. The first time I had sex with a girl, I was 18. I'd been with men for years before that. Then I had a girlfriend for a few months, off and on. But I was part of a queer community, and that really limited my ability to be with women. People thought of me as gay. I didn't really correct them. I wasn't like, "No, I'm bisexual." I was just like, "I don't care. Call me whatever you want." So I had subtle, small affairs with women over the years.

Bennett didn't correct people who identified him as gay, but honestly, even if he had, many women wouldn't have believed him, anyway – it's a common and unfortunate form of biphobia. Bennett's association with the queer community led most women in his life to see him as uninterested or unavailable, so most of his early experiences were with men. When he met his future wife, it's no surprise that they were friends for a long time before a relationship developed, almost by accident.

I was 15 when I had my first boyfriend, but that was only a few months. My first real relationship with a man, I was 23, lasted about a year. Then I had another boyfriend, that lasted two or three years. My first long-term relationship with a woman wasn't until my wife.

[My wife and I] had been friends for a year-and-a-half, which really helped, because most of my expression had been with men. I have zero game with women. I feel like I'm a 15-year-old boy with the amount of experience I've had negotiating dating, interacting on a sexual level with women – I feel years behind.

[My wife and I] were part of a very similar community: we were both artists and musicians, we were both doing these little home movies, YouTube videos of our lives and everything. Our mutual friend was like, "You guys have to meet." When we met, I was dating a man, and she was dating somebody else, so initially it was a pure friendship situation, like "We should collaborate."

But then a few months later, we both were going to a festival, and our mutual friend ended up backing out, so it was just me and her, and she forgot her tent. I was like, "You can stay in my tent." Neither of us were thinking about anything sexual at that time. But then after a day or two, somehow we started making out and she was like, "Oh, he must not be gay." And then we had sex.

In her mind, she was thinking it was going to lead somewhere. I thought we were just friends with benefits. I then got a boyfriend, so in her mind, I've totally rejected her – which I wouldn't find out until years later. In her mind, I had left her for this man. [But when] I broke up with that boyfriend, she came back into my life.

I was going through a pretty rough time. With the boyfriend, some of my more unhealthy sexual expressions were becoming debilitating, and I was depressed. She came back at a moment that really was impactful in a positive way to me. She was able to help me work through some issues I was going through. And there was this spiritual bond that was really amazing, so we were pretty much joined after that. I kicked out my roommates, and we were off to the races – it was like full on, let's do this.

Bennett already thought of himself as queer, but he didn't exactly "come out" to his wife – she was discovering his sexual fluidity in real time, as he was exploring it. Still, his queer identity played a huge role in their marriage, and at times his attractions to men were a source of conflict, even though his wife was aware of them from the start.

Nevertheless, at the beginning, Bennett felt like it was a serendipitous connection. In addition to their sexual and spiritual exploration together, they also decided to work together professionally.

I had kind of sworn off fashion, but she had been a fan of my previous clothing line, and she said that she had been disappointed and had been thinking about ways to get me to do fashion again. When we got together officially, before long she basically became my muse. She was like, "I want you to make me pretty things." I couldn't refuse. She re-inspired me. I also had a hard time with a lot of the ethics, the environmental costs, the human exploitation, the sweatshop labor. She inspired me that maybe the best way to make change was within the system.

So she did her little magic and next thing you know, we had a clothing company. That's how we started, and at a certain point, that became the thing that held us together.

Once they were together, Bennett's friends started to ask questions. Many had assumed he was gay, so this "straight" relationship didn't make sense from the outside. This experience caused Bennett to do even more in-depth research and reflection.

There was this deep, underlying confusion – people would be like, "I thought you were gay." I was suddenly confronted with this whole world of bisexuality. I started going into forums and seeing all these closeted men grappling with being bisexual. I started to develop this concept that our society has collapsed sexuality and culture in a way that is just so limiting. You have men that come out as bisexual, and it [becomes] so much more than a sexual identity – they feel like their entire cultural world changes.

That's what I experienced. My entire cultural world shifted. People thought of me differently. I stopped hanging out in queer environments. Before that, I was engaged in queer culture, like immersed, and then suddenly it all changed. I wasn't in it for years, I kind of disappeared.

I found myself starting to see just how deep this erasure is, and how deep my own internal biphobia was. I found myself not feeling accepted going to the same gay bars and social settings. I'd always oscillated between queer cultures and more hetero-centric, artistic cultures [like] Burning Man, so it was a pretty fluid thing for me, but for whatever reason it shifted dramatically.

I was also doing music, and I had a little following, and they really thought of me as a gay artist. Some of them were maybe more drawn to my identity than my music. When I got together with my wife, I definitely felt a shift. The people that were falling [off] were mainly women. I think there's this rapport with straight women and gay men where they can feel really safe, sometimes fantasize, "If only you were not gay . . . " Suddenly it felt like I wasn't this safe, gay man who was going to love them unconditionally. Suddenly I was a man who was gonna judge them sexually or judge their attractiveness.

Bennett's involvement with queer communities had initially prevented him from expressing sexuality with women, and now, expressing sexuality with women was keeping him out of those communities. Unfortunately, some people view queerness as "all or nothing", and any opposite-sex attraction is viewed as disqual-ifying. Despite this unwanted change in his social life, being with a woman helped Bennett interrogate and understand some confusing aspects of fluidity.

When I'm with a woman, I am a man, you know? When I'm the top, I am the man. And when I am the bottom, I am feminine. All that stuff is so deeply ingrained.

In a way, some of the stereotypes around bisexuality have some merit, where there were no safe people where there wasn't some kind of potential sexuality. If you don't have good boundaries, it's like, "Oh, am I supposed to have sex with them now? Do they want to have sex with me now? Am I attracted to them? Are they attracted to me?" And it can cross gender lines. So I've had issues making friends, because there'd be tension around whether I was attracted to them or not.

[With my wife], our sexual connection was super-strong. Since then I've come to realize that the way my bisexuality is manifesting is this really intense sexual attraction with women – almost purely sexual – and a more romantic attraction with men. Some of that, things change over time.

[I had] short flings with women. I joked that I had this yearly schedule where once a year I'd want to have sex with a woman. But then with [my wife], we were together for five years and I wasn't with a man that entire time.

I had something like survivor's guilt about holding her hand down the street because it felt so accepted, you know? She was attractive, and guys would look at her, and I felt like, "Oh, ha ha ha, I've got this patriarchal prize." I would almost be ashamed to hold her hand because I'd felt so many years of holding somebody's hand, having to be so considered, you know … safety, whether people would accept you or not. Holding a hand with a boyfriend felt like this act of defiance, like this political act. Suddenly I felt like it was the opposite, like I was reinforcing heterosexual domination or something.

Entering a straight-passing relationship after adopting a queer identity brings unique challenges, and for Bennett it almost felt like going "backwards" in terms of his politics. Of course, on a personal level, Bennett was actually still moving forward, expanding his worldview, and becoming a more authentic version of himself – but I can understand his struggle, especially since he was experiencing very real biphobia from outsiders. He was ashamed of how people would view his "traditional" relationship, but in a sense, he was still people-pleasing rather than holding onto his own feelings from the inside out.

With all these conflicting emotions and changes in his social life, it was hard for Bennett to process his satisfaction with the relationship itself, but with hindsight, he can see that he was ignoring some warning signs. Still, due to their circumstances, he decided to get married.

I actually didn't even want to get married. For me, it's a piece of paper. The government is not going to tell me who I love. But she has extremely religious parents, and she is polyamorous, bisexual, very liberal, and she had these fears that if she were to get in an accident, her parents would be able to take over and get power of attorney. So I went along with it.

We got married on stage in Reno, close to Burning Man, [with] a lot of [our] Burning Man community there, so we did a show and a ceremony on stage while we were performing. Then a little ceremony with our friends, and my moms came up.

But I think at that point we already should not have been together. We had some really unhealthy dynamics. I was staying around out of co-dependence, but also this loyalty, because she had helped me so much in the beginning. I was just devoted to her.

Bennet mentioned that his wife was polyamorous, but non-monogamy hadn't come up yet in our interview, so I asked about it, and the answer was, of course, complex. They had been monogamous for years, but eventually they discussed opening things up. Unfortunately, his wife's early impression that Bennett had "left her for a man" when they began dating – along with other biphobic assumptions – created an insecurity that led to very strict boundaries and ultimately, toxicity. This was complicated further by her unaddressed trauma.

She was bisexual, also. It was challenging, 'cause we were monogamous, but it wasn't like an inherent value. It was kind of circumstantial. She had a lot of boundaries that she wanted to keep, some around safety, which I totally respected. She wanted me to be friends with a guy for a year before I'd have sex with him [laughs].

We had these polyamorous ideas around somebody that would not disrupt our unit, which were totally valid, but hindered the practical application somewhat. [We] negotiated around bringing others in, and I experienced multiple men being like, "Yeah, sure, I'll try some bisexuality", when really in the end, it seemed like their intent was to be with her. It didn't seem like an authentic expression.

There was a lot of trauma on [my wife's] end. She was extremely traumatized in her early life. There were unhealthy dynamics that were just not okay. Slightly abusive. Veering into, like… she'd have these blackout episodes … where she would just freak out and … like cutting herself. I should have left a long time ago, but honestly, my bisexuality is partly what kept me there, because I just did not have that much experience with women. She would use the idea of my masculinity as an excuse for some of her behaviors. She'd be like, "Why didn't you just stop me from hitting you over and over? You're so much bigger than me. Why don't you just hold me down? Why weren't you man enough to help me? I wish you would take care of me." And I was like, "Oh gosh, maybe I'm not man enough. Maybe I do need to learn how to do these things." In hindsight it's like, no, I cannot. You can't be a therapist and a caretaker and a partner. I just didn't know any better.

She perpetuated the idea that if only I was doing something different, then she would be okay. On the one hand, that was really damaging. And then on the other hand, it caused me to do a lot of personal growth. I thought that I was the cause of this stuff, so I was like, "I'm going to learn about myself. I'm going to get better." And I did. But there's only so [much] you can help somebody. When they're dealing with that level of trauma, it's something they really have to do on their own.

I remember saying to myself, "God, if I was the girl and you were the guy, I would have been out of here a long time ago." And at some point I was like, "Well, maybe that means you should be out of here", you know?

On some level, Bennett was aware that the relationship was not healthy, but possibly due to confusion around his sexuality and needs, combined with a toxic, abusive partner and a proclivity for people-pleasing, he stayed – until he didn't have a choice.

I would have stayed in [my marriage] forever. It was really her. She brought in a third, this guy, and they basically fell in love. There was this gut-wrenching six-month process of her shifting from me to him, with a lot of gaslighting and denial of what was happening. That was just ... so heart-wrenching. I really liked him, but their connection was clearly so strong, and I could feel it.

I was living in Bali, for our company, and she had been staying with him in the Bay Area. She would go back and forth, bringing the product and selling in LA. We'd had sex together. Me and him had never had intercourse, but we'd been all three together and they'd had sex, and then me and him would make out and there was some oral, whatever. But only a few times.

Then I came for two weeks to visit him and her, and within those two weeks, it was clear. It was done. It was so torturous. It was the subtle things of how she would interact with him versus me. I could just feel her priority had shifted. At one point I was so sad about what was happening and just distraught and crying, and she said that I should probably go to my mother's house because she didn't want to disturb him ... that was devastating. I was her husband. I got in an Uber and cried all the way to my mother's house. I flopped onto my mother's doorstep, broken hearted, just devastated. I was like, "This is over."

But then I gave it one more chance. For a month I was at my mom's house. She was at his house. I kept being like, "Let's just get back together. Let's work this out." She would come to my mom's house and have sex with me, but then she wanted to stay with him. It was very confusing. I gave it one last effort on her birthday. She had gone back to Bali, and I was like, "Let me pick you up from the airport, let's just talk this out." I brought her flowers and her favorite champagne. I was like, "Please stay with me tonight", and she said, "No, I want to stay with him." I literally dropped her off at his house, sat in the car outside, just crying and crying and crying, for like an hour, completely devastated. The next day I told her I wanted a divorce. It was a really rough divorce.

I asked if she was still with that guy.

No. That lasted for a certain time, but no. But I'm so glad that it happened. It became clear just how unhealthy it was later, as I started to unpack it all.

I wasn't that happy. We were doing this fashion company, and I was working so many hours. I became a pencil pusher, dealing with manufacturing and customers and spreadsheets, and I was like, "I just want to perform." Then somehow, the universe aligned, she took the company, and I was forced to perform [laughs]. Then I started making money as a performer, so it's funny how things work out.

After her, I re-entered the gay world with a fury [laughs]. It'd been five years, and I was in San Francisco. Went kind of crazy, dyed my hair blond, feeling pretty good for 37, had really hard abs because I was so devastated and not eating from the divorce. But then it became clear rather quickly that I still had these issues and that it wasn't as much around men and women as it was around sexuality as a whole.

Bennett is clear now that getting out of his marriage was the right decision – but getting out didn't solve everything. His wife's biphobic attacks led to new confusion surrounding his sexuality, just as he was understanding its complexity. Being in an abusive relationship also prevented him from working through his own trauma and negative patterns, but now that he was out, he could finally address those things.

I'm in a 12-step program for sex. That's really helped me sort through that stuff. I'm bisexual, and these things happened, but I don't think one creates the other. But homophobia, patriarchy, biphobia, erasure, all that stuff has made it a lot harder to handle those things and to sort out what is healthy sexuality.

Going into SAA [Sex Addicts Anonymous] – they call it "acting out", the behaviors that you want to stop completely – I discovered that the ways that I was acting out were with men. Which is not inherent to my sexuality, it just is what occurred. A lot of it involved domination. It was so complex that I'm taking a step away from all of it.

It's such a classic, the sex addict bisexual, you know? There's part of me that's like, "I don't want to fit the stereotype, because when you have so little representation, every little bit matters." It's like, "Oh, bisexuals, they just want all the sex all the time." But it is what it is.

It's important to note that there are two schools of thought about what Bennett is describing: some call it "sex addiction" and view it as a disease similar to other addictions, while others call it "out-of-control sexual behavior" (OCSB) and treat it as a sexual problem, not a disorder or illness, based on sexual thoughts, urges, or behaviors that feel out of control to the person experiencing them. The latter is often not about sex but a symptom of untreated trauma or abuse, unresolved relationship issues, or other mental health issues. Some believe that the term "sex addict" adds undue stigma and leads to treating the compulsion with abstinence, which is not always healthy, while addressing OCSB focuses on addressing underlying issues. The right approach may vary for each individual, but this is an area where recovery may be affected by how the problem is named, so the semantics are important to mention.

In any case, there is stigma surrounding either label, so Bennett was nervous about playing into negative Bi+ stereotypes, but I appreciated his honesty. I believe it's so important to be truthful in our representation of bisexuality, the joys and the struggles, if we want to really be understood and taken seriously. Bisexuality does <u>not</u> equal sex addiction, and it is not a gateway to out-of-control sexual behavior any more than other sexualities – but at the same time, if we pretend that no Bi+ people have impulses that feel out of control, or that none of us ever feel wild or kinky or insecure or slutty or confused and make mistakes because of it, then we're setting ourselves up for failure.

> Recently, I've done a lot of abstinence and putting the brakes on it all to be like, "I just need to figure out who the fuck I am, without any outside influence." I'm now on day 77 of no sex. That's how I've discovered that I am truly bisexual.
>
> It's such a relief to be contained in my little bubble. When somebody is interested in me, there's nothing for me to do about it because I have these very clear boundaries now. I moved to New York, and it's been this process of discovery and healing and getting back to my art and working on my music again.

I asked if Bennett wanted kids with his wife – or in the future.

> [My wife and I] had our whole thing planned. We were going to build an empire. We discussed how we would homeschool our kids. When that relationship died, I haven't even allowed myself to think about that. I'm not opposed to it, if I had a partner and that was something they wanted. But it's definitely not at the top of my list, that's for sure. Now I'm just happy that I'm finally able to take care of myself for the first time. I finally feel like an adult at 40.

Bennett has a unique perspective, since most Bi+ men come from a straight identity first and have difficulty integrating queerness and queer culture into their lives. Bennett didn't have to overcome that stigma, but he did experience the cultural shift that comes with a perceived "change" in sexuality, and he's aware of how unfortunate this is. He wishes that gay-identified men could explore with other genders and not become outcasts of the queer community – but also that straight-identified men could do the same without being immediately seen as "gay" and having their entire world shift around them, too. I completely agree, and I often wonder why the stakes are so high for exploring sexually fluidity, especially outside the bedroom. As Bennett described, giving that freedom to men in partic-ular, who are very constrained by patriarchy and masculinity, could have positive affects in areas beyond sexuality.

> I feel so strongly for bisexual men. Especially when I [was] with my ex-wife, I was just like, "God, I want to create a world where they can be exactly as

they are." I've talked about an honest *Brokeback Mountain* fantasy, like let me just get a friend [who] I can go away with for the weekend and it's all honest and clear. You have this experience, this male bonding, and then you go back to your wife and you go back to your kids, you know? I remember seeing that movie and wishing it could be honest. It could work so well. It just breaks my heart.

One of my biggest goals in life is to help men with their sexuality. It just seems like those wounds are basically the root of all the destruction on our planet. Really healing males, and in particular furthering the cause of male bisexuality, is huge.

13

Carter on the Trans, Black, and Bi+ Experience

I was born in 1989, and I grew up in the Bay Area, in a small little red town. I am the youngest of six. I'm also adopted: I've been with my parents since I was 11 months old. I have two other siblings besides myself who are adopted. I'm also the second-youngest of my biological family of nine. So I've had an interesting childhood.

My dad worked a lot, probably by choice, so it was mainly just me and my mom and my siblings growing up, and a lot of times I played caretaker raising my two oldest siblings. My sister has Down syndrome, my brother has Down syndrome and autism. So I think I grew up fast. My mom has always been my rock and my backbone. Sometimes we don't see eye to eye, but she picks and chooses her battles wisely.

My parents are white. My dad is atheist, I think my mom is agnostic. My dad is from the South, my mom was California born and raised, so I've had the polar opposites of the hippie-esque versus the southern roots. My family has always been really open about religion and different cultures, respecting everyone, 'cause you don't know what they're going through, and most of the time they just want to be seen as human – which I think also helped me be who I was at a younger age.

I remember running around the house when I was two – my mom says I was two – saying I was a boy. And my mom was like, "Uh, okay, we'll circle

DOI: 10.4324/9781003385585-13

back to that, but you do you and keep running around and saying all this stuff", you know? Like, kids will be kids.

Carter is a Black, Bi+, trans-masc non-binary person living in Sacramento, California. Until recently, he identified as a trans man, and though he currently uses either he/him or they/them pronouns, in consultation with him and based on his story, I've used he/him for a majority of this chapter. Carter was born in the Bay Area in 1989 and was 33 at the time of our interview in 2022. He describes himself as agnostic and working middle-class, both in childhood and currently.

Carter was assigned female at birth, but he had at least some sense that he was a boy by age two. His family was generally open-minded and accepting of difference, which helps explains Carter's ability to embrace his trans identity and later his Bi+ identity, but that didn't happen immediately or without some struggle. While his mom was listening and attuned to his feelings, she could only work with the knowledge she had at the time.

As I got older, I kept saying it more firmly. My mom was like, "Okay, we'll come back to that. I hear you." Honestly, my mom tried her best, but she thought I was confused with being lesbian. She was trying to steer me, like, "No, you're a girl who likes girls, you're a lesbian." And I was like, "No, I'm a boy who likes girls." That was challenging, knowing who I was and having society already telling me I was wrong.

Then when I was 12, there was a murder in my town of a trans woman. That was the first time I've seen my town full of hate. I saw truly in that instance why it was a red town, how little of my town was actually protecting queer youth and acknowledging them and respecting them. In a juxtaposition, that's how I found out was transgender – in the article about the murder, they had a basic, rudimentary explanation, and I was like, I think that's what I am. That sounds like who I am inside.

Many Bi+ men don't realize they're bisexual until they see an example of it, and that type of visibility is just as important for trans people. But first seeing your identity represented in a murder case has got to be confusing and traumatic – a double-edged sword for Carter. He learned right away how to hold space for two conflicting concepts at once – he was a trans man, and those around him didn't respect (and sometimes wanted to kill) trans people.

Despite the latter, Carter managed to express himself authentically from a relatively early age – in fact, he was more confused by the backlash than by his own feelings.

In elementary school, I was out at a young age. I was a weird queer kid. I didn't know that was wrong. My parents always told me to be who you are and do what you want to do, which is great at home, but when I'm in society, it gets confusing and hard. I had problems, 'cause I was like, I don't understand why people are being mean to me.

I did have a crush [on] this girl in eighth grade. She was actually out, queer, and I was just enamored with her willingness to be herself and not care what anyone would think. To be so open in our little town is putting a target on your back. I remember being so in love with her, like the way she moved, the way she talked. It was hard for me just to be her friend, 'cause I wanted to be more, but I would never say anything.

Carter is not the only person in this book to admire someone who was "more out" than him growing up. Basic definitions of queerness and reading about LGBTQ+ people in a newspaper are better than nothing, but actually knowing someone who is out and thriving can be a life-altering experience. In our heteronormative society, we're constantly told that being queer will make your life harder, and while that can be true, in my experience queerness also makes life more beautiful, exciting, and meaningful. It comes with challenges, but for me, it's not only worth it, it's a blessing. (I wish I had come to this conclusion earlier than my 30s!)

Carter's crush helped him understand how he wanted to live his life, but no matter how in-touch you are with your feelings, expressing them clearly as a teenager is always hard, so Carter found himself relatively alone with his gender dysphoria until around age fifteen. Thankfully, he was in an environment where transitioning was possible – but still not easy.

I had this panic attack, and I was honestly suicidal. I was talking to my oldest sister, and I remember crying, "I like girls, and it's not something I can turn off. But I feel like I'm a boy, and I don't know how to explain that to mom and dad." I was so distraught. My sister was like, "Just tell them, they're not gonna be upset." I was like, "Easier said than done."

I called my parents in and sat them down. I was like, "So we all know I like girls, that's not news. I feel like I'm a boy. And I don't know what to do about this." My parents were like, "Okay, well what do you wanna do?" I had really, really long hair back then, and I was like, "I wanna cut my hair. Shave it down." My mom's like, "Let's think about it." I was like, "No, I wanna cut my hair. And when we go clothes shopping, I wanna go in the boys' section. I don't wanna go in the girls' section."

When I was 15, I went on summer break, I cut my hair, changed my name, changed my clothes, and came back this whole other person my sophomore year. People were like, "What?" and I was like, "Oh yeah, duh." Back then, they didn't have a lot of the laws that they have today, so it was very much trial and error by my school. The teacher was like, "That's not your name." I was like, "No, it is. That's it. This isn't up for discussion."

And then the bathrooms, my school struggled with that a lot. When I would try to use the boys' restroom, it would cause a ruckus. I wasn't supposed to be in there, but I didn't feel comfortable in the girls' locker room. The compromise we reached is I could use the admin office, which was on the other side of campus. I had to pray the receptionist was there, 'cause if she wasn't, that bathroom was locked. That was my life, running back and forth to the bathroom. I have to remind myself they didn't have the knowledge that we have now.

Carter knew he liked girls from a young age, but his first relationship (when he was presenting more feminine) was with a boy. His gender transition was a more pressing concern than his sexuality at that moment, and it complicated his understanding of sexual fluidity.

I was with someone for three years, from seventh grade to tenth grade, and he was my first love. He was amazing, really sweet and kind. When I transitioned, I remember being like, "We're just gonna break up because they're not bisexual or queer, they're straight, and it's not gonna work out." So I broke up with him after I transitioned. I was like, "I'm not gonna drag you along for this ride. I don't even know what the hell this entails. It's not fair to you", yada, yada. But after we broke up, a few months later, he was like, "You realize I would've stayed with you regardless, right? You being you doesn't change how I feel about you." [He was] not straight himself, so I had inadvertently been in a really open relationship and I didn't even know it. He was really sweet.

Despite experiencing attraction to multiple genders, Carter wasn't able to identify himself as bisexual until later in life – like many men in this book – possibly because he didn't see bisexuality as a valid option, but also because he wasn't yet fully aware that gender identity and sexuality were separate spectrums. For him, his attractions felt tied to his gender, and trying to figure out both at once led to some decisions he regrets.

I tried dating here and there. I identified as straight, so I would date the classic straight girls that were experimenting or questioning. They were always like, "You're the perfect person because you look like a boy, but you have the anatomy of girls." This is like a great stepping stone or segue, and I was like, okay. Now in hindsight, that's one of my rules dating as an adult: I'm not an experiment for you to figure yourself out. I'm a human being, and I'm not some phase, that's not my game.

I was president of the GSA for my four years in high school. My advisor was this openly gay man. He was amazing. He created a safe space in school. I would tell him about all the people I had a crush on, and he would always be like, "Why don't you ask them out?" I was like, "The girl says she's straight. Why would I?" He would always say, "Who knows? Everyone's questioning until they say who they are."

It was a lot of trial and error. I remember at one point I saw this really cute boy, and I was like, "But I'm straight." I had not understood that gender identity and sexual orientation are not synonymous, so I was like, "Why do I find him attractive?" Then I realized, "Oh shit, I may not be straight. Oh, wow." I remember saying in my head, I fucked myself over. I could have been messing with hella guys. It was like this epiphany.

It was weird 'cause I would do presentations on how gender identity and sexual orientation are not synonymous, but it never clicked until that moment. Now I understand what I'm presenting, 'cause now I'm literally living it.

Many of us go through something similar, and I've felt it myself: it's possible to acknowledge the existence of bisexuality (or queerness in general) and perhaps even become an advocate for others before we can accept it in ourselves. When we're in a box constructed by society for long enough, it's hard to break out of, even after we're intellectually aware of it, but once we take even a small step out of that box, there's usually no going back. While Carter's trans identity was clear and persistent, it took him a long time to disentangle his gender from his sexuality and to realize that sexual fluidity was possible. Once he fully acknowledged his crush on another guy, he had his bisexual "epiphany".

Still, old habits can die hard – and new interests can become overwhelming.

When I got to college, I still chased the straight girls, the ones [who] wanted a phase or an experiment. I would always chase the ones I couldn't have. I hung out with a lot of queer friends, and I had crushes on some, but I never really acted on them. I would just let them be, in fear I would ruin a friendship.

After a while, I realized I wanted to be in a relationship, and the hard part for me was, with who? I had always thought I would get married to a woman, and society said I would get married to a woman, and now I'm having these internal thoughts, like, "What if I get married to a man? This is gonna break the norm twice because not only am I trans but in a gay relationship."

I dated someone for almost five years, from [age] 20 to 24. She was my first adult love. That was a relationship where I realized that I didn't wanna hide in the closet, I wanted to be openly queer in all facets, like dangly earrings or nail polish or feminine tailored clothing, and it was hard with her, because she was so built on the machismo of like, "You have to be strong, you have to be tough." I wasn't. I was able to put up that façade, but deep inside, I wasn't those things. So we realized that it wasn't gonna work.

I dated a lot of men in my 20s. I really leaned into my era of men. It was rough. I have horrible taste in men, to be completely honest. The men I choose are gross and garbage. Like, wow, we gotta work on these standards with the men, because you really just be at that bottom of the barrel scraping, just having fun. But women, I feel like I have more of a standard, if you will.

I can't tell you how strongly this "era of men" idea resonates with me, and I know it's common for Bi+ men who come out later in life. It's like getting the keys to a candy store that was closed for decades. Sex was easily accessible, and

I wanted to try everything I had fantasized about, often repeatedly. This can be part of a natural "bi-cycle" that many Bi+ people experience, where our attractions for different genders increase or decrease over time, often in a cyclical pattern. My "era of men" was (mostly) pleasurable, but eventually it started to feel like empty calories, and I cycled back to being more interested in women.

Carter's overindulgence caused him to pull back on dating entirely, but I think it also helped him recognize what he <u>was</u> looking for in a partner when the right one came along.

> I was in two trash relationships based off OkCupid, so I was like, I'm not doing this shit any more, I'm done. My best friend, on the other hand, had gotten my OkCupid password and reactivated my account and started swiping on people for me. My now-wife had popped up in my feed a lot, but I was like, "She's outta my league. I'm gonna just act like she doesn't exist." Then my best friend's like, "Hey, I activated your OkCupid, and you got a message. You need to respond." And it was my now-wife who was asking me out for a drink.
>
> We had our first date like ten days later. We went out to a bar, and it was a three-hour date, and she did most of the talking. Still to this day, she does most of the talking. That has not changed. She was 23, I was 28. We've been together ever since.
>
> She's white. She identifies as Bi+. She's agnostic, as am I. And she's cisgender. We got married last year and we're expecting our first child. They're supposed to be born in June of 2023.
>
> My vows made everyone cry. It made her cry, too. I said, "I never thought I'd be worthy of being loved." I never thought I'd find someone, having such a shitty relationship history. Our relationship is a rarity in both of us being openly queer, being in a straight-passing relationship, being in an interracial relationship.

As discussed, I see a special relationship between the Bi+ and trans/non-binary communities. First, there is a ton of overlap, with many trans people (like Carter) identifying as Bi+. In addition, at least in my experience, Bi+ and trans people tend to gravitate toward each other in relationships, both romantic and for friendship and community. There are many trans people in my Bi+, poly, and kink communities in NYC and LA, and I've become more immersed in the trans community since coming out, especially after marrying a trans woman. I also believe that combining my bisexuality with her trans identity has strengthened our partnership. Witnessing her transition and still experiencing love and attraction throughout that journey has re-affirmed my bisexuality, helped her embrace her authentic self without fear of abandonment, and given us both a better understanding of what gender really means to us.

The fact that Carter and his wife both identify as Bi+ has certainly affected – and likely also strengthened – their bond. It has also led to deeper examination of their identities and to unexpected learning and growth. When Carter realized he was attracted to more than one gender, he had adopted a "pansexual" label, wanting to be inclusive of trans and non-binary attractions, and while his wife was (obviously) on the same page, they disagreed about terminology.

I'd identified as pansexual, and that was one of our first really heated discussions. I'm old school, what you're describing to me as Bi+ is what we call pansexual. She was like, "Yes, but times change and verbiage changes, so Bi+ is [the] equivalency of pansexuality. The plus is to be more inclusive of gender-nonconforming and trans people. We are literally saying the same exact thing, just two different labels."

So when I work with kids, I usually say I'm queer, and I'll say I'm Bi+. Pansexuality has phased out. I noticed that with more of the 18-year-olds, they use pansexual, but for 18 and younger they use Bi+.

I knew she was the one, probably after a month from our first date. I said "I love you" first, and her response was, "Thank you." But lo and behold, I got a Facebook notification saying you're in a relationship, and I was like, "What? You're not gonna tell me, you're just gonna post it?" And she's like, "This is me telling you."

Her mom said I was the first person she's ever brought home or mentioned to her. I am her first serious relationship. Her family, when she came out as bi, they had a rough time with it. They all thought she was gonna end up with a woman, so when I came into the picture, they were like, "What the hell's going on?" I'm this big burly Black person, I have tattoos and piercings, [but] I am not this machismo person by any means. I'm softer. And then they found out I was trans, and there was another added layer.

Their next question was, "How are you gonna have kids?" I told them my wife would carry, that was just the way our relationship was. I was like, I know I'm not gonna have biological children, so that's where we're at. Some of her family didn't really understand what that meant. I was like, "We'll use a sperm donor."

Carter's wife's family immediately questioned if and how they would have kids – another common thread for Bi+ people, which in this case was complicated by Carter's trans identity. Questions about kids may seem natural under heteronormativity, where procreation is often seen as the ultimate goal, but from my experience in the queer community, these are often the first questions we're asked and the only ones that seem to matter, which can feel reductive. Queer partnerships do not always revolve around biological kids, which is perfectly valid. In addition, Carter was adopted and had multiple adopted siblings, so the idea of a sperm donor was not as big an aberration to him as it must've felt to his wife's family.

Thankfully, his wife's family did the work and was ultimately accepting – partially thanks to his wife's unconditional support and boundary-setting.

At one point [my wife] called her mom and told her to tell the extended family, "[Carter's] trans, and [Carter's] Black. If you have problems with that, we will have an issue. That is not up for debate. I will cut y'all off. This is non-negotiable." I really appreciated that, 'cause I was honestly worried coming into an interracial relationship with someone who's white. Yes, I was raised by white people, but I can only code switch so much.

They did really, really well. I mean, they are great, they're amazing. They are excited for their new grandbaby. Her mom works in the medical field. She went on YouTube and watched top and bottom surgery videos and did a lot of research and asked me a lot of questions. I'm an open book, until you say something stupid or ignorant.

For queer couples, figuring out if you want to have kids can be hard to unpack, and figuring out how to do it can be even more challenging, since there are multiple options and no set script. Even once Carter and his wife decided what they wanted, actually going through with their plan was no cakewalk.

We did at-home insemination, and we have a known sperm donor. She found a Black sperm donor, which are far and few between, more scarce than we both thought. The person that we found, he's amazing, he's kind and caring. If I was a cis male, he would be like who I am. He said, "I will never understand what it's like be a queer person, but I always see the strength in the community, and it's so beautiful." I was like, this is our guy.

We got pregnant on our second try, but we had a miscarriage. Our fourth try, which was our last try, we got pregnant again, and she is 18 weeks tomorrow. I've never been so happy to not have 20 different apps on my phone for ovulation or calculations. It was rough. Everyone would see us during the conceiving process and they were like, "[Carter], you look like you're not having a good time." I was not. I'm so happy for this, but it was so stressful and strenuous and emotionally taxing.

It definitely [took] a toll on our relationship, being so frustrated and upset and trying to love one another while we're trying to do this ... and having people always ask, "When are you gonna get pregnant?" "How's that gonna work?" Half the time I was like, "Just fucking Google it. Stop asking me. I'm like in the midst of it. This is the worst time to ask me."

At the time of writing, they are still "anxiously awaiting" the arrival of their child, who they plan to raise without gendered pronouns.

Though Carter is trans and both he and his wife are Bi+ – a very queer relationship by most standards – they often pass for straight in public. Now that they're both so comfortable in their queer identities, passing has become a source of stress.

I always talk about being in a straight-passing relationship and how much I hate it. When I was younger, I would kill to be in a straight-passing relationship, for safety purposes. I wanted to be as stealthy as possible. But now I despise it. I literally wanna have an emblazoned bi flag jacket and hat so people don't think I'm straight.

Whenever we go out to queer events, we have our queer friends who are lesbian or gay, and they're walking around holding hands, and then me and my wife are like, this fucking sucks. They think we're the straight friends. I'm like, the joke's on them, we're literally part of this community. I always joke, "That's the one horrible thing about our relationship, babe, that we're straight passing and it sucks." And she's like, "Oh, I know. I hate it too."

Similar to his evolution on being in a straight-passing relationship, Carter spent most of his life wanting to pass as a man, but recently, he's come to embrace a non-binary gender identity and presentation, partially thanks to his wife. Carter now uses both "he/him" and "they/them" pronouns, depending on the situation, and in consultation with Carter, I will use "they/them" for the rest of this chapter to illustrate that progression.

I didn't come to terms with me being non-binary until like two years ago. [My wife] helped me with that a lot, teaching me gender has no rigidness, it's a spectrum. She was like, "You do whatever you please. I just want you to be happy, so whatever non-binary means to you, that's great." She's younger than me, and I had taken a step back from the community. The more current knowledge helped me so much. I worked so hard to be passing.

Carter worried that identifying and presenting as non-binary would make them less safe as a couple, but their wife put those fears at ease as much as she could.

I kept telling her, "If we go down the street in the middle of the night and someone gets mad 'cause I'm wearing dangly earrings and nail polish, are you prepared for that?" When we first started dating, I wouldn't wear any of that, so I'm adding this layer of danger. She was like, "You don't have to live in the closet just to keep me safe. No one is ever safe, honestly. Bigots are gonna be bigots regardless of polish, they're gonna find something wrong with you."

When the George Floyd riots happened, she was actually the one that got me involved, believe it or not. She definitely used her white privilege with police in order to protect us. I think that was another point where I fell deeper in love with her. I was realizing she's willing to put her life on the line to keep me safe. I've never had that, so that was heartwarming for me. We've been through a lot, a lot, a lot. She has been my rock through it all and has shown me what love is. She walks alongside me throughout this journey of different roads that I didn't even know I'm gonna take. She's still with me.

Identifying as queer lit a fire in me to be more active in social justice movements, much like Carter's wife. Once I recognized my own bisexuality and felt how much it was stigmatized, erased, and even persecuted, it gave me a new understanding of what it's like to be in a marginalized minority. Coming out connected me directly (through support groups, events, etc.) to more people of color, people with disabilities, people with non-conforming gender identities, and others. The more I learned, the more I noticed not just ubiquitous biphobia but also racism, classism, ableism, ageism, sexism, transphobia, and religious discrimination.

For once, non-monogamy didn't come up in our interview, so of course I had to ask Carter about that.

> We tried non-monogamy. It did not work out. She is jealous, which is fine. I have always been in monogamous relationships. This was the first time I've ever been open. I like it, but she made a good point: "Are you open because your relationship is lacking or because you're happy in the relationship but you just wanna have another one on the side?" At the time, we were not great, and I guess we were using that as a coping mechanism. Some of our friends are open and polyamorous, which is great, I'll be their biggest cheerleader. But that's not our cup of tea.

Carter has dealt with a lot of issues that come up for queer people, and from my point of view, they've worked their way through all of them. That doesn't mean they have all the answers, but they seem very aware of their feelings and how to approach new challenges. Now Carter is using all that knowledge and lived experience in their career to help the next generation of queer people.

> I am a "peer partner", I work for a federally qualified health center. Basically I'm a case worker, so I work with LGBT+ youth from the ages of 12 to 26 with life skills, mentorship. We do gender-affirming clothing, legal name change, school issues like Title IX, issues that have to do with gender and sexuality. I work on healthy relationships, healthy coping skills, and learning what to do when safety is the issue. If they're not out at home, and they're constantly dead-named and mis-gendered, creating safe spaces.
>
> Ironically, I have [my wife's] old job. She used to have literally the same job. She now works for [a university] as a sexual violence education prevention coordinator. She does trainings for the staff, faculty, and students.

There's nothing I find more inspiring than working through trauma and hardship and then paying it forward so that the next generation has it a little easier, and my heart is full knowing that Carter and their wife are doing this work. They've also done it within their own family.

> My half-sister had a rough time [with my queerness]. She's Christian. And my other sister, two of her three children are queer. She had a really, really rough time to the point where it fractured our family, and I wouldn't go to any family events for like two years. I think it was a struggle because they've never had interactions with queer people.

My half-sister has done a lot of work, and I've had to do a lot of education with her about stereotypes and myths. The [sister who] had the most problems is literally my safe space [now]. It's been a complete 180, our relationship has totally changed. She's done so much research, I'm really proud of her. I go to her for anything. Her kids, I sometimes feel envious of them, because the mom they have is so warm and loving and accepting right off the bat – I put in the blood, sweat, and tears for that. I would do it again in a heartbeat, but I'm like, damn, I really went through the wringer.

Carter's final thought makes me cry every time I read, so here it is, and I'll shut up now.

I usually tell [kids] that they know themselves, they know who they are. Society will tell you that you're wrong or you need to conform, [but] you have every right to march to the beat of your own drum. It won't be easy, and it sometimes can be dangerous, but you don't owe anyone conformity. No one can tell you what your journey is or if it's right or wrong. Your journey is your journey. And no matter what that looks like, that is the way it's supposed to happen for you.

14

Bisexuality and Non-Monogamy

It must be apparent by now that non-monogamy is a recurring theme among couples in this book, but it is absolutely not a foregone conclusion for Bi+ or mixed-orientation relationships. In fact, very few interviewees describe themselves as polyamorous ("poly" meaning "many", "amorous" referring to "love"), though many have explored some form of an open relationship for a period of time, and almost all have at least discussed it, even if they've remained monogamous.

This discussion often comes up only after the husband's bisexuality is disclosed, even though gender preference and relationship style are two completely separate spectrums of sexuality. Why is that? Why are these two spectrums tied together for so many people?

I don't believe there is an innate correlation, but rather a cultural one – both bisexuality and non-monogamy are deviations from current norms and from "traditional" marriage. Once you've stepped outside the norm on one spectrum and survived (and in most cases, thrived), you're more likely to question other norms and find what works best for you.

Heteronormativity is a relatively recent construct, and as I've argued in previous chapters, exclusive opposite-sex attraction has not been a historical default – in fact, it may not be as evolutionarily advantageous as a "universal capacity for queerness". Similarly, strict monogamy is a relatively recent norm, as are many other aspects of "traditional" marriage (like choosing a partner for yourself, based

DOI: 10.4324/9781003385585-14

on love). Just like I don't believe that everyone is bisexual, I don't believe that everyone is or should be non-monogamous – but I also don't think people should be monogamous by "default" or because they assume that's the "natural" order of relationships. Everyone should learn about the vast spectrum of relationships styles and decide what is best for them. To do that, it's important to put our current conception of monogamous love pairings in context and to understand how the institution of marriage has evolved (tremendously) over time.

A BRIEF HISTORY OF MARRIAGE

Most historians agree that marriage pre-dates recorded history, but in its earliest recorded forms, marriage was not about love, and it was not even necessarily about the two people getting married – it was a strategic alliance between families, for economic or political benefit. It was usually arranged, with the married couple having no say in the partnership. If love or affection developed between spouses, that was considered a benefit that could strengthen the alliance, but it was not necessary or common, and it was certainly not a factor in arranging the partnership.

Among the ancient Hebrews, Greeks, and Romans, the primary purpose of marriage was to bind women to men, essentially as their property, in order to produce offspring. Marriage theoretically ensured the biological paternity of any children that were conceived, because wives were not allowed to be intimate with anyone else. This doesn't mean that monogamy was the norm – it was just the requirement for women.

Men in ancient Hebrew civilizations often took several wives, and married Greek and Roman men were free to take lovers, have sex with prostitutes, and even satisfy urges with young men (known as pederasty, a socially accepted romantic relationship). Men could divorce their wives if they did not produce offspring. Marriage simply ensured the "legitimacy" of children born within the marriage, but it did not constrain sexual behavior or limit the number of romantic relationships (for men).

Then the Roman Catholic Church entered the picture, becoming a dominant force in the institution of marriage throughout Europe and beyond. Marriage became seen as a ceremony to bestow God's grace on the couple, or a sacrament, and a priest's blessing was necessary and soon written into law in the 16th century. Infusing religion into marriage was a benefit to women in some respects – husbands were taught to respect and cherish their wives and were forbidden from divorcing them. This was also when monogamy became seen as the ideal – Christian doctrine declared that "the two shall become one flesh", which most historians and Biblical scholars interpret as a call for spouses to join together in an exclusive and permanent union. There was a protracted battle between the Church and old nobility and kings, who still wanted to take multiple wives, but over time, the Church doctrine won out, and monogamy became the norm.

Still, marriage was arranged for practical reasons, and love wasn't an important factor until more recently. "Love matches" became popular around 250 years ago, in which love and sexual desire were considerations in arranging a marriage, but these still centered men's desires. Mutual attraction wasn't seen as important until about 100 years ago, as women gained more rights (like the right to vote, property rights, the right to divorce, and the ability to work outside the home). Though there's still enormous work to be done, the feminist movement attempted to level the playing field between men and women, making marriage more "equal", at least in theory. Arranged marriage took a backseat to choosing a partner for oneself, based on attraction and love, ideally with at least some degree of mutual respect.

Same-sex desire existed throughout history, and in some cases (like the ancient Greeks and Romans), it was accepted in society and co-existed with the institution of marriage, but marriage between same-sex partners was not accepted until very, very recently, only becoming a legal option throughout the United States in 2015. While same-sex marriage is possible (for now …), it is still far from the norm, and "traditional" marriage has a clear societal model currently: heterosexual, monogamous, lifelong, and based on love.

Growing up with these traditions, as I and most people alive today did, it can be quite hard to think outside the box and access our desire for anything else. Our culture today also stigmatizes divorce and views "successful" marriages as those that last "'til death", so there is enormous pressure to stick it out and "make it work", even if it's not working. Given the prevalence of naturally occurring sex outside of marriage throughout history – and sex with same-sex partners – I believe this idealization of lifelong, monogamous marriage forces us to repress and mutilate other desires, especially queer desires. I also believe that people tend to conflate love and commitment with sex, and while sex is often important and foundational to a lasting partnership, love and commitment are not always necessary for good sex (at least not for me).

Bi+ people who explore their sexuality gain valuable experience bucking tradition. It's not always easy, but stepping outside the "straight box" is often an illuminating and positive experience, teaching us the value and joys of nonconformity. It also allows us to practice being an outsider, and we acquire tools and learn skills that can help us step outside of other boxes, like strict monogamy.

THE INTERSECTION OF BISEXUALITY AND NON-MONOGAMY

Given all that, we might expect that bisexual people are much more likely to be in non-monogamous relationships, but that's not necessarily the case: there is only a slight correlation, if any. Overall, the vast majority of Bi+ people end up in monogamous relationships, and most studies show roughly equal rates of monogamy among Bi+ v. straight people. These results are reflected in this book, though the sample size is too small to be significant (and classification is far from rigorous), as the majority of couples I interviewed that are still together are monogamous.

A 2014 study by psychologist Kristen Mark on attitudes toward monogamy found that 78 percent of partnered bisexual men in the sample and 67 percent of partnered bisexual women were either engaged, married, or seriously dating only one person – compared to 87 percent of all men in the sample and 76 percent of all women.[1] So Bi+ people were more likely to be non-monogamous, but only slightly, by about 9 percent for both men and women. (The sample of Bi+ people was also slightly younger, which may partially explain the difference.) The study also found that 79 percent of bisexual people had been with a partner whom they believed would be their partner for life – so at least 4 in 5 bisexual people are capable of monogamy with the right person. Mark's similar 2020 study found that 79 percent of partnered bisexual people in the sample were in monogamous relationships, while 21 percent were non-monogamous, compared to 78 percent of partnered straight people who were monogamous and 22 percent who were non-monogamous – essentially identical numbers.[2]

Interestingly, even though the rates of monogamy are similar, in Mark's 2014 study, Bi+ people's attitudes toward monogamy were less positive than straight people's attitudes. Both groups were asked to agree or disagree (on a 7-point scale) with statements on the "Monogamy Attitudes Scale", some of which reflected the idea that monogamy is natural and an enhancement to marriage (like "forming monogamous relationships is part of human nature" and "monogamy builds intimacy between two people"), others which reflected monogamy as unnatural and a sacrifice (like "monogamy blocks natural drives" and "by being in a monogamous relationship, I am sacrificing my desires to have experiences with other people"). The study found that Bi+ people rated monogamy as less of an enhancement and more of a sacrifice compared to heterosexual people's ratings (and also compared to gay and lesbian people's ratings).

While Bi+ people's attitudes were different from other groups, their ratings on the "enhancement" v. "sacrifice" scales were roughly equal – in other words, Bi+ people viewed monogamy as both an enhancement and a sacrifice at about equal levels, again displaying the unique bisexual ability to accept duality. Straight, gay, and lesbian people on the other hand had higher ratings of monogamy as an enhancement and lower ratings of monogamy as a sacrifice.

These statistics begin to reveal the complex relationship between bisexuality and monogamy. If this large sample showed that Bi+ people can see both the benefits and drawbacks of monogamy at equal rates, that means that anything is possible on an individual level. This is why we see that in terms of internal orientation, Bi+ people are all over the monogamy spectrum, but I believe most of them have arrived there after more self-introspection and exploration, rather than by default. When they choose monogamy, they are more likely to be aware of the "sacrifices" it includes and the "enhancements" that non-monogamy may offer, and yet they still make that choice, so it is often more informed, authentic, and stable. When they have outside desires within a monogamous marriage, they may be more able to communicate honestly about them.

When people are monogamous by default or because they are following traditional scripts, it sometimes works out great, but it can often lead to chaos and disruption if desire for sex outside the marriage pops up, which is extremely common. (Are we really supposed to never find anyone else attractive after we say our vows? Why do so many people pretend this is the case?) Without an honest examination of non-monogamy, these desires are more likely to be ignored and repressed until a breaking point, when cheating can occur – which is also extremely common. As Jessica Fern writes in *Polysecure*:

> The divorce rate in the US is at 40 to 50 percent, and an estimated 30 to 60 percent of married men and 20 to 50 percent of married women in the United States admit to cheating on their partners ... there is plenty of evidence that the monogamous model doesn't necessarily work, with many people endorsing a proclaimed monogamy, while actually performing clandestine nonmonogamy.

When we really consider those numbers, it begins to shatter the myth of monogamy as the most "stable" form of relationships. In some ways, I feel that Bi+ people are experienced myth-busters – because we've had to be. Our attractions don't conform, so we've broken down the popular myth that heterosexuality is more natural or superior, making it easier to break down the many myths upholding monogamy, as well, and decide what truly makes the most sense for each of us.

But if Bi+ people view monogamy and non-monogamy as having roughly equal positives and negatives, why are only about 20 percent non-monogamous rather than closer to 50 percent? In some ways, I think it's analogous to the gender spectrum – if Bi+ people are capable of attractions across that spectrum, why do 88 percent end up with partners of a different gender? Is that a natural distribution, or is it due to lifelong messaging of heteronormativity and homophobia? Perhaps some Bi+ people choose monogamy not necessarily because it's their most authentic preference but because it's the best option currently in a society that still idealizes the monogamous love marriage and stigmatizes open relationships.

In addition, it could be related to openness and transparency. As discussed, about 88 percent of Bi+ men are closeted, and it's pretty hard to date men if you're not out, so it's no wonder that 88 percent end up married to women – those statistics overlap exactly. I wonder, then, if there's also overlap of Bi+ men who are not out (88 percent) and those who are monogamous (78 percent). After all, if you are unable to disclose your sexuality, you are probably more likely to keep extramarital desires – or affairs – secret.

Coming out, on the other hand, often leads to a discussion of non-monogamy – the observation that began this chapter. In the interviews I conducted, this usually happens either because the husband has also re-examined his desire to explore sex outside the marriage, so he brings it up, or because the wife makes an assumption about her husband's desires (sometimes based on the misconception that Bi+ people need to be with multiple genders at once in order to be fulfilled), so she brings it up. Thus in our current climate, this conversation is almost inevitable for Bi+ couples, regardless of individual preferences.

A conversation doesn't mandate non-monogamy, but still, the conversation alone can be scary for both partners, and the truth is it can sometimes lead to separation or divorce, which is the case for a few couples in this book. Thus, some will actively want to avoid this conversation, which could mean avoiding coming out as Bi+ in the first place (another possible reason why so many Bi+ men are closeted). But I believe that we have to be willing to risk a relationship if we want to strengthen it and make it both lasting and meaningful. It's much easier to take that risk early in a relationship, and it gets harder with each year you're together; the experiences in this book are uniquely challenging because many men weren't aware of these desires early in their relationships, so they can only bring them up later in life, when the stakes feel higher. This is exactly what happened to Quentin, Scott, and others, and their bisexuality and desire for non-monogamy became intertwined and difficult to untangle.

If talking through these issues leads to a mutual decision to break up, at least in that case it's an authentic, informed, and honest choice – and even though it may cause grief and sadness, I think Quentin, Nelson, and others would agree that it's better than keeping your emotions hidden, repressing your desires, and resenting your partner over time as you stay together but grow apart. Why can't a relationship be considered a "success" even if it doesn't last in a single shape forever?

So we have to be willing to risk everything – but with an awareness that most couples decide to remain monogamous. There are lots of good reasons to be monogamous, especially if it feels more natural to you, including emotional security, physical safety from sexually transmitted infections, and an absence of external stigma surrounding the relationship structure. At the same time, we shouldn't choose monogamy simply because it's easier, more socially accepted, or the default choice. We should be honest about its drawbacks and the sacrifices it requires.

MY JOURNEY TOWARD A POLYAMOROUS IDENTITY

I am not against monogamy, especially for others, but even for myself. I've tried both, and I've even gone back and forth – there were periods of time when my wife and I decided to be monogamous, and I liked a lot of things about it. I'm still not sure where I'll "land", if anywhere, but I'm glad I've explored both ends of the spectrum, and I'd guess I'll always be somewhere toward the middle. The idealized view of monogamy that I grew up with has been fully shattered and replaced by something more realistic, but I've also seen past the fantasy versions of non-monogamy that involve constant sex parties and relationship decadence, and I'm learning about the realities of polyamory. The more I explore, the more beauty I find in <u>both</u> realities. The mundane, complicated, messy details and the negotiation and vulnerability that are necessary to be authentic with a partner or partners are actually so much more meaningful and fulfilling than romanticized versions of monogamy or fetishized versions of polyamory. For those newer to non-monogamy, let me briefly explain how I got to this point.

I was an only child for the first 11 years of my life, and I liked it a lot. One night, my parents called a "family meeting", which felt unusually formal. They told me that they'd been looking into adopting a child, and they asked how I'd feel about having a new sibling.

I did not feel good at first. My initial reaction was to cry – a lot. I was happy with the way things were, and I thought we had a great family already. I didn't understand why they wanted to change anything. "What's wrong?" I remember asking. Was I not "enough" for them? Had their love for me changed?

My parents assured me that nothing was wrong, and that of course they still loved me as much as is humanly possible ("to the moon and back", as my mom says) and always would. But they also realized that they had "more love to give", and they wanted to share that surplus of love. I worried that their love would be divided between us, but they explained that love can grow, and it would grow to include this new family member. They predicted that the same thing would happen for me, that once I met my new sibling, my capacity for love would expand to include them, and it would not diminish my love for my parents or anyone else.

I didn't realize it at the time, but that answer changed my entire life and worldview. My parents were disrupting the scarcity model of love and teaching me about an abundance mindset at just 11 years old. They gave me the foundation to imagine love as a renewable resource that increases when shared, a muscle that grows the more you use it, and they taught me that my capacity for love was bigger than it seemed.

They were absolutely right. After that first family meeting, I quickly got on board with the adoption idea, and within a year, I had a new sister. From the moment I met her, she felt like part of our family. My capacity for love effortlessly expanded to include her, and not only was my relationship with my parents unaffected, it was actually strengthened as we took on new responsibilities and learned new ways to communicate within the family. Adopting my sister is one of the best things that ever happened in my life, it helped me become who I am, and we have a strong, supportive, loving relationship today. (She's also Bi+!) Looking back, I feel like I was always meant to be a big brother.

I wouldn't apply this to romantic relationships for years (decades, actually), but I came back to this same principle when I was interrogating my orientation toward monogamy. With this view of love, I was often confused why my partners valued monogamy so much – how I felt about other people had nothing to do with how I felt about my partner. Multiple relationships that were meaningful to me ended because I couldn't "commit", and while this had something to do with my bisexuality and not being ready to open up, I was also afraid that committing to one person meant cutting off every other possible romantic or sexual relationship I might have in the future. That was scary enough, but on top of that, I was confused as to why my partners even wanted that from me – didn't they realize that the more I used that muscle, the more it would strengthen my relationship with them, as well?

Soon I found myself gravitating toward people who identified as non-monogamous or polyamorous (around the same time I started gravitating toward Bi+ and queer people), and it just felt right. They understood my worldview about the abundance and renewability of love. Things that always felt "crazy" in my head suddenly made perfect sense when spoken out loud. I found myself much less afraid of commitment, because it was no longer tied to monogamy, and I could actually see myself "settling down" with someone, as long as that didn't end my ability to form new intimate relationships forever.

As I got deeper into my 30s and started hearing about friends and acquaintances who had cheated on their wives (sometimes leading to divorce, sometimes not), I became more aware that for many, monogamy was an illusion. They were pretending to be monogamous while living non-monogamously, and I didn't want that to be my story. I realized a fundamental truth about myself: if I ever got married, attractions outside of that marriage would happen, and pretending otherwise would only harm my mental health and create secrecy and isolation within that partnership.

Desires outside a primary partnership are often seen as wrong or immoral, but the more I've experienced them, the more I understand them as valid, beautiful, and often beneficial. I still need autonomous sexual experiences in order to fully explore and understand myself, perhaps especially when I'm feeling comfortable with a primary partner and replaying familiar scripts – even though the comfort and familiarity within that relationship are still things I cherish. I love my wife and value the affection I receive from her, but sometimes it's really nice and validating to be desired by a new person, someone who is <u>not</u> invested in our partnership and isn't "required" to affirm my desirability. I've found that having these outside experiences makes me feel more confident, sexy, and in touch with my own needs and desires, all of which benefits my primary partnership, as well.

The more I've learned and examined, the more I've realized that this relationship structure fits with my values. As Jessica Fern writes in *Polysecure*:

> People practicing CNM [Consensual Non-Monogamy] value transparency, consent, open and honest communication, personal responsibility, autonomy, compassion, sex positivity and freedom for themselves and others. Moreover, people practicing CNM typically embrace the following ideas and principles: love is not a possessive or finite resource; it is normal to be attracted to more than one person at the same time; there are multiple ways to practice love, sexual and intimate relationships; and jealousy is not something to be avoided or feared, but something that can be informative and worked through.

I agree with all of those statements, and I've experienced the value that non-monogamy brings to my life. It also has drawbacks – the pool of people interested in dating me has severely decreased, the stigma surrounding polyamory frequently has me defending and explaining myself, and the amount of effort it takes to negotiate and work through things like jealousy is enormous – but overall, I feel the benefits hugely outweigh the costs. I'm still finding my place on the poly spectrum, but I'm glad to be on that journey instead of just imagining it.

ADVICE FOR COUPLES NEGOTIATING NON-MONOGAMY

I realize that not everyone thinks the same way I do, and that's completely valid. Opening up is definitely not for everyone, but it's at least worth interrogating if your desire for monogamy is based on norms and fears or if it's truly your authentic expression. There is a wide range of possible relationship styles that often get conflated and go unexamined due to default monogamy. While I am not a licensed therapist or relationship professional (yet!), here are some of my personal observations and advice for others struggling with these issues – please take what works for you, discard the rest, and consult with a professional if you need help.

♦ First, try to separate sex from romance, love, and commitment. (In fact, try to separate <u>all</u> of those things from each other, because while they may be overlapping, they are distinct.) Many Bi+ people have sexual desires across the gender spectrum or interests in more than one sex partner at a time, but they are not necessarily bi-romantic (open to romantic relationships with multiple genders) or poly-romantic (interested in multiple romantic relationships). In fact, many Bi+ men are not interested in romantic relationships with men whatsoever (just sexual ones), and most non-monogamous couples I've met are actually "closed" in terms of love and commitment – they just have sex with other people.

   It can be hard to separate those things, but most people haven't ever tried, so they believe they can't even if they might be able to. If you try and it doesn't work, listen to yourself and hold onto your feelings, but if you try and you feel jealous, or you fear being abandoned, that doesn't mean it's not working – these are <u>opportunities</u> to communicate and strengthen your partnership. How can you talk through jealousy and use it to understand each other better? If you fear losing your partner, can you talk about that? Maybe communicating will help ease that fear, rather than avoiding what causes those feelings altogether.

♦ Remember that there are many forms of non-monogamy and polyamory (for a complete list, there are countless books and resources focused on this, like *Polysecure*). Many people who have never considered non-monogamy imagine the worst possible relationship style for them, something as far from monogamy as possible, like "relationship anarchy", a form of polyamory that rejects <u>any</u> rules and expectations surrounding relationships, has no hierarchy of partners, and no long-term commitments. While this is a valid structure that works for some, it's probably not the best version of polyamory to dive into without experience, and it's far from the norm among non-monogamous people (in my experience, the majority still have a "primary" partner, as I do, and tons of boundaries and expectations).

Exploring non-monogamy doesn't mean that everything you know about relationships has to change. You can still be committed to your partner for life while exploring sexually with others. You can still have a primary partner even if you have emotional or romantic connections with others. You can still have and raise kids with one person. You can set whatever boundaries you need surrounding relationships with different partners, and they can be unique to each partner. You can find a style that works for both of you, and your relationship has the potential to be even more lasting and meaningful, because by being honest and realistic about your sexuality and desires, you'll have diffused the ticking time bomb of outside attractions (and affairs) that plagues many default-monogamous couples.

♦ If you've started this work and still have negative feelings about non-monogamy, consider where they are coming from. Did you or people in your life have bad or traumatic experiences that you're afraid of recreating? Can you work through those feelings (with a therapist, your partner, or by yourself) rather than avoiding them? The same way I recommend Bi+ community for Bi+ people, I would also recommend joining poly communities, which exist both online and in-person. It can be nearly impossible to re-wire your early impressions of non-monogamy unless you have real-life examples of people who are thriving as poly. Being among people who consider non-monogamy "normal" can be a transformative experience and help you reframe what's important to you in a relationship. If that community isn't the right fit, you'll experience that, too, and ultimately be in a better position to decide what's best for you.

♦ In the specific case of women who are married to Bi+ men, remember that your husband may have entered into your monogamous marriage before he even realized or acknowledged that he was bisexual. If he missed his "chance to explore", it will be hard for him to figure out his place on the sexuality spectrum, what his ongoing needs really are, and which fantasies he might be able to cross off his bucket list and never try again. Try to put yourself in your Bi+ husband's shoes – he's likely feeling conflicted and scared of losing you. Can you understand his desire to explore <u>and</u> his desire to remain in the relationship? That even if he loves and cares about you, he might feel resentment for boundaries that are based on fear rather than deeply examined feelings? Can you examine yourself and your limits, and even if you come to the same conclusion, can you discuss all that with your partner so that he'll understand where you're coming from instead of holding a grudge due to a lack of communication? Or if you're open to being open, can you set up boundaries that protect your feelings and needs but that also give your partner a chance to explore his full sexuality?

The hardest part: can you accept that if your partner does explore outside the marriage, there is a chance he'll want to leave you? This is scary, there's no doubt, but if that happens, perhaps you were holding onto something that wasn't actually healthy for either of you – and if your partner stays, perhaps you can find joy in the fact that he's continuing to choose you, even after experiencing intimacy with others. Can you accept that whatever happens will be for the best for both of you, as long as you're communicating honestly throughout? Can you still value and cherish your connection and relationship forever, even if it ends in its current form?

To be clear, I'm not advocating for husbands getting a free pass to do anything with anyone, especially if their wives aren't comfortable with non-monogamy. But I do think the broader context is important, and partners of Bi+ men should at least be aware of this difficult situation and the mental health toll it takes. Kristen Mark's 2014 study also found that Bi+ men were more likely to view monogamy as a sacrifice than Bi+ women were, and while that doesn't apply to everyone, it's a valuable gender difference to note. Even if monogamy is the correct choice for your marriage, you'll both benefit if you have a sensitivity to the "unrealized" Bi+ male experience and can support your partner exploring their sexuality in safe, negotiated, perhaps non-sexual ways (like talking about fantasies, attending in-person Bi+ social groups, or watching queer porn, to name a few examples).

♦ Lastly, this should work both ways – if you can consider giving your partner space to explore, can he give you the same gift? Are there things you want to experience on any sexuality spectrum that you've never had the chance to explore because of set scripts, expectations, or your partner's needs? Can you make compromises with each other rather than just sacrifices? These arrangements don't have to be equal on both sides – you can ask for different things than what he's asking for. If you communicate openly about your desires, perhaps you can come to an agreement – and remember that these agreements can be fluid, not set in stone for life, and you can renegotiate if you try them out and they're not working.

The stories in this book can serve as a jumping-off point for finding your authentic relationship style and for beginning to have these conversations with your spouse or partner – but this book is not comprehensive or definitive, so you should do your own research and exploration. I do hope these interviews will be a reminder of the diversity of Bi+ experiences with monogamy and polyamory and prove that anything is possible.

Some men in this book have realized they need to explore sex outside their marriage, and this has ended their marriage, like Quentin and Nelson. Others have opened up after marriage and stayed together, like Gregory and William. Stanley and Christine (Chapter 17) have been non-monogamous for their entire relationship, demonstrating that when a couple has boundaries, mutual respect, and open lines of communication, non-monogamy can absolutely be compatible with a long-term marriage. But the majority of couples in this book have chosen monogamy, and most of them are still together (including Rich, Jeremy, Kaiko, Carter, and others in upcoming chapters). Though some men have expressed lingering regrets about not being able to explore, and some women have lingering doubts about the same thing, they've all at least initiated a conversation about non-monogamy and can pick it up more easily than most straight, monogamous couples.

Because sexuality is fluid, and needs can change over time, monogamy should be an ongoing conversation in order to maintain the health of a marriage, not a binary decision that is made once and lasts a lifetime. Wherever you land, openly discussing your relationship structure, your desires and fantasies, and how you view and experience love can only help you both as individuals and as a couple.

NOTES

1.   Mark, K., Rosenkrantz, D., Kerner, I. (2014). "Bi"ing into Monogamy: Attitudes toward Monogamy in a Sample of Bisexual-Identified Adults. *Psychology of Sexual Orientation and Gender Diversity.* https://experts.umn.edu/en/publications/biing-into-monogamy-attitudes-toward-monogamy-in-a-sample-of-bise

2.   Mark, K. P., Vowels, L. M., Bunting, A. M. (2020). The Impact of Bisexual Identity on Sexual and Relationship Satisfaction of Mixed Sex Couples. *Journal of Bisexuality.* https://www.kristenmark.com/wp-content/uploads/2021/08/Mark_Vowels_Bunting_2020.pdf

15

Drew and Polyamory with Two Women

I was born in the Los Angeles area in 1990. I've mostly lived in Southern California – majority of the time [it was] me, my mom and my sister. While my dad was still living with us, we did live in San Francisco for a while. I can remember those times, but that's way back when I was like four years old. I have good memories, good family times.

I feel like I'm a very shy person. Growing up, I didn't talk a lot. Unless you got to be somebody that I was close with, I did my own thing. I don't play sports. People wouldn't call me very masculine. I grew up in an environment in LA where my life could have been very different. I have cousins [who] are involved in gangs. My mom kept me out of it. I didn't want to get in trouble, I didn't want to do anything to jeopardize [myself]. I was like, I'm going to stay in my lane.

Growing up, I had a lot of people say, "Oh, you look Black, but you act white", just because of the things that I like to do. I read a lot of fiction and fantasy books, and I like to play video games. This has nothing to do with skin color. I like what I like. [But] it seemed like, "Where are you going with this, [Drew]? What do you like? What don't you like? What do you want to do? Who do you want to be with?" I had to figure all that out.

DOI: 10.4324/9781003385585-15

D rew is a Black, bi, cisgender man living in Dallas, Texas. He was born in 1990 in Los Angeles, California and was 30 years old at the time of our interview in 2020. He described himself as middle-class and not religious, both growing up and currently.

Even before we got to talking about sex and sexuality, Drew described his experience of not quite fitting in and having to "figure out" who he was. Being Black put Drew in the minority in southern California, but he also didn't quite fit in with the Black community because of a perception that he "acted white". This led to a close examination of his identity and preferences, which eventually included a search for his authentic sexuality.

Drew also grew up without many guidelines or proscriptions surrounding sexuality, so he had an unusually clean slate when he began to "figure all that out".

> Growing up, it was like, you don't talk about sex. I never had any sort of birds-and-the-bees conversation. I never had anyone to talk to. For the most part, I was on my own, I did what I wanted to do.
>
> Pretty much from five years old on, it was just my sister and my mom. I had my first girlfriend in sixth grade. She came over to my house all the time. My mom knew [her]. But we never had that birds-and-the-bees talk. I guess I would assume, as a woman, she maybe didn't know how to have that talk with me. I never really asked about it. Anything I found out would have been hearing stuff from friends, looking at stuff online.
>
> I started trying to figure out sexuality probably in high school. At the time I'd had different girlfriends and whatnot, and it honestly started as accidentally seeing gay porn. I wasn't immediately attracted to it, but it was kind of like, "Oh, I don't see anything wrong with that." So every once in a while, I'm like, "Okay, I'll watch that too. Switch things up." As I got older, it was like, "This is different. Is this okay? I don't know if it's okay."
>
> Graduating from high school, I moved out to Las Vegas with some other family, lived out there for a year, had a girlfriend at the time. I think I started watching gay porn more often but never acted upon it.

In the age of easily accessible online pornography, gay porn often plays a role in Bi+ men's awareness of their fluidity. For Drew, it was the very first clue. Porn offers a completely safe way to "try out" same-sex attraction without having to tell anyone else and often without spending a dime or leaving a trace (if you know how to clear your browsing history). The stakes of this exploration could not be lower.

Gay porn was not only the first thing that clued me in to my bisexuality, but it became a regular part of my life as a straight man. For years I did the same thing as Drew – I threw in a little gay porn every once in a while, in addition to straight porn – before I finally accepted that it might be meaningful in my life. Because the stakes were so low, it was easier to compartmentalize and minimize in significance.

I live in Texas now, so moving out to Texas, it was a new start for me. It was only myself and my mom, so I didn't know anybody at all. The first club I ever went to as an adult was a gay club in Dallas. It was like, "Okay, what is this scene like?" 'Cause I don't actually know any gay people. So I went out there. I was like, "Oh, it's just a club. They have music, we could have a few drinks."

If a gay club was Drew's first stop in Texas, he must've wanted to explore this scene, perhaps subconsciously, but never felt comfortable in a place where people might recognize him.

I've had similar experiences, especially while traveling. Alone in a new city, I felt safer to explore my sexuality. I took a few solo vacations in the years just before coming out, and though I wasn't planning on browsing Grindr and hooking up, once I got there, it frequently happened. With hindsight, it's clear I had a subconscious plan that I couldn't formally acknowledge. It felt freeing that no one from my "real life" would know – I could be a new person and try anything. Now that I'm secure in my fluidity and care less about other people's judgments, I feel this sense of freedom all the time – but I could only get the ball rolling with that illusion of anonymity and a clean slate.

It wasn't long before Drew did more than scope out a club.

I finally decided, "Okay, maybe I'll try hooking up with a guy to see if this is something I like." Awful experience. I was like, I don't think I'll ever do this again. So I kinda left it at that.

This was in the days of Craigslist – it was still a thing. Which, thinking back on it, was not the best way of meeting people. We were about the same age, I was 19, 20. I actually picked him up from work. It was an outside, like, um, oral hookup, out in some wooded area. There was no attraction, and it just wasn't a good experience. I'm a very clean person. It didn't seem very clean at the time.

[But] then I still had that curiosity. So I tried it again – still not the greatest. I was like, maybe I just liked the idea of that, maybe that's what it is, 'cause there was no attraction. I had no desire to be in any sort of relationship with guys.

The second time there was a bit of a communication barrier that wasn't obvious when we were online, a language barrier. And I don't think I was fully in the right mind to, um, be with another guy. I was like, the whole time, "What am I doing here? Why am I here? This isn't feeling good." So it didn't go very well.

Though these experiences were consensual, they were still unpleasant, and I think that's something a lot of queer men experience and don't talk about enough. When we're experimenting, especially on our own, without guidance or support, it's not always going to work out like we hope – but there can be many reasons for that, and they can be complicated to disentangle. Drew followed his curiosity and pushed through, and his third experience gave him some clarity.

> The third time when I tried, I think I was more open to the experience. It was like, I've done this a few times, I didn't like the experience, but for some reason, I keep wanting to try and figure out if this is something I'm into or not. 'Cause it was like, "Am I straight? Am I gay? Am I bi? I don't know. I've dated women. I know for a fact I'm attracted to women. I would want to be in a relationship with a woman, but then I'm on the fence about guys."
>
> So I was more prepared, and it was very clear what our intents were. That experience, it all came together and went really well. At that point I was like, "Okay, this was better. This is something that I wouldn't mind doing again." At the time I would have called it "experimenting", but looking back, no, this is just part of my life. This is something that you like to do, and there's nothing wrong with that.

Many people I've met have had bad experiences that turned them off from an entire identity. An awkward hook-up can lead people to conclude they're simply not attracted to men or women, even though there could be countless reasons why the hook-up was bad that have nothing to do with gender. Because sexuality is so often reduced to gender preference alone, many people generalize these experiences and categorize them exclusively by their partner's gender. They fail to see that other factors, like power dynamics, open communication, clear boundaries, number of partners, personality and "vibes", specific kinks and sex acts, and the environment in which sex takes place can be just as important, if not more so.

I think it's quite remarkable that even at age 20, Drew didn't take one or two bad experiences as proof that he was exclusively straight, but rather he kept on exploring. He no doubt learned much more about himself and what turns him on – which would've been the case no matter where he landed on the sexuality spectrum. He concluded that it's possible for him to be attracted to men, but masculinity alone is not sufficient – he also values cleanliness and good communication.

Interestingly, even though Drew knew "for a fact" that he was attracted to women, after that positive experience, he had a common fear for Bi+ men – that he was really gay.

> For a few years, any hook-ups were with guys, so it was like, "Okay, I'm not actively pursuing and trying to hook up with women – does that say something? Are you just not ready to say that you're gay?" And I didn't know. I did struggle with it. I'm constantly repeating this thing, but I'm not identifying as gay, so what does that mean about me?
>
> Even if I had a good experience at the time, I would still feel like, "Hmm, I probably shouldn't do this again." I think it was because I didn't know. I grew up in the church, not learning about any of this. And if I'm gay, as a Black male, how are people going to look at me? How's my family gonna look at me?

But the truth was that Drew's attractions toward women were real and valid, too, and it wasn't long before he could feel that concretely when he met not just one but two women at work who he was into. To protect their anonymity, he called them "C" and "T" in our interview.

I met C, and she's just a really cool person. I didn't normally talk a lot, but with her, I was like, "Hey, let's talk." Then I met this other girl at work, T. She had this androgynous look. She was obviously a woman, but she had that short fade haircut. It was like, "Both of these people are really cool. This is somebody I want to spend time with and make friends with." So we all started hanging out.

They weren't really sure about me, whether I liked men or women, but they were kinda like, "Whatever, he's cool." I think they kind of knew, but we didn't really talk about it too much. It was like, if he wants to tell us, he'll tell us.

One night, it was my birthday, [there was a] drag show going on. They asked if it was anybody's birthday, and they pulled me up. I don't like being in front of people, but they were like "Go", and I was like, "Okay." They asked, "How old are you? It's your birthday", blah, blah, blah. And T's out in the crowd yelling, "That's our guy!" Then they asked, "Are you gay or straight?" So I said "I'm bi." Of course, lots of times when anyone says they're bi, it's like, "Oh, you're gay." This is my first time saying it out loud, but I was like, "You know what? I'm okay." And they were really happy about it, T and C. They were like, "You actually said it. That great."

Drew came out live on stage, under a literal spotlight (something he hates), and used a label he had never said out loud before — talk about coming out with a bang! On top of that, "bi" is a label that's not necessarily easy to use in queer spaces due to biphobia within the gay and lesbian communities, and yet this unexpected public declaration felt right, and Drew still uses the "bi" label today. Sometimes we know more about ourselves than we consciously realize – Drew had done a ton of internal work already before this moment, and though he hadn't quite figured everything out, he was forced to say something, and it was a turning point in his self-awareness and acceptance.

Drew's friendship with C and T continued, and perhaps because he opened up to them and created more emotional intimacy, it soon progressed.

Me and C were friends. Then we started a casual friends-with-benefits kind of thing. The first time with T was because she moved into where I was staying. I had a king-size bed in my one-bedroom apartment, so I was like, we're friends, I don't care, I'm not gonna ask you to sleep on a couch. And we worked opposite schedules, I worked nights, she worked days.

She was very comfortable in herself and experienced. When she wakes up, she wants to have sex, but she's still half-asleep. One day, we were both home, didn't have to work in the morning, and it just kind of happened. And then it kept happening until we had a conversation like, "Hey, what are we doing?" It was like, "We're friends, and I know you're attracted to me, I'm attracted to you, so why not?"

The whole time this was happening, C's aware of it. She knows what's going on. She was out of town, but she would come back home for a few weeks, and she was staying with us. When she finally came back to stay, that's when the three of us would have those "occasionals" ... and it went from there.

By this time, T and C were dating each other. I'm still occasionally hooking up with guys. Eventually we ended up getting a house altogether, and we're in an open polyamorous relationship. I'm both their boyfriends, they're both my girlfriends, we're all together. I was with them for about five years or so. That was pretty good. They were supportive, they were well aware of what I liked, what I was into.

Regarding marriage, it's interesting. T and C are currently engaged to get married for the last three years. In Texas it is not legal to marry more than one person, so in 2018 I basically proposed and bought each a ring, and it was more of a commitment or promise. Had I been with either in a monogamous relationship, I would've considered marriage. I think our relationship may have mirrored what a "typical" marriage or long-term relationship would be in the way we communicated and how the household was while we lived together. Between the two of them, they had four dogs, so that's a large commitment in itself. We all treated each other's family as our family.

Drew never officially married C or T, but their five-year triad relationship resembles many marriages in this book. They lived together, had intimacy and sex with each other, and planned futures together, so I have included them even though it wasn't a traditional or legal marriage. Too often, we categorize relationships by their "official" label, but the experience of being inside a relationship and attached to a partner or partners is much more about the unique dynamic of those involved – and Drew's relationship with C and T, as they navigated fluidity and openness together, has many parallels with others in this book. As Jessica Fern writes in *Polysecure*:

> Secure attachment is created through the quality of experience we have with our partners, not through the notion or the fact of either being married or being a primary partner ...as the high rates of divorce and cheating demonstrate, even a monogamous marriage that typically represents the pinnacle of relationship security is not necessarily any more secure than other forms of relationship ... Allow your direct experience with a partner to be the vehicle to secure attachment instead of having certain relationship concepts, narratives or structures be the vehicle.

Drew's relationship with C and T illustrates how unfortunate it is that monogamous marriage is the only option available for many and the gold standard for most. Their story reveals how fundamentally similar a polyamorous relationship can be, as long as all partners involved are consenting and communicative.

That said, there are also important differences. Navigating a triad brings logistical and emotional challenges, and if the relationship is open to others outside the home – as many are, including this one – everything must be discussed and negotiated.

> They actually wanted me to go find a boyfriend. They encouraged that. They were like, "This is who you are, be happy about it." So any time I was with a guy, they knew about it. I went on a few dates here and there, but I never found any guy [who] I would want to be in a serious relationship with.
>
> If I was with anybody else, I had to use protection. Which for me, that's a given. And then [I had to] let [T and C] know. They'd ask, "Oh, what'd you do?" They would want details, because it would excite them.
>
> [They hooked up with] majority other guys. There were a few women, but not many. So first, I was trying to come to terms with being bisexual, and then I was in a polyamorous relationship, so that was something to overcome, 'cause I hadn't been in very many other relationships, and those were all as teenagers basically. This was my first adult relationship.
>
> People found out, and it was like, "Oh, you're living the dream" – like, no, it's a lot of communication. At that point, people didn't know I was bisexual, so they just thought, "This guy has two women." I'm like, "This is a lot more complicated than you think it is. It's not all sunshine and daisies."

This was Drew's first polyamorous relationship, and as someone exploring polyamory myself, I appreciate how complicated and confusing it can be. Many people I talk to say they couldn't imagine being poly because they wouldn't feel a sense of security – what if their partner dates someone who they fall in love with? What if they want to leave? I've experienced the same fears, but my partner and I have had many discussions about those possibilities and worked through our difficult feelings. Besides, I think that scenario is just as possible in a monogamous relationship; we're just acknowledging that reality and keeping the lines of communication open if it happens.

But I see polyamory as more than just realistic or practical; the inherent insecurity of multiple partners can actually bring unique benefits. Again, this was an area where *Polysecure* by Jessica Fern opened my eyes to new ways of thinking about relationships, commitment, and love.

> The insecurity in CNM [Consensual Non-Monogamy] can actually be a good thing in that it can keep us from taking our partners for granted or becoming complacent in our relationships in ways that are often found in monogamous relationships. Personally, I find security in the fact that when I'm in CNM relationships I know that my partners are not with me because they are obliged to be, but because they continue to choose to be. However, the inherent insecurity in CNM relationships can be grinding. This form

of relationship can bring up levels of uncertainty that many people are not yet equipped for, especially when they don't have enough internal secure attachment.

Fern's warning about the "grinding" nature of non-monogamy is important, and it's a reminder that polyamory is not for everyone. In Drew's case, though he didn't go into detail about intimacy or conflict with C and T, it sounded like they were secure in their attachment with each other – they loved and supported each other, treated each other like family, but they also maintained their individual identities and freedom – and benefited overall from their open relationship.

Drew continued to explore outside of that triad, but he soon learned that some of his limits surrounding sexuality might actually be preventing him from pleasurable experiences.

> My only hard-set boundary at the time was no one older than 32, no really big age gap. Then probably the best experience that I've had was somebody who was a lot older. It was actually a couple, and it was a really good experience. They were really good people. These two older men, one was Latino, one was Caucasian. And it weirded me out. It was like, "Why are these people so nice to me?" I didn't understand that. How can somebody that I don't know, the first time I met them, just for something very casual … like, why are these people so nice? It felt really strange to me.

Drew's confusion here feels familiar. I used to view sex as transactional and tied to relationships – some of which may be a trauma response for me, after being with women who used sex to keep me invested in relationships I was ready to leave – but coming out as Bi+ and exploring all types of sex-positive spaces with people of diverse identities, I learned you can have sex just to have sex (like any other pleasurable activity). When there's open communication and consent, it benefits everyone, and there doesn't have to be any relationship obligation.

When I began approaching sex this way, I did start to notice that people were kinder to me, and I was kinder to them, because the whole experience was more upfront and honest. Sex breaks down barriers and promotes intimacy, so sometimes even after a quick hook-up, I'd have strong feelings for someone. Having "no strings attached" actually lowered my defenses and allowed for more vulnerability and authenticity.

Eventually, Drew stopped living with C and T.

> It was a good relationship. It ended last year. We're still on good terms, we still talk.

And that's all he said about that. He didn't seem upset or express any regrets. It's tempting to wonder why things ended or what "went wrong", but as with other partners in this book who chose to go their separate ways, I don't view this relationship (or its conclusion) as negative. Our society has impossibly high standards in this area, often viewing any relationship that ends as a failure, but if there was consent and growth during, and if there's mutual affection and respect afterward, then it was a success, even if it ends.

Drew's relationship with C and T ran its course, and he's happy for what it was. Just as we should trust our intuition if we feel it's time to leave, we should also remember and honor what attracted us to someone in the first place and the connection that kept us together as long as it did. Abusive relationships aside, there is always value and beauty in the time we spend with partners we love.

Drew's bisexuality has also affected his friendships and his relationships with family members. Though he resisted labels at first, fluidity has become an important part of his identity, but he's still navigating who to share it with, when, and how. And like most Bi+ men, he's struggled to find Bi+ community.

I do not know anybody else in person [who] is bisexual and male. There is a group here in Dallas called UBE – United Black Element – and it's tailored for gay Black men. I've been out to a few of their things, but when I get into groups of people that I don't know, I hold back a little bit. I never followed up with anybody, and it's because [of] my social skills. It has more to do with that than being uncomfortable.

I used to share the experience with my friends. But if I'm talking to a straight couple or gay couple, they can't relate to the other half of me. When it comes to any sort of relationship things to talk about, you're only [understanding] half of who I am. So that was definitely hard.

Two years ago, I came out as bisexual to my sister, then my friends, and then my mom and my grandmother. I didn't actually say I was bisexual. With my friends, the conversation was very casual. I was just kinda like, "Hey, by the way, I sleep with guys sometimes." And they were like, "That was out of nowhere, but okay." And then we just kept cooking and watching TV.

Talking to my mom and my grandma, I was kinda like, "Hey, I know I'm with T and C, but I like guys, [too]. Every once in a while, I've had relationships with guys." They were like, "Is everything okay? Is everything good?" I was like, "Yeah." And that was pretty much it. No pushback. No extreme questioning. Everyone was really supportive, so that was really good.

I've come to find out some things about my mom that it'd be very hypocritical for her to have thought anything else. She's had different relationships. She has been with women before. I don't know how far that went. I was just like, "I don't really need to know the details. Do you accept me? Okay, great." This is something I didn't even find out until a few months after I came out to her.

Twist, right?! I suspect there are connections between Drew's mom being sexually fluid – but closeted – and his own confusion growing up. Not that bisexuality is genetic or even learned, but certain conditions have to be present for awareness and acceptance to occur. Drew grew up curious and open-minded, "doing his own thing", but sex was not talked about in his home, and his mother specifically shied away from a "birds-and-bees" conversation. All of this may have reflected what she was going through: she was aware that she was sexually fluid but censoring herself with others.

Drew was shy as a kid and felt like he had to figure things out and give people a clear vision of who he was – and at the same time, his mother was not open with him about her own experiences. She may have had valid reasons for not talking about this – perhaps she didn't think these experiences were important or part of her identity, perhaps she didn't think that sex was an appropriate topic to discuss with her children, or perhaps she was simply confused, ashamed, or scared – but I do wonder more and more as I do this work how compartmentalizing and omitting parts of our identity impacts those around us. If Bi+ visibility and role models are so important for those of us who have come out, the absence of those things must have an effect, as well, even if it's hidden and impossible to quantify. While creating conditions for bisexual awareness to occur is much better than nothing, I hope someday we can reduce the stigma and shame surrounding queerness so that coming out is easier for everyone and so that we can all get to know each other better – especially members of our own family.

In any case, it's clear that for Drew, coming out to his family – and their positive if muted reaction – helped him accept himself and plan for the future, whatever it holds.

Eventually, I realized I'm okay. There's nothing wrong with me. This is what I like. As long as I'm happy about it, and I'm not causing harm to anyone else, and I'm not causing harm to myself, there's no reason to not be okay with it.

I don't think I have any interest in doing polyamory again. I don't want that sort of dynamic. As far as gender, I'm open. Whether it's a man, woman, other, non-binary, I don't have something that I'm looking for. I'll be open to whatever comes my way, whatever happens.

For a very long time, I was really unsure about myself, but I think over the last few years, I've become pretty confident in who I am. I've really had to think about a lot of things. And I am who I am. I like what I like. Whoever I end up with, it's one of those take it or leave it kind of things. I'm not saying I'm the greatest person. But I'm me. And I've gotten to the point where I don't have to hide that from anybody.

16

Evan and Lindsay on Marrying Young and Evolving Together

In addition to interviewing 11 married men by themselves, I also spoke with two married couples. Their stories ended up taking a different shape – we talked less about their childhoods and internal worlds and more about their marriages and navigating bisexuality within them. I found these interviews fascinating and useful in new ways, as they offered a glimpse into how these couples communicated with each other and grew alongside each other.

I've been influenced heavily by Dan Savage, a popular queer sex columnist, who talks a lot about the stories we tell to define our relationships, which are constantly evolving. We have to repeatedly work with our partner to update the story and make sure it still fits. When two people are telling the same story, it creates a sense of safety and commitment within the relationship – but if they're not, it will likely lead to dysfunction, a lack of attunement, or possibly resentment.

In this interview with Evan and Lindsay, I watched them tell their story together, working in the moment to reconcile discrepancies that came up. They met when they were both teenagers and have been together ever since, and as they tell it, communication between them – which has evolved significantly over two decades – is what helped keep their marriage strong through difficult periods.

Evan is a white, cisgender, bisexual man from Yulee, Florida (Jacksonville area). He was born in 1984 and was 36 years old at the time of our interview in 2020. He describes himself as agnostic and upper-middle-class, raised lower-middle-class.

DOI: 10.4324/9781003385585-16

Lindsay is a white, cisgender, straight woman from Orlando, Florida. She was born in 1988 and was 32 at the time of our interview in 2020. She also describes herself as agnostic and upper-middle-class, raised lower-middle-class.

They got into sexual fluidity right away:

Evan: In the beginning, I'm thinking middle school, [I knew] that I was attracted to both girls and boys, but growing up with the mindset that you can only be attracted to one or the other, it was always a push-and-pull through my entire adolescence.

Lindsay: We have been together 17 years. When we met, I was 14, and he was 18. I moved to Yulee, which is a very non-progressive area. So even though he kind of knew these things about himself, it wasn't something he felt could be talked about. So … I don't want to speak for you –

Evan: That's definitely the case. I don't think I met a person who identified as gay until high school. It's one of those things: nobody was out. So I didn't really know what I thought.

I also grew up in a loose Baptist upbringing, going to church with my grandmother, with the whole hellfire brimstone scare-tactic thing, so I spent a lot of time struggling with religious identity within my sexuality. It was a rough way to try to figure things out. I don't think I knew what [bisexuality] was until maybe my junior year of college.

Lindsay: We had already been together years at that point.

I asked about Evan's identity and sexual activity up to the point – did he consider himself straight? They both laughed before he responded:

Evan: Loosely straight.

Then Lindsay took over to explain:

Lindsay: Everybody just thought he was gay. His family thought he was gay, people in school thought he was gay, just because he dressed well, he took care of himself. Not to be mean, but we lived in a redneck town. So for him to care at all about his appearance as a male made him stand out. But he never dated a guy. There was a time that [he] came really close, but then he chickened out.

I asked Evan to tell that story.

Evan: I used to work for Burger King through high school. I think it was junior year, before I met Lindsay. I was in drive-through, and "whoever" came through, I honestly don't even know the guy's name, got his order, came back through and ordered something extra. It was weird. Then maybe an hour or so later, my manager says I have a phone call. So I answer it, and it was this dude from drive-through. He identified that he was gay, and he wanted to meet up.

I met up with him after work. That's the first time I had ever been advanced in that way, and knowing that it was something I was wrestling with, it seemed inopportune to ignore it. I don't know what exactly I was expecting to happen, but we basically just drove around in his car for a bit. There wasn't anywhere we could park. I think that might've had a bit to do with it, because there was nowhere.

Lindsay: Very small town. You went to the beach, didn't you?

Evan: We went to the beach, the docks area, and it just … didn't work out. So he ended up taking me back to Burger King. He was from out of town, and that was more of the intrigue, because I'd never left Yulee before. So to have this outsider come in and show interest in something that I've had in the back of my head for so long …

The story ended there. Even though not much happened in the end, it was a pivotal memory for Evan, and it stood out for Lindsay, too. I think that regardless of completing a sex act, simply acknowledging to another human being that you experience same-sex attraction is a huge step and potential turning point. It becomes "real", in a way.

I often say that I came out at age 32, even though I had been exploring sex with men since age 29 – but the truth is, I was coming out to every guy I hooked up with in between, even though it didn't quite feel like "coming out". I was practicing talking about my sexuality and what I liked and disliked, unintentionally preparing myself to come out more publicly in the future.

It's also interesting that "whoever" was able to get some sense of Evan's interest at the drive-through. I used to wonder how people acquired "gaydar", and as I was coming out as bisexual, I realized: it's mostly eye contact. Straight men (and repressed queer men) do not normally make sustained eye contact with other men, but once I acknowledged my same-sex attraction and started naturally staring at guys who I thought were hot, I immediately noticed who was staring back and who wasn't. There were even a few times before I came out that guys propositioned me, only for me to declare my straightness and wonder how they "knew" I was secretly interested. The guy who propositioned Evan saw something – probably a lingering gaze – that clued him in, even though Evan may not have been aware of the signal he was sending.

I asked about how Evan and Lindsay met. It was a pretty short story!

Lindsay: We met in high school. I had just moved there, I was new in town, and we started dating basically immediately. And that was it, we were just together. I didn't really have a great family, didn't have a great home life. When I was 15, I moved out. So basically I forced him to be stuck with me forever [laughs].

It's always just been us. He never had any experience with anybody else, not male or female, aside from me. So that was always something that I kind of felt … not guilty about, but almost just, I don't know … he never got to experience anything, because we were young.

I asked if she had any experience with dating or sex before Evan.

Lindsay: One other guy. I identify as straight. I had a boyfriend for like two years. I was a mature kid. I know it sounds really terrible, I was so young, but I had to grow up. So I had experienced not a lot, but some things with him.

Evan: When I finished high school, I went to work as an electrician. Both my parents are electricians, so I fell into that. She was still in high school. She moved in with me and my parents almost a year after we were dating.

Lindsay: Then we got our own place, and I worked through high school, and we both just worked. Then we went to school, and we've literally done everything together. Always lived together, always been together.

As I was understanding my fluidity, I feared that some imaginary future wife might not accept me, but Evan – like other Bi+ guys who marry young, before they've fully recognized their bisexuality – began to fear that the very <u>real</u> love of his life might not accept him. It's extremely complicated to explore your sexuality that way, as he describes, and the stakes can feel enormous. As we've seen in other chapters, it often involves a physically and emotionally "safe" way to experiment: porn.

Evan: Probably about four years after, the only way to explore the "gay side" of my identity was through porn, and I wasn't very good at deleting histories. Some sites, the download button will be right next to the play button, so there were several things downloaded that I didn't even know were on the computer. And I think we were looking at something …

Lindsay: Yeah, I was looking through our files for something, and I was like, "What is this?" It was a shock. He tried to say it wasn't his, didn't know what it was. But within no amount of time, he was like, it is mine, and he told me that he was bi – or that he was confused, and that he might be bi.

At first, I was understanding. I mean, I was very shocked. But I was like, "It doesn't matter. I love you no matter what. We've been together four years, we've already been through so much." But we were talking for hours that day, and a lot of crying. That was the first time I ever saw him cry.

Evan: I think for me, I grew up in a small town, so my family was the only thing that I ever had. I didn't want to put that out there and risk losing the literal only connection to the world that I had. And now that Lindsay was in [my] family, it was very scary, because not only was I risking losing her, but then "What happened to Lindsay?"

Lindsay: Everyone would know.

Evan: Your family and then your friends, and then it becomes this whole thing. So it was definitely stressful.

I think I had told a friend that I thought I was bi, via a chat, and that's because she was identifying the same way. We didn't have a word for it. So Lindsay was the first person I ever told in person. And it was a lot.

Lindsay: At first, I just wanted to know if he was gay. Because all of our family thought he was gay, and all of our friends always thought he was gay. It was like, "Oh my God, I've been an idiot for so long. Holy shit." I was like, I don't know what to expect. Then the more we talked, I was understanding. But then it went the other way again.

This is perhaps the most common struggle for Bi+ married men: their wives worry they're "really gay" and not attracted to women. There's a lot to unpack there – and it's partially due to a lack of bisexual visibility, which leads to the biphobic myth that it's a "stepping stone" to being gay – but to be honest, I can understand Lindsay's concern, because it's exactly what I feared about myself.

It stems from the same biphobia, which I had internalized, but when I started hooking up with men, I worried I was deluding myself and that I had been faking my attractions to women all along – even though I'd had lots of pleasurable sex and relationships with women! It's incredibly hard to break down that binary way of thinking when our society is filled with it.

More knowledge and awareness helped Evan understand his identity – and his worldview – which was necessary before he could fully explain it to Lindsay.

Evan: Kinsey scale blew my mind. I started thinking of it as a spectrum. Before, it was either left or right, black or white, there's no in-between. That not only opened my mind on a sexual level but opened my mind on gender fluidity. Everything's on a spectrum.

Lindsay: It was a rollercoaster of understanding and not believing him that he wasn't gay. I mean, it was exhausting. I didn't know what to do or say, because I felt like I'd been lied to. Even if he wasn't gay, I felt like I'd been lied to. And it took me years, years and years, to realize that he didn't do it intentionally, that he didn't know how to express it either.

We talked for hours that night, and we ended on a very good note, and after that, life kind of continues. But then it got bad. I was so paranoid. Any of his guy friends that he would hang out with, I was questioning everything. 'Cause you wouldn't just go out drinking with a girl when you're in a relationship, so why is it okay for a guy now? It was tearing me apart.

I started eventually trying to tell friends, but nobody understood. Nobody. And nobody gave me anything good. They were all like, "I don't know how you could ever trust him. You'd probably be better off leaving. He's probably just gay", blah, blah, blah. Never anything positive, ever. Or just nothing at all, because nobody knew what to say. I felt like I was suffering in silence, while he was finally able to come out and be happy.

This is another common thread: keeping your bisexuality a secret can some-times cause a bigger rift than the identity itself. This makes perfect sense – to me, your spouse should be the person you can trust and confide in 100 percent — but there's often no way around it. Evan, for example, wasn't necessarily keeping a secret from his wife all those years, he was keeping it from <u>everyone</u> and maybe even himself, because he didn't fully understand it yet.

I've heard it over and over from queer people, especially in the early phases: "Why risk everything by disclosing something I'm not even sure about?" It's tricky to figure out whether you're bisexual, and it can be a long, lonely process. Springing it on a partner after that process can leave them feeling out of the loop, and trust must be rebuilt.

> *Lindsay*: I didn't know how to act. And I didn't want him to tell people, because I thought people were going to think I was his beard, that I'm an idiot and I didn't know how to address it.
>
> *Evan*: I didn't really start telling people until the last two or three [years].
>
> *Lindsay*: Yeah, it was a good 10 to 15 years of just us.
>
> *Evan*: It slowly evolved. I worked at [a coffee shop] for like eight years, and the guy who trained me is still a good friend of mine, [Theo]. [Theo's] gay. He's hilarious, he's my favorite, but he's a lot. We would joke around. Very early on, once Lindsay became more accepting, she would want to be included in the types of conversations I would have with [Theo], and they'd be somewhat risqué. It would all be in a joking manner, but she would sometimes see it as a threat, I'm being pulled to one side.
>
> That went on for years and created quite a bit of mistrust in our relationship, and that affected both of us in a lot of bad ways, where if I'm not being trusted … like I never cheated, but it got to the point where I was like, if I'm being accused of it all the time, and I have those urges, maybe I need to jump out and explore myself.
>
> It never came to that point. We were very good about communicating. I used to call them our "every three month fights" – we would have a four-hour discussion, lying in bed, face to face, trying to reassure her that that wasn't something I needed in my life. I don't have to be with a guy just because I'm sexually attracted to a guy, any more than I have to be with a hot chick that's jogging down the street in front of the house. It's not like that. That's something that took a while to come to terms with, and we pushed through it.
>
> *Lindsay*: [We had] ten-plus years of really hard times. It's a joke, the three-month thing, but it just always seemed like it would build to a head every three to four months. It was because I was basically sitting alone with my thoughts. I had nothing like your podcast. I had no friends who could relate to the situation. He would talk me off the ledge, but then I was always afraid that I was just a cover wife, 'cause he wasn't out to his family or anybody. It would just snowball.

When one partner is closeted, the other often is, too, by default, and both can suffer from isolation and negative thought loops – so I asked when and how Evan began coming out to friends or family.

Evan: Actually, one of the first people that I told was [Theo]. He said somebody "wasn't bi, there was no way they could be bi, they're being selfish and greedy" or something like that. The whole "stepping-stone" storyline. He had always identified me as a straight guy who was just an ally, but I was like, "No dude, that's way off base." We had a good heart-to-heart, and it opened his eyes to it. Since then, I don't know how many times he's apologized to me about that and thanked me for speaking up and letting him know that.

Once I got that from him, I really started expanding and taking pride in it, because once you get over that hurdle, that first couple of people, then it's almost shameful not to say something.

As Evan began to come out, Lindsay wanted to talk about it more, too.

Lindsay: I started trying to find things online, support groups and all that, which did not exist. I couldn't find Facebook groups. I found a stupid Yahoo group that was terrible. Everyone was too afraid to not be anonymous. Just bitter spouses who had been cheated on or hated their partners. It was basically telling me that it was going to crash and burn because I wouldn't let him be who he was, and I was holding him back, blah, blah, blah.

I finally started a Facebook group, and it sat with 20 members for like two years because nobody would join. Nobody wanted to come out, even as the spouse. I didn't understand it. It was years of not knowing what to do.

Evan: I'd say at least two or three times, it came to the point where we were trying to shove a round peg in a square hole.

Lindsay: It just felt like an impasse. I don't even know what the problems particularly were.

Evan: I think a lot of it is that I was coming to terms with who I was and wanting to connect with other people I had those similarities with. And I think that came off as a form of a threat, in that I might go too far to one side and not come back.

Lindsay: We always communicate. We trust each other. I rehash these things in my head and bring them up a million times, and he always has to reassure me, but he always does. He brings me back to earth. It's so stupid and cliché to say communication and honesty is important, but we've just always been really good at it.

We did counseling a few different times. I'm not good at counseling. I don't like counseling. I've experienced it my whole life as a kid, with all my issues. I just don't feel like a mediator benefits us. We talk about everything, so it just felt pointless. But I always recommend therapy to people who aren't good at communicating in general.

Evan: Some of the playful ways that we got through it were checking out the same guys. I remember one of our rough times, we just needed to get out of the house, and we ended up going to a wing place, and it was a super-cute waiter, the kind of waiter that has both of your eye contacts the whole time. I think we ended up leaving him a $4 tip on service, but then like a $7 tip –?

Lindsay: We wrote a note, like $7 on appearance and cute smile, or something stupid like that.

Evan: It was really just getting used to having those types of playful dynamics and loosening things up.

Lindsay: That was all I wanted, was to feel like he was including me and to not feel like I was being shut out from this whole side of him that I wanted to know, because it made me feel so much more insecure. Before I found out, we used to watch porn together. Then he wouldn't any more. He was afraid that it would send me down the rabbit hole. And it just made me more insecure and afraid because he was afraid to freak me out. So it was like over-correcting.

Evan: I tried to identify as much as possible that I was bisexual, as soon as I understood that, not so much to put myself out there, but to try to alleviate that back-of-the-head rumor that people would think she was being fooled this whole time. I tried to point out that I was bisexual and that I was married, happily.

I ended up going an entire semester for one of my writing courses not divulging anything about my home life. Letting people assume what they wanted to assume. I got the idea that everybody thought I was gay. I had an awesome professor that asked us, by the end of the semester, what is it we would stand out in the rain for.

Lindsay: Like what meant a lot to you.

Evan got choked up thinking about this memory. He tried to continue the story …

Evan: And that was like a huge thing for me …

But he got tears in his eyes, unable to speak, so Lindsay helped him out.

Lindsay: He got up in front of the class and did a whole presentation on being bisexual, and basically about the struggles from the LGBTQ community and being judged from their side, and people assuming things and erasing me from his life by assuming. And then ended it with a picture of us.

Evan: It really helped us, because the amount of research that I put into that presentation, to let people who aren't really informed understand on some scale the way that I felt and the way that I viewed bisexuality … I don't remember what YouTuber it was, but there was one that compared it to food, and I loved that analogy. I opened with that, basically saying, "Everybody in here that loves Italian food, raise your hand. And everybody that loves Chinese food, raise your hand. And everybody that loves Chinese and Italian, you raise your hand." And I was like, "Sometimes I want Italian food, and

I might be on a diet where I can't have Italian food." It was interesting to see everyone's faces, the ones who clicked, and they were like, that totally makes sense.

When I finally opened the floor to questions, people wanted to ask how that works. How could I possibly be attracted to my wife and Jake Gyllenhaal at the same time? And it was interesting, my professor spoke up during that answer time and explained it the same way that I explained it, and asked me to stay after class. And when I met with her …

Evan got tears in his eyes again. And I have to admit, sensing where this story was going, I did, too. After a moment, he continued:

Evan: It was really cool when I met with her, because she identified as bisexual. So it was important for her when I did all that, and she was holding it back, and she started crying after the class left. It was a really powerful experience, to see a professor that I admired so much connect on that level and for us to have that similarity. She was also in a seemingly straight marriage. It meant a lot to me to see that.

It wasn't the only time that putting himself out there allowed others in Evan's life to reciprocate.

Evan: My mom was somebody I was always terrified to have that conversation with. I remember when I was in elementary school, we were driving, and there were two men in the car in front of us, and they leaned in and kissed, and I remember my mom saying something derogatory.

She's since backpedaled, because once we had that conversation – I called her, I was like, this is what's going on, I don't know what to do, my marriage is falling apart – then she told me that she's bisexual.

Lindsay: And his sister.

Evan: And my sister. I was so regretful that I didn't come to terms with it sooner, because now me, my mom and my sister all joke around, when we're at like cookouts together.

We also found out at some point that my parents are swingers. We don't want that. I mean no judgment, but just randos, whatever they find, they're good. I'm happy that they're open with that. But for me, it's always been more about being attracted to a person as a whole. I can't see myself as being a "Let's go rent a boy" and see what happens.

Though they've been monogamous throughout their relationship, Lindsay expressed anxiety that Evan may have additional desires that he's suppressing. I asked how they manage that.

Lindsay: I've always offered things, because I'm so afraid of him not getting the experiences he might want but won't tell me. I'm like, I will do pegging, anything you want to do. If you're happy, I'll get off on it. But he doesn't see it that way. He doesn't just want a dick. It's more about his connection with somebody.

I have always told him that if he ever wanted to try something, it had to be a threesome, I had to be involved. I wasn't going to just let him go out and have a night of craziness on his own. He has always expressed that he didn't need it, wasn't interested, but I worry that he's just afraid to tip me down that rabbit hole again. So I am open to that. I never expected to like somebody enough, [but] we have this new friend who I am completely obsessed with. I'm not saying anything's going to happen, but …

Evan: I have a really good trans friend that I've always been attracted to. It really is the person as a whole that I'm attracted to, both in a regular relationship way and in a sexual way.

Lindsay: Which almost makes it more difficult, because sometimes it feels like it would be easier if it was just a toy situation or a rent-a-boy situation.

I don't ever worry about him cheating on me with a girl, ever. It never crosses my mind. It's always the fear of it being a guy. I can't ever be that. No matter how happy we are, what if he'll want it enough that it'll cause him to stray?

Evan: And that brings different levels to it, because how do you have male friends in a mixed-orientation relationship without it seeming like you're trying to do something?

There's no easy answer – just like non-monogamy, monogamy is complicated and layered, and it evolves in unique ways based on the people involved. To me, Evan and Lindsay's story is a good example of compatibility as a process rather than a magical state of being. To make a relationship work, you need a foundation of love, but you also need open, honest, and consistent communication – often surrounding the things you're most afraid to talk about. I expect this discussion to be an ongoing aspect of their story, even if they ultimately remain monogamous, as it helps them understand each other and their desires better.

After working through so many roadblocks common to mixed-orientation couples, they've both tried to share what they've learned with others … but not everyone is in the right place to hear their message.

Lindsay: The past two years, he started posting on Facebook during pride month, and it made me want to be like, "You know what? I want to help people." People are only finding terrible advice. I wanted to build a community of happy people, and I'm the only one still – the rest are stressed. Only people who are having difficulties seem to reach out. The hardest situations, it's a lot of "He's saying he needs this to feel fulfilled. He won't be who he is without these experiences."

People are like, "How do you make it work?" I'm like, "Have you told [your spouse] how you feel?" "Well, no." I'm like, "I don't know what to tell you then." That's where I love your podcast, being able to listen to these conversations that nobody will have out in the open.

Evan: And to hear these stories that so many of us 100 percent identify with ... It was one of the podcasts, there were several points where I knew the end of the story, because it was a portion of my story, and it's insanely reassuring to see.

Lindsay: But it's also sad, because we're all going through the same fucking thing, and nobody will talk about it. How do you ever fix it when people won't even talk about it? People won't invite their spouses to the groups. It's very hard.

We're not afraid to be who we are any more, because I feel like we are a success story, even though our lives aren't over. In my groups, they're like, "I just found out last week", "I just found out a few months ago", and I'm like, "Oh, I found out 14 years ago." And they're like, "What?" They can't believe it, 'cause nobody else is saying that.

Evan: I'm not saying it doesn't happen [differently] for other individuals, but our "coming-outs" have all been receptive, so it's encouraging to continue to do that. It really does make a world of difference meeting that one person you identify with in that way.

Lindsay has been an amazing partner in this whole situation and been even more vocal than I have been. That's really meant a lot to me to see that. And I feel like it would mean a lot to other couples.

Since our interview, Evan and Lindsay started a support group and resource guide for mixed-orientation couples. If you'd like, you can visit their website, MOR & More ("Mixed Orientation Relationships & More") at www.morand more.org.

Though I did see both a dog and a cat in the background during our interview, I didn't see or hear anything about kids ... so I asked whether that's on the agenda.

Lindsay: I have always wanted a child, and he doesn't know if he does. That's been another source of insecurity, because I'm like, is it just 'cause he's going to leave me someday? That's the final settle down, and that became a whole problem.

Evan: She knows that I don't have a good relationship with my father. He left when I was super-young. She's always known that I would never want to do that to a child: divorce or leaving or making an ugly exit. So in my narrative, if we had a kid, and I for some reason wanted to leave, then [I] wouldn't.

Lindsay: I have a shit family, and I never had anybody there. So that fear of leaving, I have it, but at the same time, I have more of a fear of never having it. Now I'm going to cry ... [crying]. I just want to create our own family, because we can create something awesome, because we're awesome. Even if we divorced, I don't feel like we'd ever not be together or friends. So that's not the worst thing in the world. I just want that. I want to put good into this shitty world.

We're at a good place with that. But we've been together for 17 years and it's just been us, and now it's scary to think about it not just being us.

Evan: It's nice when our neighbors' kids are over, and she's playing Aunt [Lindsay]. But it reaches a point where, "Okay, you guys go home."

Lindsay: It's different when they're yours. Everybody says, anyway. They'll be brats, but they'll be our brats.

I ended our interview with the feeling that by the time this book is published, Evan and Lindsay may have already started writing their next chapter together.

17

Stanley and Christine on Meeting Your Spouse at a Bisexual Play Party

A fter chatting with Evan and Lindsay, I talked to one other couple whose story is almost the polar opposite. Instead of connecting when they were young and exploring themselves alongside each other, Stanley and Christine met in their 50s and 40s, respectively, after Stanley's first marriage and after they had both already embraced their bisexuality. In fact, they never struggled with coming out to each other because they met at a bisexual play party (aka sex party), so simply by showing up, they were both out without having to say a word.

This oral history features much less back story and childhood experience compared to others, but it offers a unique glimpse into the relationship dynamics of a straight-passing couple where both partners identify as bisexual. Perhaps because they met at a play party and are in the "lifestyle" (also referred to as "swinging"), we talked a lot about sex (which I don't mind at all!). I should also note that Stanley and Christine are friends of mine – I met them at BiRequest, the discussion group in New York City that was formative in my Bi+ journey, and I serve on the leadership committee with Christine.

Stanley is a white, bisexual, cisgender man from the Bronx, New York, where he currently resides with Christine. He was born in 1961 and was 59 years old at the time of our interview in 2020. He describes himself as middle-class, both in childhood and currently, and agnostic. Christine is a white, bisexual, cisgender woman born in Bad Kreuznach, Germany in 1972 while her father was stationed

DOI: 10.4324/9781003385585-17

there in the Army – she moved to the United States at age two and lived in Minnesota until 1998, when she moved to New York City. She was 48 at the time of our interview in 2020. She grew up upper-middle-class and was raised Catholic, and she now describes herself as middle-class and non-practicing religiously.

> *Stanley*: I first questioned my sexuality when I was nine. It was boys at summer camp, sleep away, and things like that. Then later on, I was about 14 or 15, I played with a couple of guys who were older. Got to college, played with guys more my age, and a little older in their 30s. It was all good. Didn't matter. Felt good. It was fine.
>
> Then I got married to the first wife. I played a straight role, but I dabbled. I still played around with guys. She didn't know. That's how a lot of bi guys are – in the closet. Especially married bi guys, unless your partner is willing to let you do that. I had a good time with the wife in the beginning, and then things fizzled. Then I got divorced, and I went into the lifestyle to make up for lost time. We were together 23 years, but we were married 12-and-a-half.

Stanley is the only man I interviewed for this book from the Baby Boomer generation, and I think that affects the way he frames sexuality. Right away, he confirmed that homoeroticism was common in his teenage years, even though "bisexual" was not a common word or identity until the 1980s and beyond. Many bisexual men played the "straight role", as he described, got married to a woman, but also fooled around with men – which was "all good" and also "didn't matter". There is something true and interesting there, in that Stanley felt his same-sex attraction didn't affect his different-sex attraction, but at a time when any same-sex behavior indicated you were gay (a view that is still prevalent today, if slightly less so), most Bi+ men were very private about their same-sex activity, which is exactly what Stanley observed.

Stanley also seemed to gloss over large time periods with fairly short statements, and while part of that might be a learned impulse to downplay queerness, I know personally that it's also simply part of Stanley's personality: blunt, matter-of-fact, dispassionate, and sometimes unintentionally hilarious. I guess opposites attract, because when I asked Christine next to tell me about how and why she realized she was bisexual, she had quite a bit more to say.

> *Christine*: I actually started questioning my sexuality back in college. I initially started out as a straight supporter, I called it. My best friend in high school was gay, and I was very supportive. Then I started to question myself, like, "Am I being supportive, or is this because I'm bi?" I had a strong connection with women, more than just platonic, so I came to the realization that I'm actually bi and never looked back. Never a question [whether] I'm a lesbian or not; I've always known I was bi. I came out in 1991, I think.
>
> I had one girlfriend on campus, but basically just had relationships with men who identified as heterosexual. With my last boyfriend, I got into

the lifestyle. I told him I was bi, I had experiences with men and women previously, and he wanted to get into that. I don't know if you're familiar with the lifestyle, but we would swap with other couples. I would be with other women, other men. He was never with another guy.

But that's how this merges together and gets into how I met Stanley. I started getting on OkCupid and started out as straight because I didn't want to be the stereotypical bi woman, you know, "Oh, let's have a threesome." But I answered questions saying I've been with women, so they found me anyway. Then I'm like, "Fuck this. Why am I not looking to be with a bi man?" Because they have a better idea of it, they have an understanding.

When he's like, "I like to be with the same sex", I can understand, I get that, because that's what I am. I'm bi, too. So I don't see it as, "Oh, I'm not good enough." And I hear this a lot, their issue is, "You must be going that way because I'm not good enough, or I'm not enough." That's a big obstacle to navigate, because you take it on yourself. If you're both bi, there could still be jealousy issues, trust issues, whatever – but there's an understanding. I know you're not doing this to replace me. This is an enhancement. And that's how I see it, as something that adds to what we already have.

Christine was summing up what many couples in this book have experienced – because bisexual people desire more than one gender category, many cisgender partners feel like they'll never be enough because they can never satisfy multiple categories of desire at once. This attitude mistakes the definition of bisexuality, which is about the <u>possibility</u> of multi-gender attractions, not a <u>need</u> to have that within a marriage, but it's also about jealousy and self-esteem. Heteronormativity feeds us the idea that our partners are supposed to fulfill all our needs, but that's often an impossible standard to meet.

As Christine described, bisexuality gave her and Stanley a shared understanding – they each felt that their attractions to people of other genders didn't negate or take away from their love for each other, and that allowed them to trust each other. Especially when paired with polyamory or the "lifestyle", this feeling goes a long way toward dealing with jealousy and establishing honest communication – something many other Bi+ men who are married to straight women struggle with for years.

I got the sense that both Stanley and Christine were closer to 1s and 2s on the Kinsey scale (meaning "predominantly" heterosexual, but not exclusively), so I asked about their gender preferences.

Christine: I had one girlfriend for a hot second in college, but that was more platonic. We kind of kissed, but we never had sex 'cause she was just coming out. Ever since then, I've always been in relationships with men.

Stanley: Emotionally I find it better with women, but I'll fuck a guy. It don't matter.

So while both identify as bisexual, I think they'd also both describe themselves as more heteroromantic. I then asked more about what happened after Stanley's first marriage – he said that within a week of separating from his first wife, he was in the lifestyle.

Stanley: You go on Yahoo groups back then and you find things and say, "Oh, I can make up for lost time. Have sex with people and then go home." Everybody at the party was bi to a certain extent. I mean, a couple of people were bi-friendly, curious, whatever, but mostly everybody was a player. So I didn't have to worry about coming out because everybody was in the same situation. I met Christine at a party and played around and then started dating a few days later.

That's the short story of how they met! Here's the longer version:

Christine: October of 2014 is when I went to my first BiRequest, and I met "Bi [Jon]". I ended up going to his bi play party in November, and that's where I met Stanley. I'm sorry, honey, I'm going to tell him … I was one of three. Or one of five? I was one of his collection, his repertoire. But I'm like, okay, I met this guy at a play party, no expectations, just have fun. And we just clicked and we hung out quite a bit.

For me, there wasn't that awkward, "Oh my God, I have to tell him." That fear of rejection. I mean, when you are that open and exposed to someone, and intimate from the beginning, you can talk about anything. We ended up spending the night, sleeping in the same bed. We didn't do anything, we just talked until really early in the morning. Should I go full disclosure?

Stanley: Whatever you want!

Christine: He couldn't even get it up at the party. So we didn't even have true intercourse. We just had –

Stanley: Oral.

Christine: Oral. Which was wonderful.

Stanley: Because earlier in that day, I was with somebody else and we had about five hours of sex. So I couldn't get it up for the party. That was the only reason.

Christine: It was a few days later when we actually had sex. We went on a date, out to dinner, and then went back to my apartment and had fun.

Stanley: For a few hours. And then all doubt was out.

Christine: Yeah, no issues. And then it turned out to be almost every night that week.

Stanley: And then the next week it was almost every night.

Christine: Dinner and sex is basically how our relationship started. Then we just got to know each other and connected. He met my parents in early December, they happened to be visiting. It all happened really fast. We went ring shopping the end of January. It was like we knew right away. And within a year we were married. We met November of 2014, we got married September of 2015. I work fast.

Stanley: She works fast.

Christine: I wasn't expecting that, but we just clicked. I felt very comfortable and safe with him, like nothing I'd ever experienced with my previous exes. And he was very open and accepting, even though it's a different experience, being a bi woman compared to being a bi man, but there's at least an understanding. It's not like trying to go from either a homosexual or a heterosexual perspective, where they'll wonder "Why do you need or want to be with men and women?" So for me, that was wonderful.

I think the fact that both of them identified as Bi+ for a long time before meeting played a huge role in their comfort level with each other. Unlike so many others in this book, bisexuality was not a "problem" for either of them and never caused a rift between them, but rather it was an enhancement and source of mutual understanding.

But on top of that, meeting in such a vulnerable environment, where you're literally laid bare, can open you up to someone immediately. Though this is not how I met my wife, I have met other friends and partners at play parties, and that type of introduction leads to immediate intimacy. It breaks down barriers and allows you to be more authentic with clothes on, too. Christine summed it up well:

Christine: We were very open with each other. When you start basically meeting naked, just sexual, then you take your relationship from there, it's almost like the first few months of dating are out the window.

It was interesting, at one point Stanley said, "For one night, I wish we could go back and date and not have the sexual part of it." We lasted one night, until about 12:05 the next day, after midnight. Then we had to have sex. That's just our relationship – it's not all sex, but there was always a safe comfort level with that for me.

He started coming to BiRequest after a few months. At first, he was saying "I'm heteroflexible" or whatever. It wasn't until a few months later that you were like, "Okay, I guess I'm bi." Not that it matters what the label is, but I think you accepted it, because you would go to BiRequest, and we would do this together.

Perhaps this is another generational difference, but Stanley understood and accepted his sexual fluidity long before he adopted a "bi" label – he may not have seen that as a valid option, or perhaps he didn't think his same-sex activity was very "important" until he met Christine and went to a Bi+ discussion group. In my experience, many "heteroflexible" guys come to BiRequest and discuss the merits of a bisexual identity – Stanley was already comfortable with his identity, but meeting those people in real life may have helped him realize that a bisexual label made sense for him.

Knowing the answer, I asked if they identify as monogamous – and how they've navigated their relationship boundaries over time.

Stanley: We're not monogamous. That's ridiculous [laughs]. We're ethically non-monogamous. We're together, but if she wants to go and play with somebody else, that's fine. If I want to go play with somebody else, that's fine.

Christine: After we started dating, we would go to parties regularly as a couple and play with others. We've been on lifestyle cruises, until they got canceled by Covid. When we travel, we go to other parties. So we've been to a lot of parties and met other couples who are in the lifestyle. But we're not into polyamory.

Stanley: We just got enough love for each other. But we'll have sex with everybody. I mean, it's just sex. At the end, we go home together. We might bring a person in that both of us can play with, at a party or wherever we're at, but it's not like we're going to take them home and say, "Let's all get together and be a family."

Christine: For me, I don't need to introduce another partner, another romantic relationship, even though the people we've been with, we've developed some friendships. There's caring, but it's not to the point where I'm like, "Oh my God, I'm in love with them" and bring them into our family or triad or whatever. I don't need that. We're good here. So I consider myself emotionally and mentally monogamous, but physically not.

Stanley: Physically, we're sluts.

Christine: Exactly. I enjoy that play. But then we are together afterwards.

Stanley and Christine make an interesting distinction about being "open" versus "poly", and I think the choices they've made are extremely common – I suspect there are many more "open" couples like them, especially in the lifestyle community, who do not consider themselves polyamorous, which by most definitions includes multiple romantic attachments. While Stanley and Christine acknowledge that emotional intimacy can develop by having sex, they are only interested in romantic relationships with each other, always "coming home" after sexual experiences with others. Their boundaries are complex and multi-spectrum, but above all they are clear, which has helped them navigate non-monogamy safely and without excess jealousy. Christine explained:

Christine: When we started seriously dating, we had a couple of issues of jealousy, on both sides. We got into the play scene, and even though we're both open and accepting of it, it's still, "I've been with you exclusively, but now we're at a party and other people are with you." That was a little tricky to navigate.

But I completely trust him. I know that he's not gonna do anything to hurt me. We talked about it to get through that jealousy. Knowing that he's not replacing me or I'm not replacing him. Like I said, when I'm with other people, he's still the best, because he knows me. I've got that connection, that love. It's the full package. And that's just communicating and affirming. But we were fortunate enough that we already had that out there when we met, because I can see where that could be a deal breaker for some people.

As we talked more about sex and swinging, Christine described something I've experienced myself – sex with other partners doesn't necessarily deplete my sex drive with my wife but rather <u>increases</u> it by making me feel more sexy and confident overall.

> *Christine*: We'll talk about play [with others], fantasize about it, and have the most amazing sex. We'll sometimes be like "God, aren't they so hot?" We kind of create a fantasy about it, which makes it fun.
>
> When you come back, you have that sexual energy. You kind of collect it and you bring it back and you want to share it with each other. I find that interesting. And none of them are as good as him. They're good, but … you know what I mean?
>
> *Stanley*: We'd sit outside at a restaurant and watch people go up and down the street and say, "Oh, look at her, look at him. You want to do him?" And we're both looking at the same one.
>
> *Christine*: Sometimes we take it home, like, "Oh, that woman or that guy, we could have sex with them", bring them into our fantasies. So that's always fun.
>
> We've developed good friends and connections. Sometimes we play, sometimes we just hang out and have dinner. There's six of us, three couples, we're all swingers who have all slept with each other. You can imagine those dinners are kind of crazy. We're all very flirty, but I don't have any desire to go home with them.
>
> There are times where I'll sit there and watch the guys play, which I enjoy. I don't have to be "on" all the time. Or I'll play with her and they'll play together, you know? I can last longer and go with more guys. Whereas guys have got a limited time, can only come once or twice, which is fine. I've been at parties where I would go through a few men at a time, like "next, next, next", you know? But that's just the nature of being female.
>
> *Stanley*: Well you've got an "innie" and I've got an "outtie", so that explains that. Gotta make sure the blood keeps going to the outtie.
>
> *Christine*: And I completely respect that. I'm not like, "Oh my God, he can't get it up" or whatever. I get it. You find other ways.
>
> *Stanley*: Right, you have a good time some other way.

"Performance" issues are not unique to Bi+ men, but I have heard about it often, and I've experienced it myself. Unlike Stanley, who simply appears to be "tapped out" when he has too much sex, many men experience performance anxiety that feels directly related to their bisexuality, sometimes more with partners of one gender over another (especially if we're trying to "prove" our attractions, to a partner or to ourselves).

Whatever the reason, I think many Bi+ men would love to have a partner with an outlook like Christine – that it's not a big deal and that you can have fun some other way. Sometimes lowering the stakes and pressure to perform in that way can actually lead to overcoming performance anxiety. I think this attitude is overrepresented among queer and Bi+ people, because we're already writing our own sexual scripts and not conforming to the heteronormative standard of penis-in-vagina sex that ends when the guy ejaculates. I've certainly met many more straight women than queer women who have that expectation.

I asked Stanley about how the lifestyle has changed over time, especially since he started identifying as bi.

> *Stanley*: A lot of the guys we meet now are bi. They always were there, it's just that they were afraid to be there, you know? In the lifestyle, you're supposed to be a little more liberal and forward-thinking. Although some of it is not. There's plenty of discrimination against bi guys in the lifestyle. Plenty. And then you'll find women that say, "My husband is 100 percent straight, stay away" – but I may not want to do your husband. I just want to do you.
>
> *Christine*: And that's the thing, we can be with a straight couple, too. We don't have to be with a bi couple all the time. It just makes it easier and more enjoyable, because they seem to be more open. It's not always that I'm playing with a woman and he's playing with a guy. We still swap. But if that happens, that happens, and I think people feel freer, more open, if you're bi. When you're in an environment where everyone's bi, they're more relaxed.
>
> There's times where he's like, "We're meeting this couple", because he sets up all that, I let him take care of that, and I'm like, "Okay, what are we doing? Are we the straight couple? Or are we the bi couple? Which way are we going?" But everyone lately has all been bi.

It was clear they've had many group sex experiences, so I asked if they ever play separately from each other.

> *Stanley*: Sure.
>
> *Christine*: A little bit. Maybe on the cruise. But we'd be kind of in the same area. He would go off with someone else in their cabin or whatever. More of a "hall pass." That's the term.
>
> *Stanley*: It's okay to go, but make sure you come back.
>
> *Christine*: We don't go on individual dates. I don't need to hook up with guys that way or do any of that. I enjoy the parties, that connection there. I know this sounds really shallow, but it's just basically the sex. I enjoy that, and friendships, yes, great, but I don't need all the other stuff to fulfill anything.

I pressed Stanley on navigating fluidity and homophobia within the lifestyle. His answer reflected common challenges for Bi+ men – even within seemingly progressive communities – as well as gender differences when it comes to bisexuality.

> *Stanley*: Even though bi guys can be with guys, in the real world, they look gay. If they're worried about their sexuality and not coming out, they're certainly not going to want to look gay if they're bi. Plus on top of that, they

don't want to get married and then all of a sudden come out and say, "Honey, I'm bi", and she says, "That's right, as in 'bye, bye'".

Even in lifestyle, where you think they're a lot more forward-thinking, that there wouldn't be as much stigma toward bi guys – there is. It's okay if the girls are because it's really hot, but the guys who are straight don't think that it's hot to see two guys. Although their wives might.

Christine: It's almost like women in the lifestyle have to be bi, because they have to put on a show for the men. I'm not doing it to show off. Well, sometimes [laughs]. I love watching him with another guy. It's hot.

I think a lot of Bi+ men would be excited hearing this! Many of us spend years working through and shedding our internalized homophobia, and many of us have encountered women who view our same-sex experiences as a negative – but open-minded women like Christine are out there, and their numbers are growing.

Next, I asked about their gender preferences. I loved Stanley's blunt explanation of fluidity, countering the common "50/50" assumption.

Stanley: You don't have to "be bi" all the time. It's not like I gotta have a guy this week and a girl that week. I might want 20 women and not touch a guy, or play with guys and never a girl again – although that would not happen [laughs]. But it doesn't have to be even. A lot of bi guys think "I gotta have a guy and then a girl to even it out." It doesn't work that way. I'm bi, I'm bi. If I do one guy and I do 100 women, I'm still bi. It's however I feel.

Christine: On the scale, I'm more penis-centric.

Stanley: And I'm more vagina-centric.

Christine: I really love sex with men, with a penis. I enjoy being with women, but that's really what I want. Therefore, I married a man, you know? I don't feel like I'm any less of a bi woman if I'm not with a woman.

Stanley: And it doesn't make me any less bi if I don't want to be with a guy for a while. And it's not always: a guy's got a penis and an ass, [so] I want to be with him. It could be that between the ears, he's an idiot.

I asked if they had ever thought about having kids.

Christine: I'm way too old for biological kids. We talked about it when we first were dating, but right now, we're at a point where we enjoy traveling a lot, we enjoy the party scene. So I think we're kind of set in our ways.

Stanley: Yeah. It's hard to go to sex parties every week and have to bring in babysitters who can spend the night.

As we began to wrap up, I asked if they had any advice for other Bi+ people or couples, and we took a fun detour into pegging (which I also endorse!).

Christine: I do have a suggestion for women: pegging. Get a dildo. It's hot. I highly recommend it.

Stanley: It's more of a power thing than a sexual thing.

Christine: Well, honey, it's very sexual, too. She could then give him something that she could potentially feel like she's lacking. She can put on the penis and interact in a way that he may get from a guy. If he's a bottom. If he's a top, it would be different.

Stanley: Honey, I'm only verse with you [laughs].

Stanley also had some more traditional advice that reiterates the same conclusion so many other couples in this book have come to: honest communication is key.

Stanley: We met in a bi space, so everybody had their cards on the table. You talk about marriages between couples who don't know … they can't talk about it with their spouse. Or they don't understand. With my ex-wife, we had sex and then I'd turn around and go out and have sex with men. And believe me, that happens a lot. A lot of straight guys go out and play with guys and then come home and play with their wife again. For couples who are not in a lifestyle situation, they have to talk about it. That's the most important thing, talking about it and getting over trust issues.

They also ended on a familiar note about authenticity, delivered in the cutest way possible.

Stanley: I'm too old to give a shit what people think. I mean, if I'm not straight with myself, then there's no point.

Christine: Honey, you're bent with yourself.

Stanley: Stop that, honey [laughs]. Yeah, yeah. I'm straight with myself, otherwise, why bother?

18

Concluding Thoughts

A s you can see, the men in this book are leading joyous but complicated lives, and they're in or have been part of beautiful but sometimes difficult relationships. While their experiences have many similarities, most of them have felt alone for much of their journey. Even many who are fulfilled in their marriages have trouble finding Bi+ community.

Perhaps because we are so fractured, that community is in crisis. Physical and mental health outcomes are significantly worse for Bi+ people, and the vast majority of Bi+ men, especially those who are married to women, are not out, which can lead to a depressing cycle of invisibility, erasure, and shame. Despite these statistics and outcomes, the Bi+ community receives a tiny fraction of dedicated resources.

This isn't the fault of Bi+ people. Bisexuality is not only completely natural (and perhaps even evolutionarily advantageous), but it is a gift, a superpower that allows us to understand our authentic selves and connect and empathize with other people. Sexual fluidity is immensely beautiful to me, and coming out has allowed me to experience things that have enriched my life in countless ways – things that I never imagined were possible before.

Rather, the crisis we're in is due to a homophobic and biphobic society. Though the climate is getting better, there is still a long way to go. Most people still don't know a real-life Bi+ person, so stereotypes and misguided assumptions often

DOI: 10.4324/9781003385585-18

dictate how we are perceived and treated, rather than being seen and respected as human beings.

At this moment, I believe that visibility is vital to changing that dynamic. It may not be a silver bullet, but it's a necessary foundation for Bi+ acceptance and liberation.

WHAT COMING OUT REALLY MEANS

I can lecture all day on the science of sexual fluidity, but what changes hearts and minds is actually <u>knowing</u> Bi+ and queer people, understanding our humanity rather than relying on stereotypes and assumptions. This type of humanization has been happening over the past few decades for gay and lesbian people, and it has changed the landscape considerably, but Bi+ people are still trailing behind. It's a terrible catch-22 – we're misunderstood and stigmatized because we're so invisible, but that stigma causes most Bi+ people, and almost all Bi+ men, to remain closeted and invisible.

For better or worse, I believe that we – members of the Bi+ community – are best positioned to break this cycle. Many Bi+ people minimize their sexuality and pass for straight most of the time, even if they're out to close friends and family. I totally get it, for all the reasons on display in these oral histories, but that invisibility is preventing many in our community from thriving.

Coming out and being more visible is particularly difficult – and especially important – for the subjects of this book: Bi+ men who are married to women. This group is struggling more than others, perhaps because their marriages reinforce their repression and allow them to pass for straight "easily", but I hope these stories prove that passing is not actually as easy as it seems. Only when more stories like these are shared will more men be able to recognize their experience and address their identity and mental health in productive ways.

I didn't interview any Bi+ men for this book who weren't out and didn't plan to come out, and there's a simple reason: no one like that reached out to me. I would be shocked if they didn't exist – in fact, they probably exist in greater numbers than Bi+ men who <u>do</u> come out – but I'd guess that these men are not actively reaching out to a bisexual podcaster to be part of a book about bisexuality, even anonymously. Some may not be able to fully embrace a Bi+ identity for themselves. Some may be monogamous and not consider their attractions to be important. Some may simply be ashamed or afraid. I wish we could hear their point of view, but if they were open enough to talk to me for this book, they'd probably be on a path toward coming out to others, so it remains a hidden experience by definition. Still, I try to remember how common this experience is, even though we don't hear about it.

The men in this book <u>did</u> choose to come out, or have at least begun the process, and I am so grateful that they volunteered to share their stories. I applaud all of them for their openness and vulnerability and for giving others a window into one of the most hidden Bi+ experiences. Their decision to come out is extremely important – and it's equally important to understand what that decision really means.

I believe that you cannot choose your attractions – they just happen, or they don't. You cannot make certain attractions disappear, and you cannot force attraction where it doesn't exist. You can only <u>respond</u> to your attractions, indulging them or not, integrating them into your identity or not, sharing them or not. Though this can certainly affect your romantic and sexual relationships and the options available to you, the choice is really much broader than that. In many ways, you are choosing a cultural identity, and you are choosing the level of importance that your non-conforming desires have in your life. You are choosing your relationship with queerness.

Dr. Jane Ward sums it up perfectly in *Not Gay*:

> Unfortunately, the domain of culture is generally lost in popular discourses about sexual desire, which focus largely on whether homosexual activity is either "chosen" or "biological". This entire framing is far too simplistic.
>
> … People who identify as heterosexual … are generally content with straight culture, or heteronormativity; they enjoy heterosexual sex, but more importantly … they enjoy heterosexual culture. Simply put, being sexually "normal" suits them. It feels good; it feels like home.
>
> … Others … desire rebellion, difference, or outsiderness … Some of us – who typically go by the names of "gay," "lesbian," "bisexual," or "queer" – want our same-sex attractions and encounters to be taken seriously, viewed as meaningful and sometimes political features of our lives. Others – who typically go by the names of "heterosexual" or "straight" – want our same-sex attractions and encounters to be viewed in opposite terms, as accidental, temporary, meaningless, and decidedly apolitical.
>
> … It is precisely because queerness refuses normalization that [it] is meaningful to me and to other queers. The subversion is where the romance lies.

If we assume that everyone has a capacity for queerness, then coming out is not just about whether or not we experience same-sex desire, it's about whether or not we view our desires as important, as part of our identity or our politics. It's about whether we feel more comfortable fitting in or standing out. It's about whether we are happy with the status quo or prefer to push boundaries and subvert expectations.

Not everyone needs to or should come out. Whatever you choose is valid. Identifying as queer is a personal decision that deeply affects many aspects of your life. But it's important to be clear about the choice you're making and why.

Personally, after spending years wanting to fit in and be "normal", I've let go of those expectations (or at least I'm trying to) and stopped twisting myself in knots to conform. I try every day to get in touch with myself and my authentic feelings, and I try to accept and find joy in whatever I uncover. I don't have to be a certain way or do certain things in order to be loved and accepted. I'm just me, and no matter what happens in my life, there is beauty in simply being myself.

INCREASING VISIBILITY
AND EFFECTING CHANGE

For those who do come out and desire to be different, it can be rewarding, but it's not necessarily easy. By definition, you will always be in the minority, always resisting and subverting dominant culture, which can be taxing. It's important to find other people who can affirm your identity and beliefs and help you feel less alone – so we must make it easier for Bi+ people to find community and support.

As a member of the leadership team of BiRequest, the largest Bi+ community group in New York City (that I'm aware of), I can personally attest that we do not have nearly enough resources to serve everyone we should or could. Leadership is entirely volunteer-based, so we don't have the bandwidth to accomplish everything we dream of, we struggle to pay the "rent" for discussion group space at the LGBT Center and online, and we have limited ability to do marketing and outreach. Still, at least we exist – in smaller cities and especially rural areas, it can be hard or impossible to find similar community groups.

One of the great joys of my life in the past year has been joining an informal group of bi guys in Los Angeles – we meet up about once a month just to hang out. Sometimes we go bowling, or dancing, or watch a movie. Even if we don't talk about bisexuality at all, it is so affirming and fun just to be in the presence of this group. It reminds me that while sexual fluidity has its challenges, it should be joyful, and it feels that way when I'm around people who share a mutual understanding and respect of each others' identities. If it were up to me to direct funding for the queer community, I would throw a ton simply into building and supporting Bi+ social groups, all across the country.

If you can't cultivate in-person Bi+ community for whatever reason, there are other ways to connect. My podcast, *Two Bi Guys*, for example, is a decent place to start (or any other Bi+ podcast) – at this moment we have 50 episodes available, with more coming by the time you read this. I've interviewed a wide range of Bi+ people – authors, professors, artists, politicians, activists, athletes, preachers, and porn stars – so you can find episodes that resonate with your experience and figure out the unique role that bisexuality plays in your life. Our social media accounts can also help you connect virtually with guests, so you can follow their content, as well as with other listeners. You can find us by searching for "Two Bi Guys" wherever you listen to podcasts or at www.TwoBiGuys.com, you can follow us on Instagram at @TwoBiGuys, and for other up-to-date social pages and links, you can visit our Linktree at linktr.ee/TwoBiGuys.

This book is my next attempt to increase visibility and create connection. I hope that reading these oral histories has given you a better understanding of the authentic lives of Bi+ men who are married to women, especially if you haven't met any in person, and perhaps they will help you start conversations with people in your own life, queer or otherwise.

But this book is just a start. With only space for a baker's dozen interviews, there are many more experiences that I hope can be represented in the future, including: Bi+ men who are married to men, or married to trans or non-binary people; Bi+ married women; unmarried Bi+ people; trans and non-binary Bi+ people; Bi+ people from the Latinx community, AAPI community, Native American community, and other underrepresented ethnicities; Bi+ people from other cultures and outside the United States; Bi+ people with disabilities and neuro-divergence; poly and non-monogamous Bi+ people; and probably other experiences I'm forgetting or can't even imagine yet.

Thus, I plan to continue this project in one form or another. I can't guarantee another edition of a book like this (unless you and all your friends buy it …), but my goal is to share more Bi+ stories across various spectrums, both on *Two Bi Guys* and other spinoff endeavors. I hope to release audio interviews featuring both men from this book (who are willing to forgo their anonymity) as well as other men who volunteered but were unable to participate. In addition to subscribing to the *Two Bi Guys* feed for new episodes and announcements, I recommend checking out www.RobertBrooksCohen.com, which will keep you up to date on my work in this space as it evolves.

In broader popular culture and media, there is even more work to be done. Though the landscape has improved lately, with much more Bi+ visibility on television and in other media, stories like those in this book are still underrepresented, despite the fact that this is the most common Bi+ experience. For dramatic purposes, bisexuality is too often reduced to a conflict in which someone must choose between a man and a woman. This is seen as the definitive bisexual experience, but obviously, it's not. It's rarely even a top concern. There are so many more authentic, interesting, subtle, and complex challenges that Bi+ people deal with every day – like the ones you've read about here – and I'd like to see Bi+ storytelling focus on those realities.

After seven seasons of writing and producing for *Law & Order: SVU* (in which I pitched a few bisexual storylines toward the end, sadly to no avail), I am currently developing my own TV and film projects, and one of them is directly based on the stories in this book. It is tentatively titled BINARY, and it's about a Bi+ guy who comes out to his wife when she discovers gay porn on his computer (sound familiar?). It's an ensemble drama that also features a gay couple who begin to explore their sexual fluidity, as well, crossing paths with the "straight" couple, eventually exploring polyamory together. My goal is to represent some extremely common Bi+ and non-monogamous experiences so that viewers can find connections and come out of the shadows. I'm also working on a comedy about a closeted Bi+ Rabbi who reconnects with his high school crush who has since transitioned female-to-male and who works as an amateur porn performer. In addition to representing Bi+ married men, I believe we need more stories about the intersection of Bi+ and trans/non-binary identities, as well as stories that destigmatize sex work and celebrate the joys of queerness and kink, so that is what I am trying to create.

Overall, we will only see more authentic Bi+ and queer storylines in popular media when more Bi+ and queer creators are given opportunities – and when those creators are out and embrace their sexuality. We can help people understand that queerness is about so much more than sex and that it is a worldview that affects and enhances many areas of our lives – and that queer storylines can be entertaining as hell and make money for the studios that produce them – but we have to be given that chance. Trust me, a lot of the random, hidden, kinky, unexpected, and surreal experiences we've had would make great television.

FOCUSING ON THE JOURNEY, NOT THE DESTINATION

There is also work that each of us can do ourselves and within our relationships to integrate our Bi+ identities and live more authentically.

When I began this project, I was very focused on outcomes. Did the couple stay together or separate? I had an entire column for that on my interview spreadsheet. I wanted to make sure that there was a balance and there weren't too many "negative" outcomes. I didn't want to make people afraid to date a Bi+ person, and I didn't want to give bisexuality a bad reputation.

But over the past few years interviewing these men, and especially since getting married myself, my view has evolved. I no longer see the goal as maintaining a single relationship 'til death. This works for some, but it can also lead to unhappy partnerships if those involved are not being honest about their feelings and desires. I've witnessed many relationships end that are still deeper, more meaningful, and more authentic than relationships that last a lifetime. Longevity is not necessarily a positive outcome.

Rather, this project has proven to me that we should strive for authenticity, both for ourselves and within our partnerships. We can debate lots of things in a relationship – we can negotiate boundaries, we can make compromises, we can do things out of love and respect for others – but we should never have to debate or negotiate who we are. We should be able to express ourselves authentically in order to lead joyful lives. Thus, if we have a partner or partners, they don't have to accept everything we do or say, but they must accept us for who we are. It's okay if that takes time and work, but it's not okay if it never happens or isn't the goal.

If you can be your authentic self and still have secure attachment with a partner, that is a success, and it will be fulfilling, rewarding, and beautiful no matter how long it lasts. Because we change and grow as we move through life, it's normal to periodically re-evaluate whether we can still be authentic within our partnership, and if we decide that we can't, even if we could before, then that partnership may not be ideal for us in its current form.

I love my wife Moxie, more than I've loved any partner I've ever had in my life, and I value and appreciate the relationship we've developed – but I don't know what will happen in the future. We're still learning new things about ourselves every day, and we're still figuring out what shape we want our partnership to take as we move forward. Since we both identify as poly, we are both clear that we will always love each other and want to be in each other's lives, but we have not yet committed to being primary partners for life.

Sometimes this gives me anxiety, and I crave the relationship security that many of my straight and monogamous peers have. But then I remember that that security is often an illusion, and what my wife and I have cultivated, by necessity – which includes an ability to communicate honestly about extremely difficult issues – is actually quite authentic and stable, even if it does someday lead to the end of our primary partnership. My wife is someone I can be completely honest with, and so far that has given me five years of fully exploring myself while receiving love, support, and companionship. I hope that I have similarly given her the space and support to be her authentic self. If that ever changes for either of us, I will always be grateful for what we've had, how we grew together, and what we taught and gave to each other. I feel so lucky that we met, and even when our relationship is challenging, I consider it a blessing and a success, and I'd do it again in a heartbeat.

We shouldn't judge relationships because they ended or may end; we should focus on the quality of relationships and appreciate our partners in the moment, regardless of what happens tomorrow. Every conversation, every fight, every time we have sex, every time we wake up together, every gift, every hardship, every word of encouragement or support – these are the things that are valuable in a marriage, and we should be mindful of them every day.

If you're reading this book and worrying about outcomes, I get it. You might be scared to follow in the footsteps of some men in this book, because they ended up getting divorced. But relationships are messy and complicated, people change, and ultimately, you have to take care of yourself first. You have to follow your authentic path and live the life you dream of, because you only get one shot. For many, that life includes a long and loving marriage – but only by loving your true self can you truly love someone else.

Self-love is powerful and transformative. Many Bi+ men struggle with this, especially in a biphobic society. Many of us downplay our fluidity in order to conform and maintain relationships that we're told we should value. But we <u>must</u> love ourselves, and we should, because bisexuality is completely natural and beautiful. Bi+ people are worthy of love and deserve joy, even – especially – when we are messy, confused, greedy, or just plain weird.

Queerness is a gift. Bisexuality is a superpower. Once you believe that, you can truly show up for yourself and for others, and you can fully experience what it means to love and to be loved.

Index

For Product Safety Concerns and Information please contact our EU
representative GPSR@taylorandfrancis.com
Taylor & Francis Verlag GmbH, Kaufingerstraße 24, 80331 München, Germany